"I highly recommend this new edition of Bill Fibkins's book on mentoring. Over the years, I have worked closely with teachers in both primary and secondary education. In my experience the well-trained, collaborative teacher may be the one consistently responsive adult in a child's life. Retrospectively many of us credit a teacher for our own productive adult lives. Bill's prescription of mentoring is a critical asset for both experienced teacher preservation and new teacher retention. The mentor learns anew by supporting a grateful young colleague, and the young teacher grows in respect to self and chosen profession. Better yet, isolation is relieved for both. As Bill suggests, teacher and student are inextricably connected on a path to learning. For the abused and/or neglected child, the connection can lead to life long healing."
—**Charles Langdon**, MSW, consultant for schools and social services; former executive director of Children's Home Society of Washington, Deaconess Children's Services, Advancing Solutions to Adolescent Pregnancy (ASAP); and clinical professor, School of Social Work, SUNY Stony Brook University

"School reform—the *real* school reform that is grounded in each school's own reality and not theory—can only come from within, when stakeholders share the knowledge of the history of the building and of its community. What I love about this book is the no-nonsense, easy-to-read, anecdotal recounting that can be understood and applied by 'newbies' and veterans, teachers and administrators. While our roles are ever-changing, the information here is timeless and a breath of fresh air, as compared to the many theoretical but inapplicable writings that are out there." —**Stuart A. Rachlin**, EdD, superintendent of Oysterponds Schools, Orient, New York

"In this second edition of his book, Dr. Fibkins makes administrators aware of the immediate need for intervention programs to help stop the attrition of novice teachers. However, he does not stop there. He goes a step further by reminding us that a school is a community; therefore, we must all care for each other and not look the other way when a colleague is having trouble. Hence, he has coined 'No Teacher Left Behind.' Dr. Fibkins passionately emphasizes the responsibility of not letting teachers fall through the cracks by embracing mentoring for both the veteran as well as the novice teacher. Fortunately, he does not offer a one-size-fits-all approach to mentoring—he offers alternative ways to mentor both the veteran and the novice teacher. Dr. Fibkins also gives administrators the why's and how's of engaging veteran teachers one-by-one to create conditions for renewal and a second act." —**Marie J. Toto**, English department chair and Rahway High School/Kean University Professional Development School founder and coordinator, Rahway High School, Rahway, New Jersey

"Dr. Bill Fibkins, a great educator, has trained and inspired scores of teachers and now he's done it again in this second edition. Bill's work emphasizes that it is no longer acceptable for teachers to merely teach content—they need to address the needs of the whole child, especially because so many children live chaotic lives. Novice teachers need to be trained with techniques and strategies focused on classroom management by veteran teachers armed with hard-earned experiences gained after many years in the classroom, a process that offers veteran teachers a new opportunity for professional growth. The student cannot succeed without the skilled teacher, of course, but neither can the teacher survive without the success of the student. They are in it together, both connected, and they are our future. Dr. Fibkins is providing us with the blueprint, and this must be required reading for those who want to see our schools succeed." —**Gwyeth Smith**, director of guidance for Oyster Bay, New York, Public Schools

"I would highly recommend Dr. Fibkins's second edition of *An Administrator's Guide to Better Teacher Mentoring* due largely to the fact that teachers are a valuable source of indicators of child abuse. As a director of a Court Appointed Special Advocate Program (CASA), we depend on the observations of teachers at all grade levels when we investigate the educational background and psychological well-being of a child. Therefore, as Dr. Fibkins suggests, it is important for novice teachers to have the opportunity to gain knowledge and wisdom from 'seasoned' teachers in order to intervene with at-risk students before serious problems emerge. Teachers mentoring teachers is an innovative approach to bringing all teachers on board and not letting any children fall through the cracks. Dr. Fibkins's visionary program sheds a whole new light on the old '3Rs' . . . it's now refresh, react, and reboot!" —**Betty Wirth**, director, Northern Neck , Virginia, CASA

An Administrator's Guide to Teacher Mentoring

Second Edition

William L. Fibkins

ROWMAN & LITTLEFIELD EDUCATION
A division of
ROWMAN & LITTLEFIELD PUBLISHERS, INC.
Lanham • New York • Toronto • Plymouth, UK

Published by Rowman & Littlefield Education
A division of Rowman & Littlefield Publishers, Inc.
A wholly owned subsidiary of The Rowman & Littlefield Publishing Group,
Inc.
4501 Forbes Boulevard, Suite 200, Lanham, Maryland 20706
http://www.rowmaneducation.com

Estover Road, Plymouth PL6 7PY, United Kingdom

Copyright © 2011 by William L. Fibkins

British Library Cataloguing in Publication Information Available

Library of Congress Cataloging-in-Publication Data
Fibkins, William L.
  An administrator's guide to better teacher mentoring / William L. Fibkins. —
2nd ed.
     p. cm.
  Includes bibliographical references.
  ISBN 978-1-60709-676-4 (cloth : alk. paper) — ISBN 978-1-60709-677-1
(pbk. : alk. paper) — ISBN 978-1-60709-678-8 (electronic)
  1. Mentoring in education—United States—Handbooks, manuals, etc. 2.
Teachers—In-service training—United States—Handbooks, manuals, etc. 3.
School administrators—United States—Handbooks, manuals, etc. I. Title.
  LB1731.4.F53 2010
  371.102—dc22   2011039706

™
⊖ The paper used in this publication meets the minimum requirements of
American National Standard for Information Sciences—Permanence of Paper
for Printed Library Materials, ANSI/NISO Z39.48-1992.

Printed in the United States of America

Contents

Acknowledgments

This book is dedicated to my mentor, George Forbes, former principal of Bay Shore Junior High School, Bay Shore, Long Island, New York. Bay Shore Junior was a large school with a population of over 1,600 students and a multicultural population. Given these large numbers of pre-adolescent students at the school, it was not an easy setting to administer. However, George helped create a safe, caring, and hopeful learning environment. He was a kind but strong administrator who believed in collegiality and involving every staff member in the education process. George also understood what good teaching was all about and he didn't hesitate to address poor teaching and discipline practices. He did whatever was necessary to help prevent his teachers and students from drifting into failure patterns. He wanted everyone to succeed.

As such, he had finely honed mentoring skills; he successfully modeled these skills in every school venue. He knew how to listen, be nonjudgmental, and encourage new ideas and approaches. But he also could accept criticism and understood how to overcome resistance to new projects. He was available to his staff, students, and parents in times of professional and personal crisis.

George understood he couldn't be a model and mentor for every teacher on his staff. He delegated responsibility and helped other staff members gain needed leadership experience and exposure. In my case he encouraged me to develop a school-day teacher-training center in conjunction with the State University of New York at Stony Brook. In a real sense he invited me to become his partner in training teachers in the school. He was not threatened by my new role or the involvement of a university. He understood the need for a shared intervention if the teaching staff was to grow professionally and avoid burnout. He couldn't do the job on his own and without help.

In closing let me say that George's intense involvement with teachers, students, and parents probably came at a cost. Being accessible, available, and continuing to know and understand each staff member as they move through the various stages of their careers takes great energy, will, determination, and time. When teachers find a mentor from whom they can get help and support and develop new skills, the floodgates open. Word is spread among the faculty that "really he listens and understands what is happening in my. . . ." Teachers no longer feel alone or without support. In this mentoring process, my guess is that George had to give up some of his personal life so he could complete his mission of helping each teacher and student be all they could be. The good news, and the reward, is that he succeeded with me and my colleagues. Who knows what would have happened to our careers if a George Forbes weren't around to teach, advise, and guide us.

Foreword

Since the middle of the 1980s, public attention has been drawn to the debate over the quality of America's schools. One repeatedly used indicator, common to every public, private, or parochial school in our nation, is the effectiveness of the classroom teacher. An effective teacher, in the minds of many Americans, is one who enables students to learn while simultaneously advancing individual students to the next tier of their achievement. Perceived as a collective, renewable resource, teachers continue to be upgraded through a deliberate and thoughtful process defined as a professional development continuum, a guided sequential progression that begins with mentoring.

Research documents that teachers who know a lot about teaching, and who work in environments that allow them to know students well, are the critical elements of successful student learning. The question plaguing school boards and administrators today is how best to elevate beginning teachers to a satisfactory level of effectiveness while stabilizing attrition rates. One educative solution is offered by Bill Fibkins in this book, a process plan for total school involvement in an expanded and enriched set of experiences designed to nurture, support, instruct, and incorporate an entry-level teacher into the working life of a school and district. He does not suggest that mentoring is easy or a quick fix; however, he does reiterate that it is worth doing.

The goals of Bill's book are to give direction to the selection and preparation of mentors, design a mentoring curriculum, and monitor a school-based mentoring program. It is a focused, practical approach to establishing a mentoring program, a logical approach to a longitudinal process, one of many to be sustained and managed by a building or district administrator. Yet a mentoring process is a program that will demonstrate annual gain as incentives for retirement become available and as pressure builds on local boards of education to reduce class size. While a greater need for novice teachers continues, so does the need for an induction program, a complex set of tasks both social and instructional in nature. Mentoring as a school improvement initiative, which is Fibkins's thrust, is based on the logic of mutual benefits among and between the major constituencies active in the public schools: teachers, administrators, parents, students, and unions. It is a process expected to benefit others in the school organization by improving the quality and ownership of decision making, reducing resistance to change, and ultimately impacting student achievement. Mentoring grows ever more important as alternate teacher certification programs expand and teachers, entering classrooms without the benefit of supervised field experiences, are expected to perform at levels of competency.

Discouraged and disillusioned, many teachers quit, with half leaving the profession within five years. One purpose of mentoring, aside from offering support, encouragement, insight, and practice, is to retain new teachers within the education system. The residual effects of teacher-mentor programs most often are related to the quality of the mentor–mentee relationship, a relationship with an intense and specific life expectancy. During that designated time a mentor is expected to encourage the beginner to reflect upon the professional, social, and cultural issues of the school community.

Attributes and characteristics of an effective mentor include the ability to provide clear and frequent communication. Communication includes feedback, listening, and responding, useful skills to support the transition of teachers into their professional capacities within a school and skills that are essential to developing and sustaining rapport with students. This verbal and, on occasion, written give-and-take tends to work particularly well when communication centers on the improvement of student learning and achievement.

School leaders and university deans continue to explore ways in which they can partner in the preparation of pre-service and in-service certificated teachers. One such partnership might revolve around mentoring and supporting the beginning teacher, helping to dispel the professional loneliness that comes with the job while providing opportunities to expand his or her knowledge base of best classroom practices. Other partnership activities might include school-based teacher education programs, cohort placements of field experience students, and preK–12 teachers co-teaching university courses.

The twenty-first century brings its own brand of teacher recruitment, hiring, and retention as budgets are defeated, state aid cut, and teachers "riffed"—precluding the hiring of fresh, motivated teachers. Instead, there is a reported surplus of teachers, with an oversupply of substitute teacher, currently so many that districts refuse their applications. Employed teachers await a buyout and stay longer in this atmosphere of financial uncertainty.

Mentoring will not solve these ills of the American education system. This, too, with time will pass. However, mentoring is a process that continues to make a difference in the life and work of new teachers and inspires experienced teachers to grow consistently in their chosen profession. It is a life-long learning process that makes a deliberate and sustained commitment to the education of educators.

Martha M. Mobley, Ph.D.
   Director, Teaching Performance Center
   Kean University

Chapter One

The Pressing Need for Administrators to Take on a New Mentoring Role

We live in a world in which mentoring, coaching, team building, and empowering have become standard practices for many successful corporations and corporate leaders. Concerned and committed employees want to learn how to be successful and play an important role in building their company. They expect their CEOs to make ongoing training easily accessible in order to prepare them for their ever-changing roles.

As Michael Hammer and James Champy suggest, ongoing training to constantly assess the needs of customers and to learn new skills to address these needs are top priorities for successful corporations.[1] "Change is constant" is a frequent theme. In fact, many Americans work in a rather democratic setting in which skill is what counts, not dress, degree, or background. Collegiality, the sharing of authority among colleagues, is promoted, as is the theme that each member of the corporation must be a constant learner if the organization is to thrive.

This process, embraced by so much of corporate America, needs to be adopted by future-looking educators as well. If any place has constant change, it is America's schools. Students, parents, and community members look to schools to solve the academic and, increasingly, nonacademic or personal problems of students. Education opens doors; it is the ticket to a seat in our highly competitive society.

Yet ongoing mentoring for teachers—investing time and money in their professional development—has not caught on in the same way that it has in corporate life. Some would say the reason for this lack of a national effort to establish school-based teacher mentoring programs is a lack of funding and

1

resource allocation. They have a point, of course, because schools always need more resources.

However, more complex reasons keep local schools from establishing ongoing mentoring programs led by successful and respected local educators. Here are five reasons:

1. Many school administrators are very busy people. They rightfully say they do not have time to mentor every teacher in the school. Resolving crises, preparing budgets, overseeing curriculum development, and carrying out state education department testing mandates are just a few of the many complicated tasks that are the responsibility of school administration. When teachers and community members think of the role of the administrator, these are some of the tasks they associate with the role. Like it or not, many administrators are locked into a traditional role in which convention dictates that they are primarily business leaders and problem solvers, not mentors of teachers.

   Unfortunately, this limited conception of the duties of administrators keeps them from developing a mentoring program to better prepare teachers to meet the needs of their changing customer population—students and parents. Don't administrators have enough on their plates already? Assuming total responsibility for another major program, one in which they would be mentoring every teacher in the school, may seem too much for beleaguered administrators. And they are correct. Given the limits of their time and ability, they alone cannot institute a mentoring program.

2. Many administrators also rightfully say that even if they had the time, they would still lack the necessary training and methodology to acquire skills to help them become effective mentors. Many are not accustomed to working in intimate, one-on-one relationships in which they help teachers, a situation that calls for behaviors and skills such as building trust, being patient in order for change to occur, and offering ongoing support. While much literature exists about teachers as mentors for students, I believe critics pay less attention to what it takes for administrators to be effective mentors for teachers.

3. There are few role models for administrators to emulate if they indeed did have the time to become effective mentors for their teachers. How does the administrator as mentor behave? The role of an administrator is a powerful role that involves quick reactions, decision making, and politicking. Mentoring is different. It is a shared role that requires delicate and caring intervention and feedback. It is a slow process built on mutual trust and self-respect. It works only when both parties, the mentor and the protégé, clearly understand the areas that need improvement and how the mentor can be useful.

It is a teaching position carried on in the classroom setting, a far cry from the administrator's often crisis-centered and chaotic office. The mentoring setting is not without the conflict or resistance that comes with helping teachers change, but the conflict is subtler. It requires new, tactful approaches and skills. Mentoring also requires the belief that change is possible with patient and trustful intervention.

4. If the administrator had more time, opportunities for skill acquisition, and a model to follow to become an effective mentor, would he or she be willing to take on this different role? In all likelihood, teachers, students, parents, and community members at first would be confused with this new mentoring role, and resistance could run high. People may talk, saying things such as, "Why is the administrator spending so much time helping teachers? Doesn't he belong back in the office?" Change is difficult, especially when the head of the school begins to take on a new role that is not in keeping with tradition, assumptions of the past, and conventional wisdom.

5. Even if all of the above needs are met, administrators need to come to terms with the issue that providing mentoring for every teacher is a serious move. It is not small change. Will they get the support and resources needed from the central office? Being out of the office trying to forge new mentoring relations can take administrators out of the political issues of the school. While they would be more visible to teachers, they would be increasingly out of the office, not dealing with the self-promotional aspects that are key to survival in the highly politicized world of school administrators.

They may even learn to value mentoring above the more crass aspects of their work that politicization requires. Shining one's light all day can be draining, but being out of the picture can be dangerous to one's career. Making mentoring a major part of an administrator's work can be risky business if pursued with too much enthusiasm.

These reasons are all valid. Administrators are busy. Many lack mentoring skills and a model to follow. A risk is involved in taking on a different administrative role that may leave them vulnerable to those who want a more traditional, office-centered administrator. But I believe these risks are overshadowed by the growing public demand for teachers who are well prepared. These demands are a driving force in helping administrators take a hands-on role in retraining their teaching staff.

David A. Gilman and Barbara Lanman-Givens suggest that school districts need to restructure the principals' role to allow them to focus on student learning and instructional leadership and to face fewer demands for management tasks.[2] Principals will be able to devote more time to improving instructional leadership and student learning when they can delegate some managerial duties to an assistant principal or office manager.

But change is slow and sometimes requires small, incremental steps. School administrators can proceed to play a major leadership role in developing a mentoring program without totally restructuring their daily job requirements and becoming completely immersed in a new role. Here is how:

- While administrators cannot do much about the demands of their job and time requirements, they can teach themselves mentoring skills. They can prepare themselves for the mentoring role.
- Knowing they cannot establish and maintain a mentoring program alone, administrators can form a mentoring team made up of an assistant principal, department chairperson, teacher leader, and counselor leader. The administrator will have a place in the mentoring process but will be joined by a competent team made up of educators who are known and respected in the school.
- The administrator can train this team to be effective mentors and ongoing sources of support and training for each other.
- The administrator can lead the way in promoting the mentoring program. In selling the program, simple questions work best. For example, "Wouldn't it be better for our staff to be well-trained and better prepared than to be resting on our laurels, waiting for the next crisis?"
- The administrator can encourage teachers who have been mentored to take on a mentoring role with colleagues, thereby widening the mentoring circle and creating new opportunities for renewal. This process creates a new role for teachers—mentors for colleagues as well as teachers of students.
- The administrator can encourage the mentoring team to pass on their skills to support staff and students, thereby creating a school-wide mentoring process in which all members of the school community have the opportunity to be learners and begin a new way of operating, leaving past failures and setbacks in the past where they belong.

This plan allows administrators to create a mentoring program and thereby escape the self-defeating illusion that they are the only resource for training and renewal in the school. This mentoring plan can create a freeing process for administrators, altering their role in a subtle but clearly defined way. In the process of being a mentor leader and mentor, the administrator moves away from a traditional supervisory role and acts as a facilitator, an enabler, and someone whose job includes the development of people and their skills.

The mentoring program is also an acknowledgment that America's schools are experiencing a time of great change and that the roles of educators must change with these demanding times. In turn, the role of teachers in today's world is multidimensional and dynamic. It is a role that requires intellect, a desire to learn and take risks, emotional and physical wellness, and openness to personal and professional change. This is not a slot that can be filled by just anyone with a degree, completed coursework, and certification—a "warm body," as they say on the front lines in the schools—sent naively into the battleground of the classroom.

Effective mentoring tears away the faulty assumption raised by critics that teachers' work involves simple, easily achievable tasks. A teacher is a warm body, not exactly a rocket scientist, some would say. To the contrary, as any effective teacher knows, teaching involves interacting with many, sometimes hundreds, of students and staff each day.

Much of this interaction is complicated because it requires the teacher to know the needs of the many students he or she is trying to serve and how to make use of the best skills to meet these needs. To be effective, the teacher must be aware of each student's personality, home life, motivation level, physical and emotional condition, relationship with peers and other teachers, and most importantly, the student's goals and dreams. Each student has his or her own story that needs to be understood and respected.

Contrary to the public's widely held vision of a soft job with summers off, teaching is a very demanding role. Teachers need to be in excellent physical, intellectual, and emotional shape if they are to do this important job well. They also need a mentor who is able to listen to their needs, concerns, and fears, a mentor who can help keep them up to date and master the skills they need to be at the top of their game.

Initially, teachers themselves often are reluctant to become involved in professional renewal development programs. In the busy world of teaching, teachers are constantly dealing with the present, with the daily issues of students, parents, colleagues, and administrators. Learning new skills that can help them deal with emerging issues is not a reality in most schools because there is no mechanism in place to make it happen.

While many teachers admit that they feel the need to learn new skills, nothing much happens unless schools make clear, easily accessible, attractive, ongoing, and trusted intervention programs available. Also, teachers' skills do not stay the same, but get better or worse over time. Leaving teachers without opportunities for mentoring is hazardous and undesirable.

Leaving teachers without opportunities for mentoring is not cost effective. Poorly trained teachers can be problematic and even harmful. As a result, administrators in some schools continually find themselves in a reactive mode of trying to dig themselves and their staff out of ill-advised interactions between teachers and students. It is a daily, time-consuming, and dismal practice trying to right problems related to poor—sometimes inept—student disciplining, parent communication, and staff relationships, and to unprofessional practices.

Rather than taking a proactive role in mentoring and training teachers, many administrators find themselves caught in a catch-22 situation: they have no mentoring program in place, so they have no proactive mechanism to help troubled teachers become effective.

The constant stream of rectifying the problems caused by teachers who, as one would naively expect should know better, is debilitating. But in fact, some teachers do not know better and it is not their fault. They are, for the most part, simply untrained to handle the problems and issues that are part of their duties in America's changing schools, whether they are new, midcareer, or veteran. Untrained teachers are problems waiting to happen, and everyone in the school—administrators, fellow teachers, students, and parents—usually knows their plight.

Here is an example demonstrating what often happens when teachers are left without effective intervention and mentoring. Anyone who has been a classroom teacher knows teaching has many emotional pitfalls. One can easily lose one's way going down new roads without experience and direction. As Dr. Seuss suggests—and it certainly applies to the lives of teachers—"You will come to a place where the streets are not marked. Some windows are lighted . . . but mostly they're darked. Simple it's not, I'm afraid you will find, for a mind-maker-upper to make up his mind."[3]

When teachers enter the field they are often unaware of their own conflicting values and feelings about students. It's new territory, and they have no past experience to guide them—the "windows are darked"—except for their own limited personal and professional backgrounds. Teachers tend to make their job comfortable by spending more time with students who are like them, avoiding students who are different and whose physical appearance, background, personality, or behavior inexplicably stirs up unwanted, hostile feelings in them.

Spend time observing teacher–student interactions and no doubt you will see many teachers directing their questions and gravitating toward certain students, usually the brightest and the best behaved. They seem at home with these students because they pose no threat.

When teachers gravitate toward a certain type of student, this means that there are many other students who they seem to avoid, seemingly afraid to make contact for fear of rejection. What do teachers do when confronted with students who may reject them, who are not willing to play their game? They hesitate and stumble, looking for the right response, which usually doesn't come, drawing a line between them and the resisting student.

A sort of battle begins, and teachers are usually alone with the problem. Do they share it at a faculty meeting or in the faculty room? This usually is not the place they can get help with their problem, so they think it is better to keep it to themselves. Maybe no one will notice.

In many schools, teachers know they are on their own. Help and intervention are things they talked about in college courses. It is not a reality for them. Once again, the role of a teacher reminds us of what Dr. Seuss says, that at times you will be "all alone! Whether you like it or not, alone will be something you'll be quite a lot. And when you're alone, there's a very good chance you'll meet things that scare you right out of your pants. There are some, down the road between hither and yon, that can scare you so much you won't want to go on."[4]

Being alone, these teachers watch the clock, waiting for the period to end, telling themselves to keep the students busy and under control. Tomorrow is Friday. TGIF! I've survived another week. June is three months away. Maybe next year's classes will be easier. The other teachers say this is the toughest class in years. Maybe it's not me. Maybe it's them.

This example is all too common in our schools. Is this a natural condition? Yes. The classroom really is a battlefield. It is a place to test the teacher's skills, courage, will to win, compassion, and endurance against some students who by nature resist and act out.

Yet it is the teacher's responsibility to win these students over and get them on track to a good education. It is the teacher's ballgame to win or lose. It often is not peaceful, calm, and correct. It is a heated chess game. The teacher makes a move and the students counter it. If the teacher is unskilled or lacks the will to win or the compassion and the endurance to go the distance with these students, problems will arise. Courage plays an important part.

Teachers invariably experience a classroom situation that can, as Dr. Seuss depicts it, scare them and make them not want to go on. Doing battle and losing can bring about surrendering and letting the students do what they want. One hears from a teacher, "It's not my job to straighten them out." Often, crying, burnout, and casting blame on the students can be all too easy.

Finding the courage to regain control in difficult classroom situations is not easy, especially when the teacher is alone or does not know how to ask for help when the ship is sinking.

Left unaddressed and unresolved, a hostile classroom limits the positive impact the teacher can have on all of the students in the class. To be effective with all students, the teacher needs to understand complicated student–teacher interaction and learn the necessary skills to make contact with each student in the room. It is important to understand that all teachers bring their own biases into the classroom that either enhance or interfere with the teaching and learning process.

Factors such as the students' gender, race, culture, personality, and behavior can unexpectedly set off conflicting feelings within the teacher that spring from personal biases and limited background. These conflicting feelings often go unspoken. The myth that teachers are supposed to like—even love, some say—and support all of their students usually prevails in the schools and hides the real mentoring work that has to be done.

Spending too much time with some students and avoiding others is not a cost-effective strategy and does a disservice to each group. The students who are unconnected and left out may personalize the rejection and consider it their own problem, not the teacher's.

Effective mentoring can help teachers develop a set of skills that will help them avoid the classroom polarization that usually sets in when they are unaware of and unprepared to deal with students who come from different cultures and ways of behaving.

Traditionally, many schools have not made mentoring and supervising teachers and investing in their continued improvement a top priority. The mentoring process that exists usually involves a few classroom observations followed by a conference and written evaluation. It is a process to get out of the way as fast as possible for both the administrator and the teacher. In their meetings they often engage in little or no conversation about how to improve the teacher's skills and do not point out specific teacher–student interactions that need to be addressed over time.

They seldom discuss the teacher's own fears and concerns, for example, why is this teacher uneasy with certain students? Why does he seem to discipline certain students more harshly? Why does she lecture so much and leave little time for students' participation? In this hurried evaluation process, the teacher and administrator do not ask questions that would bring the hidden concerns and needs of the teacher out in the open to be addressed without judgment.

Most likely these schools do not have time set aside for the administrator to model new classroom techniques and approaches and suggest other sources of support and training within both the school and community—truly to be a teaching principal.

What does take place in these so-called supervision and mentoring conversations often focuses on what I call the business aspects of teaching. The administrator makes sure that the teacher has enough materials, is current on testing schedules, is ready for parent conferences, knows when grades are due in the office, and so on. To use a basketball analogy, the administrator does not blow the whistle unless there is some flagrant violation going on with students and parents. The administrator is there to make sure that everything is under control and keep things from getting out of hand.

The process is often apologetic: "I'm sorry, Tom, I hate to intrude, but you know I have to make these yearly evaluations. Let me come in for a few minutes during third period. I'm sure there are no problems."

When it takes this form, teachers often view supervision and mentoring with sarcasm and dark humor, a game to be played but without much substance. It becomes an interaction guided by the words, "Let's not make this a problem for each other; we are busy people." Clearly this is not a model that creates conditions for helping teachers identify problem areas and learn new skills.

This is not to say that administrators in this role are not caring or that they are disinterested in their teachers' professional development. Of course not. But the mentoring role described above keeps them in an observing, not a teaching, role. It is a process in which both the administrator and the teacher settle for less. What presents itself as an opportunity for real dialog and change is downgraded to a chore. It is a lose-lose situation for both the administrator and the teacher. Teachers remain stuck using skills that are out of date and tend to produce failure. It is a bit like giving them World War II rifles to fight a war in which the opposition has modern electronic weaponry. Administrators remain stuck as well, using supervisory skills and a process that robs them of real interaction with teachers.

These conditions can be changed. An effective mentoring plan can alter the way teachers continue to grow and learn, and it can also bring needed change to the way administrators view their role in improving their teachers' performance.

The potential for professional growth involved in effective mentoring is not just for teachers. In developing a trusted mentoring role with teachers, administrators also create a teacher–learner climate in which they, too, become open to examining their own skills. Where are their strengths as a mentor? For example, are they an effective listener, nonjudgmental, able to offer constructive feedback or successfully model the behaviors they are asking their teachers to take on? Just as important, where are their skills lacking? What areas do they need to improve? Remember, the skills of the administrator, like those of his or her teachers, do not stay the same. They either get better or worse over time.

Without reflection and positive, nonjudgmental feedback, administrators can get stuck as well, using and relying on skills no longer relevant in today's schools. In this intimate mentoring relationship, they, like their teachers, become aware of the barriers that threaten and undermine their work. For example, they become aware of those teachers who they avoid and who seem to threaten their role as administrator. And like teachers with their students, mentors need to work hard to overcome these barriers by being in touch with their teachers; their personalities, home lives, motivation levels, physical and emotional well-being, and relationships with peers, colleagues, students, and parents; and most important, their goals, dreams, and fears.

Most teachers dream of being something special in the classroom. In the mentoring process, the administrator begins to become aware of these dynamics and focuses on the new skills he or she needs to get teachers committed to the process. Also, administrators usually don't receive truthful and direct feedback concerning their work. Being a mentor opens up the possibility of direct feedback from teachers.

Clearly, mentoring is an extremely useful and helpful way for administrators and teachers to stay on top of their game. In pragmatic ways, mentoring also helps define where educators need to put their resources: in teacher improvement. By zeroing in on a way to provide teachers with ongoing skills acquisition and renewal throughout their careers, they are avoiding vague, elusive definitions such as "school reform."

Michael A. Ballin—president of the Clark Foundation, a foundation whose mission is to help improve schools and the education of children—questions whether the millions his foundation has spent on large-scale reform programs have had lasting impact:

> Talk about something that is hard to do . . . try to change a system. Even under the best of conditions it can absorb or co-opt the energy of the reformers. It matters relatively little whether we can craft great institutions out of existing schools. Schools, after all, are institutions; education is the work of educators, not the work of schools. Good schools help; great schools help more; but great teachers are a far more precious commodity.

> As the Clark Foundation has discovered, addressing the system rather than the specific actions of individual teachers leads us to commit the cardinal sin of educators . . . confusing treatment with the cure. For the Clark Foundation, for the massed armies of school reformers . . . I have only one bit of advice to aid escape from the futilities of school reform. Stop trying to make schools great schools and take up the task of trying to make teachers great teachers. We engage in school reform teacher by teacher.[5]

Mentoring also provides schools with a way to avoid teacher turnover and attrition. As the National Education Association (NEA) suggests, more than a million veteran teachers are nearing retirement.[6] Twenty percent of first-time hires leave their teaching jobs within three years. In urban districts, nearly 50 percent of newcomers leave the profession during their first five years of teaching.

America will need two million new teachers in the next decade, and experts predict that half of the teachers who will be in public school classrooms have not yet been hired. By 2006, America will educate almost three million more children than it does today—more than fifty-four million youngsters. We will need intervention to help new hires and also cut down on unnecessary turnovers.

The NEA recommends that newly hired teachers be assigned a mentor who will assist them with everything from classroom management to student assessment. An effective mentoring program can also address turnover and attrition. A report issued by Public Agenda, "A Sense of Calling: Why Teachers Teach," found that 76 percent of the nine hundred teachers polled contend that they are made to be "scapegoats" for problems in education.[7] Moreover, a majority told pollsters that they don't see opportunities for career advancement, nor do they feel appreciated for the work they do. The teachers also reported that their jobs are made more difficult because they lack the skills to maintain classroom discipline. Six in ten teachers said that most take over classrooms without the requisite experience in handling them. The study found keeping capable teachers in the classroom depends on improving each educator's quality of life during the school day rather than increasing their paychecks.

The issues raised in the Public Agenda report—scapegoats, feeling unappreciated, little opportunity for advancement, lack of needed skills—can be addressed. If they are left unaddressed, we should not be surprised by the fact that 20 percent of new teachers flee the classroom after three years and that 50 percent leave urban schools after five years. Teachers are telling us what they need, not only to survive but also to become great teachers. Let's give them what they need: skills, accolades, support, and career novelty. Mentoring can help produce this change.

I believe David C. Berliner captures the value of mentoring when he suggests the following:

> Mentoring programs are promising for two reasons. First, they cut the dropout rate of teachers from roughly 50 to 15 percent during the first five years of teaching. Without mentoring our [teacher] shortages will grow. The second reason we need mentoring is a moral, not a pragmatic, one. We must not abandon beginners who have been placed in the complex world of teaching. Through apprenticeships novices can learn from masters. Mentoring helps new teachers think about their experience and it helps them to handle the emotional side of teaching. Teaching is an emotionally draining experience. Teachers get caught up in the lives of kids and their parents. They need to know what a healthy response is and when to put up boundaries. They need clear advice about how to do something better or different the next time they teach it.[8]

There are two additional benefits from the mentoring process. Well-trained mentors are also ideally positioned to advise and guide midcareer and veteran teachers who run into difficulties as their careers evolve. Renewal opportunities need to be available for all teacher groups in the school setting. Secondly, master teachers benefit immensely in their new role of advising and guiding newcomers. They are able to use their hard-won classroom experience in a positive way, instead of being isolated in their classrooms with no opportunity to be a teacher of teachers.

Teachers as mentors of colleagues can act as catalysts to reinvigorate experienced teachers and create a sense of novelty and change, a chance to show others how they have learned from many setbacks and failures over time. This is a major change.

Berliner also accurately describes where we are in developing school-based mentoring programs when he suggests:

> Mentoring is not widespread enough. Here at Arizona State we mentor more than 1,000 teachers in their first two years of teaching. About 300 teachers from the school districts mentor these new teachers. . . . Every state really needs a program like this. It costs a few hundred dollars per teacher per year for the first two years of the teacher's professional life. It's the pragmatic and morally right thing to do.[9]

The same applies for midcareer and veteran teachers as well. The mentoring process presents school administrators with a unique opportunity to help every teacher become more effective in his or her classroom. How do they proceed in this important mission? An important first step is to better understand what it is like to be a competent teacher.

Administrators need to observe master teachers to help them identify a model of an effective and competent teacher. This understanding can help educators focus on what kinds of teacher behaviors and skills create, foster, and support these models.

It is important for educators to understand how professionals in other fields such as music, dance, and sports become successful in their craft. What can we learn from their successful careers? What barriers and obstacles do they face? What are the parallels between their successes and those of teachers?

NOTES

1. Michael Hammer and James Champy, *Reengineering the Corporation* (New York: HarperCollins, 1993), 28.
2. David A. Gilman and Barbara Lanman-Givens, "Where Have All the Principals Gone?" *Educational Leadership* 58(8) (May 2001): 73.
3. Dr. Seuss, *Oh, the Places You'll Go!* (New York: Random House, 1990).
4. Ibid.
5. Quoted in Peter Temes, "The End of School Reform," *Education Week*, 4 April 2001, www.edweek.org/ew/ewstory.cfm?Slug=29temes.h20.
6. National Education Association Teacher Quality Fact Sheet, "Teaching," (20 April 2001) www.nea.org/teaching/shortage.html.
7. Julie Blair, "Teacher Idealism Tempered by Frustration, Survey Finds," *Education Week*, 31 May 2000, 6.
8. David C. Berliner, "Improving the Quality of the Teaching Force," *Educational Leadership* 58(8) (May 2001): 10.
9. Ibid.

Chapter Two

A Vision of the Competent Master Teacher

Before we proceed to examine how administrators can understand and implement a teacher mentoring plan, let us consider the qualities of the model teacher we are trying to create in an effective mentoring process. What is our picture of a competent teacher? What are the parallels between a competent teacher and performers in other fields such as athletics, dance, music, stage, and film? What can we learn from other professionals about issues related to skill acquisition, renewal, failure, success, commitment, aging, courage, and the ongoing battle to ward off extinction?

Teachers and administrators are, after, all, performers. They work live on stage each day. Their performance is closely watched and critiqued by colleagues, students, parents, and community members. This audience assesses the teacher and forms an opinion and, like criticisms of Broadway actors and actresses, some are not kind. Teaching, like other performing arts, is risky business.

If teachers fail to deliver a good performance, their worth and value are diminished. They may keep their job, but skill-building opportunities and chances for renewal are not always easily available or desired. Dr. Seuss reminds us that "unslumping [ourselves] is not easily done," and it is no easier in teaching and the arts.

Stephen Sondheim, the great American composer, suggests, "What I found out in my work is that everyone is talented. It's just that some people get it developed and some don't. Developing your talent takes work." [1]

Here is a vision of what competent teachers look like, the hard work that they must put into the process, and the realities that they must face to ward off the ever-present forces of failure and extinction. This picture hopefully adds to your understanding of why the leadership of school administrators in the mentoring process is so important. Not letting one teacher fall through the cracks of failure is an achievable goal, one made easier with the recognition that the craft is demanding and requires ongoing hard work and commitment. There are no easy days.

Teaching, like the other performing crafts—music, acting, dance, and athletics—requires a special set of skills that are honed and refined over a professional's lifetime. Teachers who successfully develop their craft understand that the process is evolutionary and includes many experiences of failure in the search to become an effective teacher. It takes a skilled craftsman to know how to connect the dots of the past and the present—the visible and the hidden—and find the pattern.

In the classroom, teachers use their craft to show their students that the world is safe, even with all the violence, and manageable. The students may come from homes that are abusive, even violent, but in the classroom (literally a home away from home), they fit, they are safe, and they belong. The teacher, for the duration of the school day, is the parent or mentor they need to show them the way. He or she gives students the necessary skills to move through life's challenges. A teacher makes students feel useful, optimistic, and confident that they have a role to play in the world.

A competent teacher's daily work is meticulously crafted, from the first hello in the morning until the yellow school bus heads home after class. If one observes teachers closely, one sees a form to their work and a process in how they go about creating a classroom climate in which every student can learn. Of course, they are affected by events beyond the classroom—calls for education reform, budget battles, issues the administration has with the union, family problems that affect students, and cries of teacher burnout from colleagues. But their main focus is the classroom.

Successful teachers know they have to shield themselves from the external distractions that are kindling outside the classroom. They discipline themselves so they do not fall prey to these distractions that may sap their energy and spirit. In a sense they are like athletes intent on getting to the Super Bowl, the World Series, or the Final Four. They must tune out the external noise, conserve their energy, and stay focused.

Of course, teachers are not at all immune to events in the school, the district, or the educational community, or to the struggles of fellow teachers to be more effective in their work. They just do not allow these events to rule their life and get in the way of their major goal—to be the very best teacher each day for the students and to serve as a role model for peers—some who say they want to better their craft and others who seem satisfied to be less than they can be.

Teachers understand that peers, many of whom have settled for mediocrity and rebuff every effort to raise their level of skill, can be coached into more training given the right intervention. The teacher does not reject or judge these peers. He or she is available to help these teachers and include them in the ongoing work of improving the craft of teaching. Teachers make sure to avoid cynicism and the debilitating effect it has on their craft.

They are akin to dancer Twyla Tharp when she says, "Cynicism is very de-energizing. And dance needs energy to go on. You have to believe that what you are doing is important . . . so there is no point in being cynical if you want to dance. So get over it."[2] Teaching also needs energy to go on. The model teacher walks a fine line, being available to peers who are cynical about teaching but not taking these words to heart. Good teachers can't afford cynicism. They get over it.

In the laboratory of the classroom, model teachers view themselves as having the skills and desire to teach every child who enters the classroom. They continually work at their craft and over time develop a unique style, one that showcases their talents. When it comes to education reform, competent teachers listen but do not stop their work or change their style to wait for the next round of proposals. They do not hold their breath and wait for change to come to them. Instead, they see themselves as agents initiating change in the place where it counts most: their classrooms.

For teachers like Ana England, a sixth-grade math teacher in Watsonville, California, little is expected to change in the current debate over education reform. "I've looked at the state standards [in science and math] and the things the Board has crossed out are words like 'analyze' and 'explain your thinking.' But there's nothing in the standards that says you can't teach that. A good teacher is going to do that, in addition to teaching the basic skills."

Nathan Tarkov suggests that any attempt to dictate a solution (to teachers) is doomed: "Whatever the curriculum, ultimately it comes down to the teacher, especially the teacher's energy and character, and sense of humor and ability to relate to young people, and not just the policies the teacher follows."[3] The question successful teachers always ask when it comes to innovation and reform is, "How does it improve learning in my classroom?"[4]

A teacher's own failure and resistance are also major factors in developing a unique teaching style. Much of what teachers do each day results in failure. Becoming better at the craft leads a teacher down many roads, some of which are dead ends. Failed lesson plans, failed approaches to resolving a student's personal problems, the discouragement of a bad day when everything seems to backfire—all of these can lay a teacher low.

Getting some students to do what they don't want to do—work harder, get better grades, have hopes and dreams—is no easy task! It is tough work, a demanding labor not unlike the assembly line's constant pressure. Even the best teachers can lose their way and face a dead end. Constant reassessment of what is going on in the classroom—is what I am doing right now working?—is a critical skill for the competent teacher.

Becoming a successful teacher is an evolutionary process that requires work, discipline, focus, overcoming failure, developing a style, and refining that style so it continues to work. It means continually searching for new approaches and giving up what once worked but is no longer effective. It is a constant, though not always conscious, process of addition and deletion. It means taking risks and giving up the tried and true for a glimpse of a distant vision.

Effective teachers are like musicians who are constantly improvising with new lyrics and notes so they don't become outdated. The career of the competent teacher is no different from that of other performing artists and athletes. Teachers improvise to meet the individual needs of each child and create the conditions under which each child can learn. In the words of jazz pianist Keith Jarrett, "When you are improvising, you can play anything, and you can make it work somehow."[5]

Changing and improvising take work, practice, and discipline. As composer Stephen Sondheim suggests, it is a process that one works at to become better. Sondheim reports that the first music teacher he had at Williams College, Robert Barrows, "made me realize that all my romantic views of art were nonsense. He taught me that art is something to be worked at." And so is teaching. Many teachers have talent, but some get developed and some don't.

Woody Allen, actor and director, suggests that to stay at the top of your craft, "You just have to work. You can't read your reviews."[6]

Frank Sinatra, perhaps the greatest popular singer of our time, gives us a glimpse into his work at developing the Sinatra style.

> I began swimming in public pools, taking laps under water and thinking song lyrics to myself as I swam holding my breath. Over six months or so, I began to delineate a method of long phraseology. Instead of singing only two bars at a time . . . like most other guys . . . I was able to sing six bars, and in some songs eight bars, without taking a visible or audible breath. That gave the melody a flowing, unbroken quality, and that's what made my sound different.[7]

Much the same can be said of the sound of the great trumpet player and singer Louis Armstrong. It is often said that his singing is a direct extension, a kind of mirror, of his playing. In fact, he never sang out of tune or put accents or notes in the wrong places. He knew how to articulate and how to set each song, no matter how trifling, into focus. And so do competent teachers. They too know how to articulate and set each lesson plan, no matter how trifling, into focus.[8]

Performing artists, like teachers, face bouts of failure and self-doubt throughout their careers. Some overcome these barriers and move on to fulfill their promise. Others get stuck and finish out their careers unfulfilled and jaded. Visit any school and you will find teachers who have overcome barriers and are seen as stars of their craft. You will also find teachers who got stuck and have not developed.

Here are examples of how the battle to stay at the height of one's career is fought by famous performing artists and athletes. Their stories of achievements and setbacks can help would-be mentors understand the precariousness and risk that are a part of the craft of education as well. Performing, being in front of the crowd, doing it well—this is hard work. Done daily, five days a week, invariably leads to some wrong roads, misdirection, and even breakdowns among the successes.

- *Frank Sinatra, singer and actor:* Frank Sinatra suffered a series of setbacks in the early 1950s. No one would hire him. "I was in trouble. I was busted . . . I did lie down for a while and had some large bar bills for about a year. Then I said, 'OK, holiday's over . . . let's go back to work.'" But his comeback was slow. In an age of rock 'n' roll he had to travel—to Australia in 1959, the legendary Melbourne concert—to work and stay connected to a live audience. He even announced his retirement in 1970. But he began to hit his stride again in 1973 with the release of the aptly titled album *Ol' Blue Eyes is Back.* His comeback was complete when he gave a concert, "Sinatra: The Main Event . . . Live," to a sold-out crowd of 20,000 people at Madison Square Garden on October 13, 1974. His opening comments at the concert are poignant: "Thank you. It's my great pleasure to be back in New York and to be able to work again. . . . I'm ready and I'm set."[9]
- *Twyla Tharp, dancer and choreographer:* Tharp is troubled and a little exasperated by a dark mood that has seemed to settle over dance recently:

> My business is simply the work I do . . . but I must say I have little patience for what I basically think is the disregard for the abundance of good things that we've had from the dance world in our lifetime. The depression in the dance world is totally debilitating. I can't afford it. I've worked too hard my entire life to have to endure at this point. I'm not interested in seeing dance die. . . . You have to believe that what you are doing is important.

> You really have to believe that you are of some use to people and that what you have to offer has something good for them. I've always believed that a dance evening energizes an audience, that an audience goes out feeling chemically stronger and more optimistic. This is what I understand about dance. And this is an important thing. We need this. Our culture needs it. Cynicism is very de-energizing. And dance needs energy. You have to believe that what you are doing is important. So there is no point being cynical if you want to dance. So get over it.

- *Pete Harnisch, baseball pitcher in recovery from depression:* For Pete Harnisch, free agency could not have come at a worse time. Harnisch missed most of the 1997 baseball season with the New York Mets after falling into depression in April. After his return to the Mets in August, he was traded to Milwaukee. Interest in Harnisch had been lukewarm, as he explains it. "I'm in kind of a 'prove it' year. I know what I've got to do and I'll go somewhere and pitch 200 innings and make my start. Obviously, I would have hoped to be signed by now."

Harnisch was not sure whether his bout with depression muted interest in him. "It wouldn't surprise me if there was some concern, but I don't walk around every day wondering if it's going to happen again." Harnisch said dealing with depression was the most difficult thing he had ever been through. "But in a way it makes you stronger. I know it's kind of a cliché, but now it's like, what's worse out there? You can't hit me with anything else."[10]

- *Louis Armstrong, singer, trumpet player, and first black superstar:* Near the end of his career, Armstrong was senselessly overbooked and overworked. His trumpet playing became stenciled and tired. The wear showed. He was down a wrong road that sapped his energy and talent. But still you knew that when you went to see Armstrong, you were listening to the great Louis Armstrong, the first black superstar, and you'd better pay attention because he might suddenly stop you with an impassioned "Sunny Side of the Street." Sadly, celebrity status, as in Armstrong's case, is often mindlessly conferred when the celebrated can no longer do what makes him famous or when what he invented has become buried and forgotten under accumulated applause.

- *Cecil Taylor, jazz pianist:* In a conversation with jazz historian Nat Hentoff, Taylor reported that he had some terrible times when he first started playing as a professional. Hentoff reported, "He told me he hadn't worked in six or eight months. He said he held imaginary club sessions in his room, to keep himself from forgetting what it is like to play in public. . . . "[11]

- *Keith Jarrett, jazz pianist:* "If I play a poor concert, I'm ruined. I've given myself toxin."[12]

- *Miles Davis, trumpet player:* Davis, world-renowned trumpet player, presents a vivid picture of himself as a craftsman who hit a dead end when he began using drugs. "I lost my sense of discipline, lost my sense of control over my life and started to drift. It wasn't like I didn't know what was happening. I did, but I didn't care any more. I had such confidence in myself that even when I was losing control I really felt I had everything under control. But your mind can play tricks on you. I guess when I started to hang like I did, it surprised a lot of people who thought I had it all together. It also surprised me."[13]

- *Phil Simms, sports announcer and former New York Giants quarterback:* "Sometime in your life, you're going to experience something difficult, like being a back-up quarterback. The thing is never to get comfortable with not playing. If you do, it'd be hard to keep your skills. By not playing, there's a greater chance of things going downhill."[14]

• *Chris Mullin*, basketball star for the Indiana Pacers and recovering alcoholic: For Mullin, the secret to fulfillment no longer comes with what he is capable of doing inside the arena: "You know basketball is very unbalanced . . . you win, you feel good. You lose, you feel bad. I can't rely on that. I've been through so much the last four years, so much insecurity, that basketball isn't the rock. It isn't the foundation for me right now. I find it hard to get excited and upset. A lot of times it's just an empty feeling . . . I know time will make it better, help me focus. I can't say I see the light at the end of the tunnel. Maybe I can see the tunnel."[15]

• *Neil Young*, singer, songwriter, and actor: Young's career was always subject to surprises and unpredictability, mainly because of his frequent shifts of mood and mind. Every statement Young makes, he may someday retract; every style of music he plays, he may eventually disavow, only to return to it again in the future; every musician he plays with, he may someday desert. The only sure statement one can make about his next step is that it won't be anything like his preceding one. As Young suggests in his famous song, "Hey, Hey, My, My," "It's better to burn out than fade away."[16]

• *Jason Robards, actor:* The popular actor Kevin Spacey saw Jason Robards as a mentor figure. He says, "Actors know a great performance when they see one because inside every actor is a great performance. A thousand things come between most actors and their dreams. There are only a handful like Jason who are given the chance, and have the courage, to give audiences the best and the worst of themselves. Again and again. So actors live through a performer like Jason Robards. He was brave. He adored the craft of acting. He clung to it and honored it. Actors can tell the difference between those who respect the written word and serve the material and those who set out to serve themselves. Jason fought to be the best."[17]

• *Bob Brookmeyer, musician:* "I've got a wonderful band and I'd like to write about three CD's worth of large-ensemble jazz music for them. They've given me a fresh palette. There's another place waiting for me. I don't know where it is yet but it's where I have to move."[18]

• *Paul Schrader, film writer:* "Having done fairly early on work I thought was valuable and I thought would endure was an enormous relief. I knew that I had done something in life. I know people my age who still have not had the sense of personal artistic rewards. And it gets to be a hard and bitter thing in your 50's and 60's never to have had the sense of 'I did something.' . . . Most artists have seven hot years and then there are seven shadow years. And the rest of their lives are living off that. Except for some. Some artists are able to reinvent themselves with second lives."[19]

- *Carl Yastrzemski, baseball player:* Walter Hriniak, a close friend of Carl Yastrzemski and Boston Red Sox batting coach, had this to say about Yastrzemski: "He worked at hitting practice until his hands bled. In the rain, in good weather, at 8 o'clock in the morning before anyone was out in the ballpark, at age 38, 39, 42. Younger players saw it and will never forget it."[20]
- *Andre Previn, pianist and conductor:* "There are many evenings, though, when I come home and start talking to the furniture. I'm offered invitations but usually I can't accept. I spend my evenings studying, working, preparing, and the times I have a casual evening off are rare. A career in music, when you get to a certain point, it takes all your efforts just to stay there."[21]
- *Merce Cunningham, dancer and choreographer:* Cunningham was asked why audiences no longer see him in his famous plastic bag routine. "Because I was in it once," he replied. Because I was in it once. For Cunningham, dance remains a continuing exploration of movement, a process rather than a fixed and reachable goal. "Every artist should ask, 'What is the point of doing what you already know?'"[22]
- *Don Sutton, Hall of Fame baseball pitcher:* Sutton was willing to move to pursue his art and passion, willing to accept being third or fourth or fifth pitcher on his staff. That's how he got to win 324 games. He pitched in a style he called "crafty."[23]
- *Larry Bird, former Boston Celtics star:* "In high school my coach told me, 'Larry, no matter how much you work at it, there's always someone out there who's working a little harder. . . . If you take 150 practice shots, he's taking 200,'" Bird recalls. "And that drove me. In the pro's, that someone was Magic Johnson. In my head, in my dreams, he was the one I was always competing with."[24]

For the competent teacher, there is always the fear of extinction, insignificance, and running out of energy, ideas, and emotional gas. In a real sense the risk of diminishing or losing the essence of one's craft is what drives the competent teacher to take risks and discover new approaches. A good teacher is on the edge and can go either way: drift away like Miles Davis or rebound like Frank Sinatra. Yet the adapting, refining, and seeking new approaches to fuel one's creativity is a slow process. It is a continuous process of asking, as Merce Cunningham does, "What is the point of doing what you already know?"

It is also a process, as artist Bruce Nauman points out, of "avoiding what is too easy."[25] Cecil Taylor describes the process well: "Sometimes I will work on my material two years before I play it. I get rid of some pieces right away, because they aren't very good. I put some away for a year, then go back to them and see how they sound. I am relaxed with the idea that not every piece I write is perfect. You improve in the smallest steps. At the end of a year, maybe you've developed an inch."[26]

Competent teachers, like Cecil Taylor, develop by inches. When you walk into their classrooms you sense the slow development that is characteristic of the competent teacher. What you observe is a setting that belongs uniquely to that teacher and defines what his or her work is all about. The furniture, the pictures, the sense of activity—all contribute to the choreography of that classroom. It is impossible to imagine this room without his or her presence and command.

A competent teacher is like the dancer Merce Cunningham: "He is not a figurehead but a doer . . . even when offstage, he stays in the back of your mind, wise and discreet, an inscrutable observer, without whose supervision everything would fall apart."[27]

One has to adapt to succeed at a craft. John Cassavetes, the late film director, put it well when he said, "You have to fight sophistication. You have to fight knowing, because once you know something, it's hard to be open and creative."[28]

Some teachers, through a process of self-analysis, awareness, understanding today's children, and constant skill building and seeking new approaches, evolve into competent teachers. This evolution is both a tangible and an intangible quality that observers see and feel when they walk into the teacher's classroom. It is tangible in the sense that they can see the skills the teacher is using to motivate the students to learn. It is intangible in the sense that the observer feels the excitement, energy, and element of risk as the competent teacher pushes, pulls, confronts, and cajoles students to stay engaged in the learning process.

No one is exempt; everyone is in the game. Everyone is seen as a valued learner and participant. Everyone has a place and is safe.

It is a physically, emotionally, and intellectually demanding craft—no different from that of musician, actor, dancer, or athlete—that often leaves the teacher spent at the end of the day. It goes on five days a week, eight to twelve hours a day, with preparation, teaching, advising, and teaming with colleagues.

As Nathan Tarkov suggests, the success of the craft depends very much on the teacher's energy, sense of humor, and ability to relate to young people. These vital qualities are not givens for every teacher entering the teaching field. They have to be attained and nurtured through a daily regimen of self-care, self-awareness, and ongoing professional development.

Surprisingly, when we talk about education reform and encouraging teachers to increase their level of competency, there is little mention of the important need for teachers to be in excellent physical, emotional, and intellectual condition throughout their careers in order to get the job done each day.

Often, competent teachers succeed in an environment where some peers reject their all-out zeal, their giving 100 percent. What competent teachers do in the classroom seems beyond others' skills and creativity. These teachers react, naturally, by being defensive and distancing themselves from the competent teacher model. They allow and even encourage distractions in the school's politics to become the main focus of their daily work.

The classroom and the students take on a secondary role, becoming a place that the teacher has to go to. It is like playing for a last-place team: you play the game but you are never a winner. The work is drudgery and the only relief comes outside the classroom, perhaps in the faculty lounge, where the talk often is about burnout, school politics, the next teacher contract, or notorious student behavior.

A major, often overlooked reason for the seeming lack of hard work and commitment to improving skills on the part of many teachers is that the craft requires much more physical, emotional, and intellectual energy than they expected when they first entered the profession. Keeping up, let alone getting better, requires personal and professional discipline. It requires a commitment to self-care, such as being in good physical condition and keeping one's personal and professional life in order. It requires self-awareness so one can remain flexible and open to new directions and approaches when needed. It also requires taking advantage of ongoing opportunities for professional development. It requires a willingness to say, in the words of Frank Sinatra, "I'm ready and I'm set"—every day.

Many of these seemingly disinterested teachers long to be more like competent teachers, to acquire the skills they need to be successful in their teaching role. They want to better their craft, to view themselves and to be viewed by their colleagues as gifted and talented teachers. They want to be shown how, not told how.

There is no more painful scene than to observe a teacher failing to teach and communicate with students. The teacher knows failure is setting in and the students are aware. Everyone in the classroom watches the clock. When will the torture end? Students act out and learning gets lost in the teacher's battle for control and survival.

Many teachers experience this situation every day. The class period and the school day can't end soon enough for them—or for their students. They are looking for ways to become better, not failures. Too often, any help available to them takes the form of telling teachers how to correct what is not working.

But telling does not show them how to go about improving their craft. This action is unsubstantial lip service, not being "our brother's keeper," not taking him by the hand and leading him through the steps, not teaching by example. Supervision, whether it is administrative or peer supervision, does not work if it is limited to telling someone what to do rather than showing him.

The mentor's task is to find ways to help teachers reach their goal of improving. It is a worthy goal. In a real sense mentors are their brother's keeper. When educators see fellow teachers and their students floundering, it is their professional responsibility to help them better their craft. When students are performing poorly, we tend to do whatever it takes to get them back on track. Teachers are learners, too, and when they experience failure, we need to get them back on track.

There are a few naturally competent teachers, but most achieve a high level of competency by hard work and effort. Competency doesn't come easy and, as the saying goes, "no pain, no gain." Those who truly master their craft do so because they understand that they are involved in a career-long creative process. Like successful musicians, actors, dancers, and athletes, they understand that the process to get good and stay good takes dedication and commitment to ongoing skill acquisition.

A competent teacher possesses some specific characteristics. Here is a summary of those characteristics:

- He works hard, understands that his craft is very demanding, and he is physically, emotionally, and intellectually ready each day.
- She develops a set of skills and a style that works to help her students learn. She sees her classroom as a laboratory in which she must experiment and change.
- He sees himself as having the skill and desire to teach every child who comes through the classroom door. His mission is dedicated to helping all his students be successful.
- She understands that failure, resistance to change, and embeddedness are necessary experiences in developing her craft.
- He experiences self-doubt and needs affirmation and feedback about his work from students, peers, parents, and supervisors.
- She is able to relinquish outworn approaches and seek new ones.
- He is focused and disciplined and does not allow detractions and events outside the classroom to interfere with his and his students' work, growth, and creativity.
- She is wary of too much good publicity about her work, which can lull her into complacency.
- He seizes every opportunity to be a mentor for colleagues and include them in his work. He has the skill, as musicians do, to perform solo so that his peers can observe firsthand how the competent teacher goes about his work. This means not rejecting colleagues who rebuff his interventions and believing that every teacher can be brought to a higher level of performance.

- She is loyal to her colleagues who are floundering and getting more than their share of criticism. The work of the competent teacher is to help them get better, to build on their existing skills and uniqueness. Ineffective teachers need to feel safe and nurtured before they can set out to risk new approaches.

The musician, craftsman, and jazz pianist Cecil Taylor puts it well: "It's rare to find musicians who are loyal and protect you and give you the space to be yourself. You learn to value them highly and give them the same space they give you. Each musician has to play his world in the framework you design for him. Improvisation is the blood that makes music go. It's a way to prepare yourself to talk responsibly with others in a musical community."[29]

- He is tough, has the will to win and the fire in his belly, but can be soft when needed. The classroom is an environment filled with cross-currents—who is in control, who is competing with whom, who is well liked, who is on the outs. It is often not a civil, orderly place, in spite of our efforts to make it so. It is explosive, as one would imagine when one puts twenty or thirty students together in one room. The competent teacher understands this phenomenon, embraces it, and avoids the naysayers who constantly wish it weren't so. Having the skill to get students to learn amid these cross-currents is a must.

- Like dancer Twyla Tharp, the competent teacher understands that "You have to believe that what you are doing is important, that you are of some use to people and what you have to offer has something good for them."

We have many competent teachers in schools throughout the country. But usually we don't hear the stories of how they developed their craft and made it work. How did they arrive at a stage in their teaching career in which they were able to look at their craft with pride and say, "I've created something and done something significant with my life"? How do they face tough classes, students, and failures, and still manage to press on? Let's match a real-world persona with our model of a competent teacher.

We have such a teacher in Irmgard Williams, a teacher in South Heights School in Henderson, Kentucky. What is she like? A semifinalist in 1995 for the Teacher of the Year in Kentucky, Ms. Williams typifies what it takes to be a competent teacher. She may not identify herself as a competent teacher, but I believe the label fits her very well. Following is a snapshot of Williams's personality, skills, and approach to teaching:

- Williams says, "I'm here to do a job . . . whatever you give me, I'll handle it. I really feel like my classroom is my ministry." And her dedication has rewards. She was semifinalist for Kentucky's Teacher of the Year award and was selected as Kentucky Education Reform Act (KERA) Fellow, a faculty member on loan to other schools in the state.

- Williams acknowledges that her teaching methods are different—better, she thinks—than they were years ago. She attributes it to a combination of new ideas generated through staff training and her own instincts about what works best for young children. She doesn't follow education reform like a zealot, however. She prefers a balanced approach that doesn't ask her to toss out tradition with the trash.

- Williams believes, "If some children can't learn one way, they can learn another."

- Like a talented artist, Williams knows that good teaching requires a continual refinement of the craft, an ability to adjust techniques as circumstances change.

- In her classroom (a multi-age primary program with twenty-four students, mostly six- and seven-year-olds, among them a child with spina bifida, a child with autism, three children with attention deficit hyperactivity disorder, four children taking Ritalin, and one child with, she suspects, Tourette's syndrome), Williams, standing five feet, two inches tall, barely rises above some of her students.

    Yet she is clearly in control. She sings, she dances, she even dons costumes on occasion, but she never lets fun and excitement give way to disorder. Like many grandmothers, Williams knows that children often need a soft lap to sit on and a homemade cookie to soothe their hurts, but they also need a steady hand to guide them. When a child misbehaves, Williams pulls him or her close to her side, cupping the child's chin in her hand with a gesture that mixes affection with discipline. She is effusive with praise, almost jolly at times, as she moves among her pupils, and she is always proper.

- All her colleagues didn't praise her success as a classroom teacher. "Well," one teacher sniffed, "how did you get to do that?" The letter Williams received from the state about not winning the Teacher of the Year award was polite but perfunctory; it didn't provide the extensive feedback that Williams so desperately wanted. "I keep wondering what I did wrong," she said. Like so many of her peers, Williams was so unaccustomed to praise that she clung to every word.

- Whatever pats on the back Williams missed in her years of teaching, she wasn't stingy with her praise for others. "You can have the mechanics, but if you don't have teachers with heart and a passion to teach, what do you have? From the top down, there ought to be something we do to show people we're proud of them. It might make better teachers if more recognition were given."[30]

Ms. Williams embodies many of the characteristics present in so many of the competent teachers:

- She works hard. She says, "I'm here to do a job."
- She believes she can teach any child who walks through her classroom door. She says, "If some children can't learn one way, they can learn another."
- She has commitment and passion about her work, referring to the classroom as her "ministry."
- Her teaching methods have improved over time. She knows that good teaching requires a continuing refinement of her craft.
- She trusts her own instincts and experiences about what works best for the children. She doesn't rely solely on the advice of education experts.
- She is in charge. She is the chief choreographer in her classroom.
- On top of these characteristics, she is human and has self-doubt. She is hurt by snide comments from peers—"How did you do that?"—and by a lack of praise and affirmation from her administrators and KERA officials. Education leaders in Kentucky tended to take the loyalty and the morale of converts for granted and concentrated their efforts on resisters. As a result, active reformers such as Williams often received few strokes, and trivial snubs became magnified.
- She is cognizant of her fellow teachers and wants to help them improve their craft. She understands the importance of affirmation in this process.

How can a team composed of a principal, department chairperson, teacher, and counselor leader mentor teachers so they evolve into competent teachers like Irmgard Williams? The following chapter focuses on the characteristics of an effective mentor. Clearly competent teachers and mentors are more alike than different and operate with similar skills. They work in different contexts—teachers serve students and mentors serve teachers—yet a common thread runs through their efforts.

NOTES

1. Stephen Schiff, "Stephen Sondheim," *The New Yorker* (8 March 1993): 77.
2. Jennifer Dunning, "Twyla Tharp Finds Virtue as a Cause for Dancing," *New York Times*, 12 January 1995, C1, C13.
3. Jacques Steinberg, "Class Wars: Clashing over Education's One True Faith," *New York Times*, 14 December 1997, sec. 4, 1.
4. Ibid.
5. Andrew Solomon, "The Jazz Martyr," *New York Times*, 9 February 1997, sec. 6, 35.
6. John Lahr, "The Imperfectionist," *The New Yorker* (12 September 1992): 68.
7. John Lahr, "Sinatra's Song," *The New Yorker* (3 November 1997): 77.
8. Whitney Balliett, "King Louis," *The New Yorker* (8 August 1994): 69.

9. Lahr, "Sinatra's Song."

10. Steve Jacobson, "Complex Illness Hit Harnisch," *Newsday*, 6 August 1997, A71.

11. Whitney Balliett, "Cecil," *The New Yorker* (5 May 1986): 104.

12. Solomon, "The Jazz Martyr," 34.

13. Whitney Balliett, "Miles," *The New Yorker* (4 December 1989): 156.

14. Bob Glauber, "Simms: I'd Retire If . . . ," *Newsday*, 19 October 1991, 85.

15. Harvey Araton, "At Age 30, Mullin's World Takes Strange New Twists," *New York Times*, 14 January 1994, C6.

16. Steve Erickson, "Neil Young . . . On a Good Day," *New York Times*, 30 July 2000, sec. 6, 26.

17. Kevin Spacey, "An Example, a Mentor, an Actor Above All," *New York Times*, 4 January 2001, AR6.

18. Terry Teachout, "Still Full of Jazz, Still Pouring It Out," *New York Times*, 19 December 1999, AR44.

19. Bernie Weintraub, "Looking Back at Two Classics," *New York Times*, 23 January 1998, E8.

20. David Faulkner, "For Yastrzemski, the Fire Still Burns," *New York Times*, 14 October 1986, C3.

21. Helen Routtencutter, "Andre Previn," *The New Yorker* (12 January 1983): 43.

22. Alastair Macaulay, "Happy Hooligan," *The New Yorker* (27 April 1992): 89.

23. Steve Jacobson, "A Complement to Sutton's Life," *Newsday*, 7 January 1998, A75.

24. Ira Berkow, "The Legend Continues . . . Bird Shoots for Coaching Greatness," *New York Times*, 10 August 1997, sec. 8, 1.

25. Andrew Solomon, "Bruce Nauman," *New York Times*, 5 March 1995, sec. 6, 28.

26. Balliett, "Cecil."

27. Ibid.

28. Philip Lopate, "Learning to Love the Ardent Chaos of Cassavetes," *New York Times*, 17 August 1997, H11.

29. Balliett, "Cecil."

30. Holly Holland, "KERA, A Tale of One Teacher," *Kappan* 79(4) (December 1997): 265–271.

Chapter Three

Characteristics of the Effective Mentor

The major goal of a mentoring program should be to help every teacher be highly skilled, self-aware, inclusive, energetic, and creative, and to carry a zest for teaching into the classroom every day. These are big goals and not easy to achieve. Nevertheless, they are important goals if we are to help all children be all they can be—intellectually, emotionally, and physically. Perhaps it is easier to put a face to these goals by describing what a successful classroom looks like. Visual descriptions help because they give concrete meaning to the word *teacher.*

Here is a vision. When you walk into a successful teacher's classroom, there is no aura of giving up, boredom, lesson plans yellowed with age, or a teacher longing for retirement. These enemies of good teaching are not present. If by chance they emerge, as they are sure to do on occasion, the teacher fiercely challenges them because they are hazardous to effective teaching. In an effective teacher's classroom, you sense the slow development of a building art form, a continuous process of trying out new material and discarding old. You observe a setting that is uniquely the teacher's and defines what his or her work is about. The furniture, pictures, flowers, space for quiet time, sense of activity and of something important going on—all contribute to the choreography at work.

The teacher is in a real sense the choreographer at work. His or her words, actions, and focus all convey a message, a lesson to be learned. He or she is not unlike the dancer Merce Cunningham, whose presence and power are described by Alastair Macaulay in Chapter 2: "He is not a figurehead but a doer . . . even when offstage he stays in back of your mind, wise, discreet and an inscrutable observer, without whose supervision everything would fall apart."

This picture presents a person involved in something worthwhile and important, a person with a gift for creating conditions in which students feel at home, energized, and committed to learning and to each other. Without this teacher's presence—in the hands of a less skilled, less caring, or less committed person—everything would indeed fall apart.

Teachers have a great responsibility to be prepared for the many challenges that arise each day. Children are our greatest natural resource. Our work as educational and community leaders is to make sure they are well prepared and up to the task of learning. This also means not letting one teacher be less than excellent because of lack of skill, support, or encouragement. School leaders talk a great deal about not letting one student fall through the cracks. Why not do the same for teachers? Many of them, as every reader of this book knows, need intervention and help to improve. Teachers want to be successful with all their students, even those who are openly or covertly resistant to help and training.

All teachers go down wrong roads and experience failure and burnout. Teachers make mistakes because of inexperience, lack of skill, or faulty assumptions about children, parents, colleagues, and school culture. But as film director Mike Nichols suggests, we must keep in mind that "nothing is written . . . it's all in the future . . . things can change . . . shift your weight . . . believe in change."[1]

Teachers can overcome their lack of experience, skill, and self-awareness with caring intervention by mentors who can dignify their worth and at the same time help them learn new, effective approaches.

The focus of this book, then, is on tackling the question of how to develop and nurture effective teachers within the school setting. We must take it "rung by rung." It is about how we can proceed to make mentoring easily accessible to teachers so they can learn how to maintain a high level of skill, an ongoing commitment to their own professional development, and a caring zest for their important work. It is about creating mentoring opportunities for teachers in every career stage—beginners, those in midcareer, and veterans in their final years of teaching. We must remind them that they share a common bond: a desire to be at the top of their professional life and successful in educating all of their students.

Teachers are more alike than different. Novice teachers, those at midcareer, and those finishing their careers all have one thing in common: the desire to be effective and recognized as people who make a difference in the lives of children, parents, and colleagues.

Ongoing mentoring of teachers at all career stages is the best way to help all teachers be master teachers. Just what is a mentor and why should this role be championed by administrators and others in leadership positions in the schools? What is the interaction like between a mentor and a teacher?

What are the key elements in the process that a successful mentor must understand to guarantee success?

Webster's Dictionary defines a mentor as a wise, loyal advisor, a loyal friend, teacher, and coach. Each of these words—wise, loyal, advisor, friend, teacher, and coach—represents a critical aspect of the mentoring role. This chapter discusses the central role wisdom plays in the mentoring process.

THE WISE MENTOR

What are the characteristics of wise mentors?

1. They are people who have experienced and understand the realities of teaching and classroom dynamics. Clearly every teacher could benefit from having a wise mentor in his corner throughout his career, someone he can count on to be there for him in good and bad times. He needs a supportive and intimate relationship with a mentor who knows firsthand the struggles, failures, and fleeting successes that mark the daily life of a teacher—someone who has been in the trenches, has the battle ribbons, and is a frequent visitor to and observer of the real world of teaching.

Mentors should be people who are known and welcomed—bearers of gifts, not grief; someone who knows the sounds and smells of the classroom without abandoning the reality that a teacher's day involves many different and demanding responses: confrontation, care, deflection, encouragement, reprimand, and more.

Mentors might best be described by lyricist Stephen Sondheim in his *Follies* hit song "I'm Still Here." Remember the lyrics? "Good times and bum times, I've seen them all . . . and I'm still here."[2] The wise mentor knows how to create a successful classroom environment and is aware of the dangers that can befall well-intentioned but poorly prepared teachers. Her own career probably has had failures and low points. It helps a mentor to speak from real experiences that helped her come to terms with her own lack of skill, prompting her to reassess and learn new ways of teaching. It does take one to know one.

2. Mentors are people who understand that teaching is hard work and that renewing oneself is not easy. On the path to becoming effective, teachers may succeed for a while without hard work but it will catch up with them. The actress Charlotte Rampling puts it well when she suggests, "As you go through life there are cycles you have to live through. There is so much apprenticeship about life that quite a lot of time you're walking in mud. Everything seems to go wrong but you keep on walking because you have to survive. Then there is a moment when things come together, as if by magic, though it's not magic. It's mostly hard work."[3]

It is hard work that has a special risk to it. The French actor Phillippe Torreton has the right idea. Torreton has a starring role as a kindergarten teacher in the film *It All Starts Today*. He suggests that being an actor prepared him to perform in front of a class but being a teacher was more challenging. He says, "A teacher is never forgiven. As actors, we perform in front of people who have bought tickets and even if they're bored, they're unlikely to make a fuss because they have paid good money. But for a teacher facing pupils who don't want to be there and are thinking only of recreation, the smallest mistake, the tiniest slip of attention, is punished. It's terrible exposure." [4]

3. Mentors are people who know that improving one's skills calls for taking risks and forging new directions. The wise mentor knows that in the work to change old habits and acquire new skills, the familiar, trusted ways of doing things are tenacious foes. Teachers, like all people, resist change. It is a normal state of mind. As in a bad marriage, we often stay with what we know even if it is not working. As the late film director John Cassavetes advises, "You have to fight sophistication. You have to fight knowing because once you know something it's hard to be open and creative." [5]

It takes courage, even being afraid that the old ways are killing you personally and professionally, to change. And the reality is that when we begin to try out new ways and new lessons, we often stumble. Our minds and bodies refuse to cooperate. We should not be surprised by this reaction. We are, after all, accustomed to the old, worn ways, like that mothballed sweater we refuse to throw away. It may be threadbare but it's comfortable and ours. The wise mentor understands that trying out new ways can be upsetting, even traumatic. It can make one afraid, anxious, and unsure.

As Dr. Seuss suggests, "You will come to a place where the streets are not marked. Some windows are lighted but mostly they're darked. A place you could sprain both your elbow and chin. Do you dare stay out? Do you dare go in? How much can you lose? How much can you win?"

Yes, change can be perilous, but that is not necessarily bad. Remember Cy Coleman's advice: "If you're going to last you can't make it fast." Change requires some upheaval. If we can ask our students to change, how can we stand by and ignore a teacher's need to change? As actor Kevin Spacey suggests, "If I am afraid, there is a good shot I'll take the part because I know it will stretch me to do better work."

The dancer and choreographer Merce Cunningham, when asked why he no longer did his famous plastic bag routine, replied, "Because I was in it once." He's done it, and now it's time for renewal and new beginnings. Mentors understand that they must continually raise the bar for their protégés by asking what the point is of doing something they already know. Is this what you want to be doing a year from now, or five years, or twenty? They know they must encourage their teachers to avoid practices that are too easy.

In a sense, the words of poet Anne Carson are the central core of an effective mentoring relationship. Carson puts it well: "You don't learn anything when you are still up on a window shelf, safe. The other way is to jump from what you know into an empty space and see where you end up. I think you only learn when you jump." [6]

Carson also suggests that "the major task of a lifetime is to avoid boredom and trafficking in the inessentials of life such as lusting for retirement and spare time." These are the enemies of every competent teacher. But taking risks is scary, so we all need someone to hold our hand as we navigate through new territory.

4. Wise mentors are people who understand that teachers all arrive in the classroom with biases, premade judgments, and prejudices. Teachers are human. They arrive at the classroom door with the mental and emotional baggage from their background, training, and learned ways of looking at the world. Mentors understand that this is not something to be afraid of or keep hidden.

The wise mentor knows to shine the spotlight on a teacher's dark side, recognizing and accepting it to set teachers free of self-imposed barriers that keep them from connecting with all students. Be human, have feelings you don't like and accept them, but don't isolate students because of color, gender, behavior, physical appearance, and so on. And don't spend all of your time with students who are more like you and are not threatening.

The wise mentor makes teachers aware that even they do not like every one of their students. Many teachers, when asked the question, "Which students in your class threaten or unnerve you?" will often answer, "Not a one. I like and respect all my kids." They may believe this or be truly unaware of their own feelings, but in fact certain students threaten and unnerve teachers. Teachers silently hope that those students are absent, move, or transfer out of their classes.

But effective mentoring helps teachers understand that their greatest potential for growth comes from accepting students who rebuff their good intentions and overtures. It is the teacher's job to figure these students out—to sweat, try new approaches, fail, be tough, be soft, do whatever it takes to win over these students.

With careful mentoring, teachers learn not to shirk off the responsibility for their lack of success with certain students. They learn to avoid an easy way out for their lack of success—blaming the parents, blaming society, asking the guidance counselor to transfer the student to another class, and so on. With effective mentoring, teachers learn to face their demons and fears to be more effective for all their students. In the process, the lessons they learn in terms of being more accepting of differences, of not attaching negative meaning to them, are not lost on the students. Efforts by the teacher to be inclusive are a major stimulus in helping students accept the variety of people they encounter in the real world.

5. *Wise mentors are people who understand that bad times, failure, or burnout can happen to every teacher, even the most successful ones.* Sometimes being a star can kill the teacher professionally. Dr. Seuss suggests that many of us land in a "useless place" and experience difficulty trying to get out. The urge to settle down and get comfortable is always with us.

Teachers may use the same lessons year after year and watch them turn yellow with age. They may allow themselves to become part of faculty-room conversation that focuses only on the negative—topics such as turbulent kids, tired teachers, pressures from parents, administrative lapses, lack of respect for teaching, and the overall lack of rewards. They may find themselves, as Ann Carson suggests, trafficking in the inessentials of life, lusting for retirement and spare time.

The wise mentor understands that by lying fallow, teachers are allowing themselves to slide into sameness. Each day becomes a repeat of the one before, and teachers begin to count the days until June and the last day of school. Thoughts of September, a new beginning, remind them of just another year.

Failure and bad times come, often unexpectedly, to even the best and brightest teachers. These negative experiences—bad days, bad years—are not reserved for teachers who do little or teachers whose kids are out of control and breaking down the classroom walls. The wise mentor knows that even the most successful teachers fall victim to failure and burnout. These can be the star teachers, looked at throughout the school district, perhaps even nationally, as models to follow. They are certainly not the types of teachers the community would expect to run into trouble professionally.

Wise mentors also understand that becoming an expert can take the teacher away from the central focus: the kids in the classroom. If teachers write a book, present at conferences, and spend more time away from the real world of the kids, they're not in the real game of school any more. They become known as the guy who got out—out of the classroom and on his way to fame and fortune. In the process, he may be losing his skills and the taste for classroom teaching. His fame and newfound accolades are based on what he did before, not what he is doing now. His currency is past experience—who he was. He has begun to read and believe his reviews. He has landed in Dr. Seuss's "useless place" but at first doesn't realize it.

It becomes easier to write and speak about teaching than to actually do it because it doesn't force him to take risks. The conference circuit—hotels, the buildup as he is introduced, the book signings, and cocktail parties after his speech—may make him soft. In politics they say, "The man is an empty suit." He finds that his craft, what he invented as a teacher, is being buried and forgotten under accumulated praise.

Wise mentors know that teachers can't be star conference presenters on the circuit and still be effective teachers. Being a star is antithetical to being a creative teacher. Stardom demands the validation, worship, acceptance, and accolades of the audience. In contrast, becoming a competent teacher requires the awareness and skills to avoid placing too heavy an emphasis on the validation, worship, acceptance, and accolades of students and parents. Applause is not always the friend of the competent teacher.

The work of the teacher is to help her students value learning. It requires creating demands and expectations for students and helping them move on, well prepared. Students need teachers who push them to be better. It is often a battle, an ongoing confrontation. Students don't need teachers who are buddies or friends.

Effective teachers need to satisfy their own need for validation themselves, not through their students. Once teachers become stars or experts, the tables get turned in the way they view their professional persona. Instead of having the focus of their work be on students looking to them for direction, they focus on looking to them for validation and praise. This is bad medicine for any teacher.

Mentors tell teachers in this situation to be cautious when leaving their classroom on a regular basis to be a presenter. They may be leaving behind the skills and the joys that come with the everyday world of teaching.

6. Wise mentors understand and value loyalty and the privacy of their protégés. Effective mentoring requires a trusting and loyal relationship. When a teacher opens the classroom door and exposes his or her teaching style and classroom persona for critique, observation, and feedback, it's often a new and risky undertaking. Having a mentor observe every aspect of one's interaction with students and parents is, as any teacher knows, a little like walking a tightrope.

Many questions emerge, as they should: "What will my mentor think about me after he sees the real me in action? Will he pick up on areas and subtle problems I have with some of my students? Will some of my students embarrass me by acting out? How much of what he observes will become a formal part of my record? Having a mentor sounded like a good idea but now that it's a reality, I'm not so sure."

A major element in creating a safety net for anxious and uncertain teachers is for the mentor to remain very trusting and loyal. What goes on in the observations, feedback, and dialog between the mentor and teacher remains between them and not a part of any formal record. They share any written assessments and then discard them. The real work of mentoring is in the observation, assessment, and setting of achievable plans to learn what new skills the teacher needs. As such, all interactions between the mentor and teacher remain private, just between them.

In a sense, the casting of this loyalty and privacy net creates a new way of doing business in the schools and a way for teachers to get the renewal they need with dignity. Being listened to, getting feedback that is useful but kind, and learning new skills even though there can be failure and setbacks involved represents a welcome change in our schools. Trust and loyalty spark renewal and allow one to take risks.

If the teacher fails there is support and a caring mentor to help, to grab the teacher so he or she doesn't fall through the cracks. This safety net represents a breath of fresh air blowing through the hallways, sweeping away the heaviness and isolation that comes with being independent as a teacher. Schools, after all, are notorious for spreading gossip and leaking private information about teachers who are having trouble. Gossip, rumors, and voyeurism feed into a negative school culture.

Teachers learn early on to keep the focus on their colleagues and off themselves. They learn early on to keep their needs, questions, failures, and successes to themselves. To share openly how one feels and the problems one has with certain students, to ask a colleague for help, and to share one's successes are not acceptable in most schools. It's simply not done. To do so is to risk being labeled as needy, soft, at risk, or burning out. It is raising the red flag and asking for sarcastic rebuttals. Teachers also learn not to shine the spotlight on themselves and talk about their successes with students. The rule is, "Don't ask for help and don't promote yourself."

Imagine for a moment a teacher sitting in a crowded room and asking for help from colleagues. "Joe, you're a veteran teacher here. People respect you. I know you're free third period. Can you come into my class and give me some clues as to why these kids are acting out so much?" Imagine teachers saying out loud that they are uncomfortable with certain students and they would like to learn how to be more accepting and tolerant.

Can you visualize a teacher talking about what a great lesson she had this morning and inviting colleagues to come in and observe her good work? In my experience, help is not forthcoming in the venue of the faculty room. It is not a priority. It is gossip, sports, and finger-pointing territory. "Spare us your needs and accomplishments": This is the faculty room mantra.

Mentoring helps reshuffle the deck, so to speak, by allowing teachers to reveal themselves and ask for help. They can right behaviors that are destroying their classes. To change, they need protection, safety, a kind ear, credible feedback and advice, models for change, and ongoing support in the process. Schools are often quick to give students who are encountering difficulties this kind of support. Why not the same for teachers?

7. Wise mentors are people who understand that the personal and family problems of students can be very painful for teachers. A wise mentor doesn't shun or ignore the impact that personal problems have on a teacher. Students from every economic level come to school looking for a safe harbor, a refuge from turmoil at home.

The most well-off students are sometimes more difficult to help because they are supposed to have found the good life in the right neighborhood. They hide their pain well. Sometimes help comes more swiftly to the poorer students because they show their needs—little money, poor clothing and nutrition, health problems, little parental support. They get the teachers' attention.

Any keen observer of school life understands that teachers experience stress as a part of the struggles of students and the students' parents. This is true for teachers in every school—urban, suburban, and rural. Personal problems of students and their families know no geographical boundaries.

The number of personal problems they confront each day often takes beginning teachers off guard. Some are lucky; they have some training in how to react and get their students the proper help. Others, though, are ill prepared for this reality. They say, "It's not my job to help," or "I wasn't trained to deal with this." Some teachers literally push needy students aside with responses that imply that the students should get help elsewhere. They shut down their own emotional reactions to the pain they see the student experiencing. Unfortunately, this response often gets support from veteran teachers who, after many years in the classroom, still remain untrained in addressing the personal problems of their students.

These veterans advise novice and midcareer teachers not to look too closely at their students and to keep a safe distance. They suggest that if the teacher responds by connecting with kids in need, he or she will be in dangerous and unknown territory. These streets are unmarked, as Dr. Seuss suggests. And maybe these veteran teachers are right because, after all, they have no training in personal intervention and the institution does not expect that they get involved. In turn, they can't be blamed nor held responsible, can they?

In the end, intervention is the responsibility of a few overwhelmed counselors and school psychologists who can never really address the needs of all the students. The result? Students' problems don't get addressed. Teachers look the other way or defer. It's a no-win situation. They know very well that the outdated system of a few counselors trying to help all the kids doesn't work. Everyone loses: the needy kids, teachers who may want to help but are untrained to respond to specific needs, and counselors who know that they can't solve all the kids' problems alone.

Wise mentors understand these dynamics. They understand that teaching is a painful business and one can never be fully prepared for what the day brings. How does a teacher respond to the personal and nonacademic issues of his students—the tears from divorce, a swollen eye from a beating, soiled clothing from lack of care, steady absences from chronic and unattended health problems, and the look of fear of being unsafe in a child's eyes?

The wise mentor knows these are issues to be addressed, not overlooked by claiming that teachers and administrators cannot do everything. He or she knows there is much teachers can do to help kids in need.

Teaching teachers to intervene and support the personal needs of a student is something every mentor can learn. The key is showing teachers that the process of addressing the personal needs of troubled students provides them with a way to get those students back into the academic fold. Students who solve their personal problems have renewed energy to devote to learning.

8. Wise mentors understand that teachers may also have problematic personal relations outside school that impact their ability to be successful. Mentoring—observing, listening, helping teachers learn new skills, developing a trusting relationship—creates conditions that allow a teacher to talk about personal issues that may be affecting daily work. It is an unexpected and significant part of the mentoring process.

Once a mentor creates a sense of trust and loyalty, it becomes apparent to teachers that anything, including their worst fears and problems, can be put on the table and discussed. It's a logical extension of the mentor and protégé's conversations. To be successful, teachers need personal lives that are intact and relatively stable. When teachers' personal lives are unbalanced their classroom performance is affected. They suffer and so do their students.

Should mentors listen to a teacher's problems that are external to the classroom? Of course. A mentor should address any issue that affects the performance of a teacher. Life's problems hit us all. Family problems, divorce, death, poor health, unruly children, alcohol and drug abuse, and career setbacks can weigh heavily on a teacher's mind. Often there are few outlets in the school for sharing these concerns. Silence is usually the keyword among coworkers, but beneath the surface a troubled teacher always gives off signs: increased sick days, isolation from colleagues, arriving late and leaving early, new and erratic classroom behavior, confrontations with students and supervisors, and addictions that he or she can no longer hide.

A wise mentor who has refined his or her listening and empathy skills allows for time and opportunity to open doors to these issues. As a human being who has experienced the travails of life himself, he is not immune to these issues and, while not a therapist, he can hear concerns, offer sources of help, and be a monitor and confidant to observe the toll these events may be taking on the teacher and his students.

Not every overture for help works. Getting help requires ongoing mentoring conversations that clearly allow the opportunity for personal issues to come to the surface. Sometimes teachers are ready to reveal and discuss a problem. They want help. Simple words work best, such as "Jim, I noticed that you've been very short, almost angry, with your kids today. It's not like you. You're usually so relaxed and having a ball. You mentioned you and your wife are splitting up. Is there anything we can talk about?"

A simple question may start your troubled teacher on the road to help. Helping teachers resolve personal issues as a way to improve teaching performance is a worthwhile investment for mentors.

Are there cautions to be addressed in this process? Of course. The primary function of mentoring is to improve teaching performance. Helping teachers resolve personal issues is a critical consideration but it should not dominate the conversations. Mentors are not therapists or counselors. If personal issues are the dominant theme, then the mentor must encourage outside help to assist the teacher, and himself, in the mentoring process.

9. *Wise mentors understand that by its very nature a successful mentoring relationship changes over time.* As a protégé grows in skill and knowledge, the mentoring relationship will change. The protégé will gradually acquire a teaching persona and stature of his or her own, and eventually be prepared to become a mentor for others.

What is it like for a mentor to nurture a new teacher and then have to move out of the way so the talent of the protégé can shine? John Lahr aptly describes the process of what happens when a mentor is no longer needed in the same way in his description of the relationship between the playwright August Wilson and Lloyd Richards, head of the Yale Drama School.

Richards says, "August was very receptive in the early days. He had a lot to learn and knew it. He was a big sponge, absorbing everything." Richards sent Wilson to the sound booth, to the paint shop, to the lighting designer. "As he learned structure . . . playwriting, really . . . he was also learning everything else," Richards said.

But as Ben Mordecai, managing director of the Yale Repertory Theater, suggests, "as Wilson grew in confidence, craft and stature, it became increasingly difficult for him to play the protégé in the partnership. The two of them artistically began drifting apart, which was, I think, a natural thing. The collaboration wasn't happening at the level it had in earlier years." As Wilson saw it, "Lloyd slowed down." But it was just as true to say that Wilson grew up.[7]

The eventual maturing of the protégé into mentor should be a cherished goal. A successful mentor should be able to freely share wisdom and skills without selfishly remaining in charge, keeping the maturing teacher stuck in the protégé role. The mentor should know when it's time to step aside and let go. Giving the protégé freedom to move on and integrate the teachings of the mentor into his or her own persona is what it's all about. The mentor must recognize when it is time to welcome the protégé into the club as colleague.

Will teachers in mentoring relationships be ready to take on such a role? No, some will resist moving into a mentoring role even though they are ready. They are comfortable as the protégé. They need to be encouraged to be on their own. That is true of any mentoring relationship. August Wilson grew up in his relationship with Lloyd Richards and he had to move on.

But we are not all Wilsons. Sometimes it seems easier to stay even though we know it is time to move on. A major theme in this book is that people tend to stay with what they know. Teachers stay with what has worked in the past. Protégés in the mentoring process tend to stay subservient, in awe of their mentors. Moving on means leaving behind what we know and are comfortable with—the aged, threadbare sweater. It is the only choice if we are to continue on the road to success.

Knowing when to end the mentor–protégé relationship is a two-way process. Mentors must be aware when the time has come to disengage. They know that to attempt to maintain the status quo of the relationship diminishes and undermines the power of the mature protégé who is ready to help others. Mentors also know that to remain as is undermines their own need to move on and mentor others. The protégé, too, must be aware of and trust his or her own feelings of being ready to move on. To stay keeps the protégé in a lesser role, forsaking a mentoring role for herself.

Disengaging is a difficult task and becomes even more difficult when the relationship has something worthwhile and life giving in it for both the mentor and the protégé. Knowing how to disengage is really what schooling is all about. Teachers have to disengage from students each June, when suddenly the school year is all over.

Teachers build close relationships with students throughout the year, and then all at once they're gone, disappearing down the hall into a yellow school bus. They may see some of the students the following year, but the students will have moved on. Teachers can try to hold onto the relationship, and some do, or they can let go, accepting the endings and committing themselves to new beginnings with new students in September. In the same way, the mentor and protégé must acknowledge the need for ending old relationships and beginning new ones as well.

10. Wise mentors understand that not every teacher will embrace mentoring. They anticipate resistance and are not surprised when the first shot is fired across their bow. They must proceed slowly.

In a sense, open, spoken resistance helps shape the leadership of a newly formed mentoring program. It gives the individuals involved a glimpse of who is opposed and what the issues are. It makes administrators aware of what teachers' perceptions are if they question whether mentoring is just another ill-planned program to get more work out of teachers. It allows administrators to gauge the depth of teachers' resistance and suggests ways of going about convincing them of the benefits to themselves of a mentoring program.

Other teachers may resist quietly, saying they support the project but still harboring a certain ambivalence. They leave themselves an open door to back out. Tacit resistance is problematic for leaders of a newly formed mentoring program because it is hard to judge where this kind of opposition stands. It is very important for mentors to engage not only those resisters who are openly opposed but also the silent resisters. Ignoring this group and failing to engage them in dialog early on can cost the program in the long run. Unanswered resistance doesn't go away; it looms over a program, always ready to raise questions of authenticity and credibility.

Why shouldn't leaders of a newly formed mentoring program be surprised by resistance? Teachers work in an environment with little novelty and change, often remaining in the same grade level and classroom for their entire careers. They work in an environment where the focus is often on the negative—which kids are misbehaving, which teachers are burning out, which parents are creating chaos, which administrators can't be trusted.

It is typical school culture that would rather point fingers at teachers' kids who aren't making it rather than engaging in promoting the notion that all teachers need to be learners and involved in ongoing mentoring and support. When invitations come along for something new like mentoring, a mentor should not be surprised that many teachers will be, and probably should be, skeptical of any plan to "mentorize" them. They are used to the humdrum, gossip, and isolation of their daily lives. They will ask, "Why do you want to help me become a better teacher?"

Many teachers have been sold on programs that were ultimately not in their best interests and benefited only outside experts. Many have a history of negative involvement with reform efforts. They have legitimate reasons to be distrustful and resistant. Wise mentors and their mentoring teams understand and accept the responsibility of getting teachers to participate in the energizing process of mentoring. Their work is to convince teachers, one by one, that it is in their own best interest to become involved.

A part of this effort to overcome resistance is also to subtly speak to the dangers involved if the school and the teachers simply drift along without any ongoing opportunity for institutional and professional renewal such as mentoring. The mentor's message is that teachers do burn out without renewal opportunities. It can happen to any staff member. We are all vulnerable if we have no mechanism for self- and institutional improvement. Institutional reform emerges when teachers become better trained and more successful in their work.

But as Dr. Seuss suggests, "un-slumping yourself is not easily done." Overcoming resistance to a mentoring program requires a clear plan. Mentors should include opportunities for teachers to openly voice their concerns; an acceptance and appreciation of these views, however negative and sometimes hurtful; a clear and proactive response as to why teachers should participate; a strong will; tough skin; and the hard work involved in continuing to sell and guide the program through periodic setbacks. Quiet persistence, keeping open the potential for change, and being available are the ingredients for success.

Requiring participation in mentoring is not enough. Teachers must see this process as helpful and be willing to give themselves over to it professionally.

11. Wise mentors possess highly developed communication skills that can be used in a variety of interactions with protégés. Mentors know how to listen, be nonjudgmental, and provide useful feedback and modeling that can act as a guide for improvement. They know how to assess the classroom skills of their protégés, join with them in a dialog on how to improve their skills, and remain an active source of support as they inch along the road to becoming master teachers.

Successful mentors know how to intervene, listen, be nonjudgmental, give constructive and accurate feedback, confront failure-causing behaviors, support successful and failed efforts to change, be available for counseling on educational and personal issues, and be a general advocate for their protégés. They know how to offer hope and encouragement and, at times, critical assessment—for example, needed feedback to address behaviors that may be destroying the teacher and the class. They know how to say the right words to help teachers become aware of these behaviors and the work that needs to be done to make corrections.

Why is caring and supportive feedback so important? It is hard for teachers, or any worker, to improve in an atmosphere that is caustic. A Gallup Organization study completed in 2000 shows that most workers rate having a caring boss even higher than money or fringe benefits. In interviews with two million employees at 700 companies, the study found that how long employees stay with a company and how productive they are there is determined by their relationship with their immediate supervisor. [8]

Caring involves speaking the truth and giving feedback that is direct. Sometimes it becomes apparent that a teacher needs to think about a career change or retirement. The wise mentor knows that the potential to improve one's skills professionally is a necessary component of a job. Seymour Sarason suggests:

> The ingredients of job satisfaction . . . are many and interacting, but there is one which tends to have devastating effects, and that is when one's work is no longer challenging, or interesting, or unpredictable; one knows from one day to the next, from one month to the next, what one will be doing and this stretches into an indefinite future. It matters little if what one does is valuable to others or even if others regard it as interesting and even fascinating. If one has mastered one's task, if that mastery does not lead to new challenges, if one's job no longer is experienced

as interesting, if one feels one has learned as much as one will in that job, one is in trouble and it compounds difficulties from any other sources.

I am talking about not only so-called lower-level jobs but higher ones as well. I have seen too many professionals who are bored by their work to exempt them from those generalizations. Conflicts within a setting around power, status, and money are in some measure a consequence of the fact that people no longer find their jobs intrinsically interesting. [9]

Jean Ciavonne, a retired teacher from Colorado Springs, Colorado, describes how sometimes the enchantment related to teaching fades. She says, "For more than eighteen years, teaching was a wonderfully satisfying experience and I loved every minute of it, almost. How did I know when the enchantment disappeared? For me it was not a sudden revelation. Correcting papers began to seem like drudgery. After parent conferences I was not cherishing remarks from gracious parents. I didn't suddenly dislike children. It was just that the things that some of them did annoyed me more." [10]

Mentoring veteran teachers almost always involves issues related to retirement and the decision to stay or to go. Like Ciavonne, teachers encounter a growing sense of something changing in their responses to children. The options of renewing or reinventing themselves or leaving altogether become a daily consideration. Questions such as these usually are not raised in the faculty room or administrator–teacher supervision meetings. Wise mentors need to be attuned to such questions and help veteran teachers talk out loud about the choices available, to say it's OK to have these thoughts and to ask, "How do you think you should proceed?"

The mentor's feedback takes many different forms. Some of it is very pragmatic. As John S. Holloway suggests, "trained mentors help novice teachers plan lessons, assist them in gathering information about best practices, observe the new teachers' classes. The novice teacher reflects on their practice and applies what they have learned to future lessons." [11] The mentor advises and guides them on how to take care of the nitty-gritty aspects of classroom life that, if unattended to, will create mischief.

Holloway also suggests that the ability of mentors to frame their discussions with protégés around the issues of teaching and learning is a vital part of the feedback and learning process. He reports on a 1999 study by Giebelhausa and Bowman of a large-scale mentoring program, Pathwise, a formal induction program developed by the Educational Testing Service (ETS) for prospective teachers and their mentors.

The purpose of the study was to learn whether a specific model for framing discussions on teaching and learning would nurture and develop teachers' pedagogical skills. Data analysis indicated that prospective teachers who were assigned mentors trained in discussion demonstrated more complete and effective planning, more effective classroom instruction, and a higher level of reflection on practice.

Honest, accurate feedback calls upon mentors to create a climate that encourages their protégés to talk about issues beyond the everyday details of classroom life. These might include issues related to career development, retirement, and one's personal life and well being, issues that impact on the protégé's daily performance. There are different kinds of discussion, more personal discussions that have a deeper meaning for the protégé and require an approach from the mentor framed by gentleness, acceptance, caring, and support. Caring, direct feedback is often necessary in helping protégés deal with emotional and health issues.

The movie *Wit,* directed by Mike Nichols and starring the actress Emma Thompson, gives us insight into how mentors should and should not behave. This is a story about Vivian, a literary scholar, and her last battle with cancer. The play begins with Vivian's doctor staring into the camera in extreme close-up, blurting, "You have cancer." More indignities quickly follow. In the hospital Vivian encounters a young doctor who is callow and insensitive. These are certainly not helpful mentors.

Vivian also meets a nurse, Susie, who has great compassion for her. Near the end of her struggle, Vivian is visited by her aged mentor, E. M. Ashford. Played by Eileen Atkins, Ashford climbs into bed with Vivian, cradles her, and reads from a children's book. Ms. Atkins' fragility and gentleness make the scene shattering and heartbreaking. [12]

Get the picture? Caring feedback is not always in the words spoken. It is also in the compassion, the eyes, shown by the Susies of the world toward a person whose world is suddenly falling apart, and in the spontaneous acts of people like Ashford to make contact and be part of what the protégé is experiencing, even in death. Being fragile and gentle are skills to be remembered, honed, and used by every mentor when the time is right.

12. Mentors are people who know how to take care of themselves. They know how to confront their own anxieties about the enormous responsibilities involved with mentoring colleagues, and in turn are physically and emotionally up to the mentoring task. A major message mentors impart to their protégés is teaching them that self-care is an important part of ongoing professional development. The mentor's message is, "You can't be a master teacher if you're not physically and emotionally prepared for the hard work teaching requires every day." Not being ready for the daily demands leaves teachers at risk and vulnerable to poor performance, ill-timed reactions, and burnout.

Mentors are people who know how to take care of themselves. They understand that it is difficult for educators to lead and be models when their own personal issues control and overshadow their efforts. They must be constantly vigilant, working to keep their personal life, health, and emotional well-being under control. They know how to confront their own anxieties about the enormous responsibilities involved with mentoring colleagues, and in turn are physically and emotionally up to the mentoring task.

A major message mentors impart to their protégés is teaching them that self-care is an important part of ongoing professional development. Not being ready for the daily demands of teaching leaves teachers at risk and vulnerable to poor performance and burnout.

Effective mentors also understand they are not, and never will be, skilled in every area of mentoring. Some areas of interaction with protégés may test their communication skills. But they are aware of their humanness and, like their protégés in relationships with students, vulnerable to reactions that may surprise and even threaten them. For example, there will be teachers in the mentoring process to whom mentors have difficulty relating.

Mentors, too, arrive at the mentoring door with the emotional baggage of their life experiences. While they are aware of their own biases and the people and issues they tend to avoid, mentors, like teachers with students, find communication with some protégés difficult.

Knowing and accepting oneself, the positive and the dark side, doesn't eliminate the threatening feelings one can experience in relating to others who are different and difficult to help. It requires ongoing discipline and focus. Mentors know that they can't help teachers relate to students who are different and difficult to help if they themselves are unable or unwilling to go through the same process with a protégé. Simply put, you have to walk the walk, not just talk the talk. Talking to protégés about how they should behave without having to do it themselves isn't fair, is it?

In order to maintain a high level of self-care, awareness, and insight into interactions with protégés, it is important to have easy access to credible feedback. That means having a mentoring team in place made up of fellow administrators, teacher and counselor leaders, and mentors themselves who serve as a support group for each other. People in leadership roles need easily accessible resources alongside which they can compare their experiences. They need to continually assess whether they are communicating effectively with their protégés or allowing themselves to create barriers that will cause trouble within their relationship.

Mentors need to observe and take notice of each other—be their brother's keeper, so to speak. When a mentor observes or hears a fellow mentor becoming combative, he or she needs to intervene and help the colleague sort things out. What are the issues causing the conflict? Is there another direction to take? This is not therapy. It's simply helping each other stay focused and on course.

13. Mentors have a keen understanding of aging and career development. Teachers often find themselves stuck in the one classroom/one school/one district career trap. Looking forward to a professional life in which one will remain in the same geographical place with little opportunity for novelty and change can weigh heavily on one's enthusiasm and zest for teaching.

Unfortunately, the reality for many teachers is that this is the way they will live out their professional lives. Skilled mentors understand that they need to be alert to teachers' comments about aging and lack of career change.

Effective mentoring can be a positive force in helping teachers redefine their careers without necessarily having to move into new job areas such as counseling or administration, where their teaching talents might not be well suited. Helping teachers focus on what they are doing well, giving them praise and acknowledgement for their good work, helping them reassess their skills and select new areas for skill acquisition, and helping them mentor other teachers may in fact provide a much more exciting way of viewing their work than abandoning the classroom for what seems to be a new direction.

Many administrators and counselors who have left the classroom, as they labor in intensive and pressured jobs, often long to return to those days when they worked with students. Clearly, helping teachers learn how to mentor other teachers keeps them active in their own classrooms but also gives them a new status in the school and community. It has a nice ring: a teacher of kids and a teacher of teachers.

Novel career change does exist. The Career in Teaching Program in the Cincinnati public schools is living proof that this kind of process is doable. As Susan Keiffer-Brown and Kathleen Ware suggest, teaching remains one of the few professions where novices have the same responsibility as twenty-five year veterans. [13]

This situation poses problems on two fronts. Prospective and beginning teachers are overwhelmed by the challenges of working with students and experienced teachers have only one option if they want broader professional responsibilities and substantially higher salaries—to leave the classroom for administrative positions.

The Cincinnati Career in Teaching Program addresses these problems in a systematic way. The Peer Assistance and Evaluation Program assigns all new hires to consulting teachers, advanced or accomplished teachers in the same subject or grade level who are released from classroom duties to work with up to fourteen teachers.

Consulting teachers orient inductees to the district schools, assist them with curriculum and content development, and mentor their teaching skills. Experienced teachers who exhibit serious teaching deficiencies may also be assigned to the consulting teacher. Consulting teachers collaborate in planning lessons, team teach, and hold monthly groups on issues such as managing diverse classrooms, teaching toward the district's standards for learning, and creating multiple forms of student assessment.

In this way, new teachers receive support from both the consulting teachers and colleagues. This approach points to the underlying philosophy of the program. Teachers in the district receive the support and mentoring necessary for professional improvement.

Holly M. Bartunek wisely suggests a model that offers mentors a useful resource in understanding the developmental needs of teachers. This model views a teacher's career as moving within a cycle that includes the following stages:

Pre-service
Induction
Competency building
Enthusiastic and growing
Career frustration
Stable and stagnant
Career wind-down
Career exit[14]

These stages are dynamically influenced by personal environmental factors such as family demands and organizational and environmental factors such as societal expectations. This model can help remind effective mentors that novice, midcareer, and veteran teachers do indeed have different issues to confront. For example, a novice teacher needs safety, routine, and set boundaries. However, these same parameters may be the kiss of death for experienced midcareer teachers who need novelty, risk, and a career alternative such as mentoring to remain energized and committed. Being "stable and stagnant" has the smell of decay for them.

Veteran teachers nearing retirement need a mentoring process that encourages them to reflect on the help they gave to literally thousands of students and parents. They need to be reminded that their presence mattered a great deal to many people. Veteran teachers also need support to map out where they are headed next. A new career? A move to a new locale? They need gentle questioning concerning what's next.

Poor retirement planning can leave newly retired teachers suddenly alone without the safety, routine, and set of boundaries they once knew. They need support in how to say goodbye, walk out the door, and embrace their new space. Honoring and remembering retired teachers can help prepare them for a positive exit, helping them not to look back

14. Mentors have finely honed political skills and can sell the mentoring program to others and convince them to get involved. Effective mentors must have good selling skills. They are, after all, selling a new product. They want teachers to open up their hearts and their minds to this proposal. In a sense, their mission is to go out among the people, door-to-door if you will, and, like a politician, speak the words that make it easy for teachers to say, "I'll join."

They have to clearly spell out what is in it for people. They have to use every forum and venue—faculty meetings, team meetings, coffee klatches, faculty room dialog, going to a local bar for a drink, phone calls to teachers at home, and the like—to communicate a core element of the program: the mentoring process shouldn't be confined to one room in a school.

It's a lot like running an election, in that mentors need to try to turn out as many positive votes and as much enthusiasm for the project as they can. Mentors have to believe in the program and believe that the staff really needs mentoring to help them be better teachers. Mentors have to believe that every teacher, even the most resistant and arrogant, wants a way out of being ineffective. The beauty of selling a program like mentoring is that it offers everyone a chance for a new beginning.

15. Mentors understand that sometimes mentoring relationships don't work out. Perhaps both sides, the mentor and protégé, have both worked very hard to relate but in the end encounter barriers too difficult to overcome. These are relationships that might have worked out with more awareness, understanding, and intervention skills, but for some reason never successfully got off the ground. Maybe there was too much intimacy, contact, and reliance involved in the failed relationship.

Too many of these characteristics on the part of the mentor, the protégé, or both can create a problem and prove to be a risk to the ultimate goal of mentoring—readying the protégé to be self-reliant. Mentors—like teachers who seek spend too much time with their favorite students while ignoring the needs of other students—can easily find themselves too involved with protégés who court their favor and involvement.

The reverse can be true, where the mentor unconsciously courts the favor and involvement of the protégé. In these situations, a relationship is established early that is comfortable, safe, and enjoyable. Risks often hide in these relationships that become too intimate because they can easily move from being relationships with professional boundaries to a more personal relationship in which the goals of a mentoring program are secondary to the friendship the mentor and protégé form.

The mentoring team needs to reinforce the dangers involved in becoming too involved with protégés, and they need to intervene when they observe a mentor going down that road. In some cases mentors need to end the relationship and a protégé has to be reassigned. Is this a common problem? No, but it can happen in any mentoring program. It's best to be prepared and immediately address the issue with training and ongoing monitoring.

The match between mentor and protégé brings together two people with different backgrounds, cultures, and ways of looking at life. At first, these relationships might seem like poor matches. Sometimes the mentor's personality and mentoring skills simply don't work in relation to the protégé. The mentor's intervention seems to raise resistance rather than to create openings for positive communication.

An honest assessment by a mentor aware of the problem would rightly focus on ways he or she has to learn new skills to save this floundering relationship. Not all mentors have this level of awareness or are connected to a mentoring team that could help them think through new alternatives, and the mentoring relationship may end because the differences between mentor and protégé are never solved. Mentors are perhaps flawed as a result because they fear they are likely to repeat this negative performance with another protégé whose different culture and background could threaten the relationship.

These are mentoring relationships that don't have to fail. Education, awareness, new skill acquisition, and monitoring by colleagues can quickly turn these relationships into success stories. Failure to act and leaving these mentors to wrestle with their own problems results in failed mentoring relationships that might have succeeded.

We learn more about ourselves and improve our skills when we are at last able to connect with colleagues and students who come out of a different experience from ours. In the process we learn to understand them and accept them and become a more caring school community.

16. Mentors understand that the mentoring process involves huge professional and personal benefits. Effective mentoring works both ways. It helps teachers become more aware, trusting, effective, and valued by themselves and by colleagues.

But the process also helps the mentor. Engaging teachers in one-on-one dialog about their work, offering useful suggestions, and supporting efforts to change can be very animating for mentors. It provides them with the opportunity to know teachers in an intimate and personal way that no supervisory or faculty meeting could offer. It also gives mentors the opportunity for teachers to know them—their skills, the way they try to improve and renew themselves, their professional and personal goals, and their own successes.

It also provides mentors with the opportunity to get direct feedback from teachers on how they are doing as a mentor. Is the mentor an effective listener? Is he or she nonjudgmental? Is he or she able to give positive feedback? Is he or she able to model effective teaching skills? Is he or she able to help teachers confront sensitive issues such as gender and race? Is he or she caring and supportive?

In the mentoring process the mentor too becomes a learner and opens himself to feedback from his protégés that will help him be more effective. It no doubt comes as a surprise to teachers that mentors also considers themselves learners and want feedback about their performance so they can improve and renew themselves, as well.

Too often in the supervision process the only people who are observed and get feedback are the teachers. There is no place or opportunity for administrators, department chairs, and teacher leaders who do supervision work to get feedback for themselves from teachers. Some may not want feedback; it is not the usual way of doing business. But it does cut them off from growth and real contact with the people they are presumably helping. Elizabeth McCay, assistant professor of educational leadership at Virginia Commonwealth University, suggests:

> Recent efforts in school reform have focused more attention on the professional development of teachers than on the learning needs of school leaders, especially principals who direct the process of change. The isolation that many principals feel often hinders their ability to learn. Feedback from colleagues within the district is often not objective. The staff may fear retribution. Principals need objective, safe . . . feedback. . . . Before principals can take on the dynamic challenges of school reform however, they must become active learners, willing to change their own thinking and practices as they lead others in implementing reform. [15]

In the mentoring process the deck of learning is reshuffled. Mentors, whether they be administrators, department chairs, teacher leaders, or counselor leaders, now become co-learners with their protégés, echoing the promise that mentoring can indeed help every educator in the school setting be a continuous learner throughout his or her career. Everyone is in the game of renewal, an idea that, when accepted throughout the school, leads to a personal, professional, and institutional breath of fresh air.

John S. Holloway describes research in which both mentors and their protégés responded favorably to the mentoring process. Neil Scott analyzed the effects of the Beginning Teacher Induction Program in New Brunswick, Canada, and found that 96 percent of beginning teachers and 98 percent of experienced teacher mentors felt they benefited from the program. The experienced teachers were enthusiastic because they believed that mentoring allowed them to help others improve themselves, receive respect, develop collegiality, and profit from the novice teachers' fresh ideas and energy.

When mentors—whether they are administrators, teachers, or counselors—become co-learners it creates an opportunity for career and personal rebirth. In becoming co-learners with their protégés, they too jump off their isolated ledges into the excitement of personal and professional renewal.

17. Mentors understand how to help teachers find and define their best teaching selves. In a real sense, the role of mentors is to help their protégés find their best teaching selves, the professional persona that works best for them. It is a process that encourages the evolving teacher to look within herself, identifying strengths as well as areas that need improvement in order to find her own teaching voice.

Mentors encourage teachers to observe colleagues and borrow techniques, but not to blindly become a clone. Building a teaching self modeled on the skills and performance of colleagues is risky. As Arthur Combs suggests:

> The good teacher is not one who behaves in a given way. He is an artist, skillful in facilitating effective growth in students. To accomplish this he must use methods appropriate to the complex circumstances he is involved in. His methods must fit the goals he seeks, the children he is working with, the philosophy he is guided by. . . . The good teacher is no carbon copy but possesses something intensely and personally his own. [16]

Donald Cruickshank addresses the need to have teachers find their best teaching selves. He cites Robert Travers, who suggests that teachers must be always ready to modify their role and search for material and sources within themselves through which the modified role can be achieved. Travers calls for a mentor or "role trainer" to help teachers gain insight into their role by encouraging them to be like actors and become totally immersed in their unique role rather than simply saying the correct words and performing the correct actions. He cautions against becoming a robot or a clone and following the role modeled by a particular teacher. The critical question asked by the mentor is, "What do you, as a unique person, bring to our students, staff, and school, and how can we help you to shine this light?" [17]

18. Wise mentors understand that an important task of the mentor is helping protégés clarify the many roles they play in the classroom, school, and community. The mentor understands that teaching is not an easy job and is not one easily mastered without help. Teachers must play many roles and show many faces. Donald Cruickshank highlights some of these roles that have emerged from school reform proposals:

- A *competent teacher* is a teacher who knows what good or effective K–12 practitioners do and they are able to demonstrate these abilities.
- A *student of teaching* is a teacher who is reflective; that is, he or she gives careful consideration to the act of teaching.
- A *community builder* is a teacher who is humane and who enhances the self-image of students and members of the community.
- An *artist* is a teacher who knows who he is, what he is like, and how he can use his unique talent to enhance student learning.
- A *concerned teacher* is more concerned with the needs of students and less concerned with her own needs.
- An *actor* is a teacher who understands the role of effective classroom practitioners and has acquired the abilities to perform it well.
- A *problem solver/decision maker* is a teacher able to resolve problems and make decisions in a way in which benefits accrue to all parties.

- An *enlightened teacher* is well educated and concerned primarily with students becoming well educated.
- A *culturally responsible teacher* is ready and able to work with diverse students in diverse communities.
- An *inquiring teacher* directly engages in inquiry related to teaching and learning.[18]

Cruickshank's data serves to remind us that becoming a competent teacher requires the acquisition of many different roles and skills. This process of acquiring roles and skills also requires motivation, encouragement, and on-going opportunity to sustain and improve these skills throughout one's career. Clearly, most teachers cannot develop these roles and skills on their own or overnight. They need mentors to teach and support them.

19. Mentors understand that they must bring some joy, energy, humor, and lightness to the mentoring relationship. It is important for mentors to keep in mind one axiom about a good school: it's a fun place to be and people—students, teachers, parents, and even administrators—are having a good time. Maybe not every day; after all, crises and bad times do come to the best of schools. But overall there is a lot of laughter, celebration, and hanging out when the work of the day is accomplished. We see students, staff, and administrators being themselves, not aloof professionals clinging to their degrees and professional status. Mentors need to foster this kind of climate with their protégés. The work of teaching is serious and the consequences of our actions are vitally important.

But taking ourselves too seriously, forgetting that it is fun to be around kids, and living totally by the rules can result in a big dose of teacher boredom. What student wants to go to a class where everything is serious, where no laughs are allowed, where the day is all about getting ready for SATs, state tests, and finals?

An important aspect of the work of mentoring is teaching protégés to be balanced—not too serious, yet not too undisciplined. That means encouraging protégés not to have too many rules. A mentor's mantra—and consequently, the teacher's—is, "Leave room for play, for the unexpected, for the Catch-22, M.A.S.H., One Flew over the Cuckoo's Nest issues that take place in a school every day."

One way to get this message across to protégés is for the mentors not to have too many rules themselves, both as a school leader and as a mentor. What is this kind of behavior like? Herman Edwards, former coach of the New York Jets football team, put it well when he said:

> I don't believe in too many rules. I believe in high expectations and making those known individually. I expect people to handle themselves and if they don't then we have to talk. I believe in an open environment because it's good for the team and

good for the game. I believe in having coaches who are teachers and who display energy. I believe that players are the system and that coaches can play a greater role in ensuring that players do not fail. I always want our players to understand that everything we do here will be designed toward them being able to use their talents. It's almost like if you go to a park and watch kids play. They only have a couple of plays that they drew up in the sand and they use their talents from there. Sure, we can make it as complicated as we like, but the key is to simplify and let the talent surface. Coach to their talent and strengths. We will do that here and off the field. . . . I believe in these words. . . . Be you. It's good enough. [19]

This is good advice for mentors and teachers. Keep it simple. Let the talent surface. Don't let students and teachers be caught up in complicated rules and overly high expectations. In Edwards' words, "Be you. It's good enough."

Mentors need to be balanced in their training with teachers. They need to arrive at the mentoring sessions ready for interaction that is serious while at the same time being prepared for lightness and a few laughs. Focus on the nuts and bolts of improvement but leave room for a little self-deprecation and learn to laugh at your mistakes and yourselves.

This is how teacher lore is created, with stories and tales from the classroom that teachers remember because they are so bizarre that they have to laugh at themselves or cry. Every teacher has some of these experiences. Wise mentors know laughter sometimes softens bad landings.

20. Mentors understand that their lack of knowledge about every subject and grade level does not reduce mentoring effectiveness. In the real world of mentoring, it is not possible to match a protégé with a mentor who is completely knowledgeable about his or her subject matter or grade level issues. This lack of knowledge should not be a barrier to effective mentoring. What really counts is the mentor's understanding of classroom dynamics and effective teaching. Skilled mentors see clearly when a teacher is zeroed in on his or her lesson and students, and knows when students are into it—zoomed in on the teacher and his or her delivery. There is a sense of excitement, rhythm, and risk in the air, an atmosphere that says "We all want to be here and we're loving this moment." The subject matter or grade level becomes irrelevant. What matters is that learning is taking place for both the students and teacher.

On the other hand, mentors also see clearly when teachers are not zeroed in on the lesson and their students. Instead of excitement, rhythm, and risk in the air, the classroom becomes a disjointed, even unbalanced climate in which the teacher and students are at odds, finding no middle ground or harmony. Teachers and students look for a way out, an early exit from the stress of the classroom. They are like symphony musicians who have never practiced together; their music doesn't connect. Here the subject matter becomes irrelevant; it remains elusive. The class never seems to get to the point where knowledge and learning take place. The classroom lacks safety, routine, respect, and boundaries.

Many classroom management issues need to be addressed before the students become learners. It's like an abusive family acting out. Order and safety must be restored before any semblance of family life—caring, respect, and love—can emerge.

Yes, knowledge of subject matter is useful, but I believe that understanding what constitutes effective teaching is a higher priority, a priority that helps mentors support what is working and see it clearly. It is a priority that requires mentors to intervene when they observe what is not working, when they see an imbalance that needs to be corrected.

21. Wise mentors understand that they have to teach their protégés how to create ongoing sources of support—a social network—to enhance learning and renewal, and in their mentoring role create "mentoring hubs" where informal learning and exchange are ongoing and easily accessible. At some point, mentoring reaches a conclusion. The mentor and protégé must part company and move on to other tasks. It is critical for the protégé to have established his or her own support and learning network: colleagues he or she likes to spend time with, talk about new ideas with, and seek expert advice from.

Many teachers lack a supportive network. They spend time with students, in faculty rooms, and at meetings, but often lack informal, ongoing contact with colleagues who can be supportive. Laurence Prusack and Don Cohen, authors of *In Good Company*, make the case that successful businesses pay loving attention to commonplace conversations and everyday life. They suggest that telling and listening to stories, chatting, and sharing a little gossip are the main ways that people in organizations come to trust and understand one another.

Because successful businesses rely on a foundation of trust, commitment, and novelty, these authors have concluded that they possess an enormous but untapped asset in the wisdom accumulated by workers over decades of experience. The challenge is creating an organizational setting in which workers come together on a regular basis to exchange conversation and pick each other's brains.

Prusack and Cohen point out that in 1998 Alcoa, the aluminum giant, made a physical investment in social capital by moving its headquarters from a thirty-one-story tower to an eight-story building that featured open offices, glass-walled conference rooms, and escalators instead of elevators. Each floor had a family-style kitchen to encourage workers to mingle. Executives at Oticon, a maker of hearing aids, noted that people often paused to talk as they passed on the stairs, so Oticon rebuilt its office to create broad stairwell landings with coffee machines and places to sit. [20]

But as Malcolm Gladwell suggests, while innovation and the best ideas arise out of casual contact among different groups in the company, getting people in a workplace to bump into people from other departments is not as easy as it looks.

Gladwell describes the work of a researcher at MIT named Thomas Allen who conducted a decade-long study of the way in which engineers communicated in research laboratories.[21] Allen found that the likelihood that any two people will communicate drops off dramatically as the distance between their desks increases. A worker is four times more likely to communicate with someone who sits six feet away than with someone who sits sixty feet away. People who sit seventy-five feet apart hardly talk at all.

Allen also found that when people weren't talking to those in their immediate vicinity, many spent time talking to people outside their company. He concluded that it was actually easier to make the outside call than walk across the hallway.

There is a subtle but powerful message in this data that speaks to the difficulty isolated workers like teachers face in their desire to be lifelong learners. If you constantly ask for advice or guidance from people, you may risk losing prestige. Colleagues might think the teacher is incompetent. The people teachers are asking for advice might get annoyed. Calling an outsider avoids these problems. Allen's engineers were far too willing to go outside the company to ask for advice and new ideas. I believe that is the case with many teachers.

The wise mentor understands the need to help his protégés to identify where and from whom to get advice. After all, many schools, particularly secondary schools, have huge campuses, some with student populations of 2,500 or more. Mentors need to query their protégés on whom they spend time with, whom they talk to about new ideas, and where they get their expert advice.

In other words, mentors should ask teachers to describe their network for support and where they go to get this exchange. Teachers should describe how they overcome the barriers that keep them isolated and dependent on themselves or, as in Allen's case of engineers, an outside person who doesn't really understand their work setting. The positive results of successful mentoring can quickly dissipate without supportive networks in place.

Finally, mentors should work to create informal gatherings and forums where colleagues can easily come together to exchange ideas. I call these gathering "mentoring hubs" because they are an extension of the one-on-one mentoring process. What are these mentoring hubs like?

Schools don't have the resources to build new settings, like Alcoa did, that encourage more face-to-face exchange. However, teachers can be invited to before-school and after-school coffee klatches, lunchtime brown bag discussions, and school meetings featuring topics related to teacher renewal.

The idea is to help teachers stay in close contact with each other in diverse environments and to create hubs that foster professional exchange and growth, places to try out new ideas with colleagues and ask each other, "What's stopping you?"

To accomplish this task, mentors need to look at their schools in new ways, not just as a series of classrooms and offices, a physical space. They must create a personal vision of where, when, and how ongoing learning and renewal can take place, and gain the necessary support for such interactions. They must create places that have a professional feel where people of service—and that is what teachers are—can gather, places of opportunity that can open new doors, the antithesis of the professionally eroding conversations of the faculty room.

Creating hubs of learning in the school setting can be a simple undertaking on a small scale. As Emitai Etzioni suggests, in order to increase a sense of community and connectedness, "we need to provide people shared space to mingle. It does not require a grand social science study to note that when chairs are placed in empty spaces in many public buildings next to elevators, people are often found there 'visiting.' The same holds true for other places to sit, from park benches to lounges in public libraries."[22]

In schools this means creating new ways for people to come together by turning an empty office or classroom into a lounge area with a new or used sofa, chairs, and a coffeepot—a teachers' place to launch new ideas.

In a real sense, then, mentors are the pulse-takers of the school. They have direct links to the many teachers and formal and informal networks these teachers create. In the mentoring process, one-on-one meetings with teachers elicit a great deal of data about their work experience. Teachers raise issues such as lack of trust, boredom, being trapped, and a strong desire for novelty and stimulation. This data provides clues as to whether the school setting is meeting the needs of teachers. In other words, is the school setting providing conditions that allow teachers to experience growth, differentiation, and diversity throughout their careers? Mentors are well positioned to translate this data into ongoing hubs of learning that provide opportunities for novelty, communication, and testing of new ideas, places where teachers go to get and give information in an environment that allows easy access and exchange.

22. Mentors have a sense of the history of the school and the good work that has gone on there. One of the most troubling aspects of modern school life is the lack of tribute and respect for former teachers. There are usually no pictures of teachers who have served in the school, no brief history of their contributions—where they served, subject or grade taught, extracurricular activities such as coaching, degrees awarded, not even a memorial wall listing their names. It is as if they vanish when they retire or leave the school for another position.

The same can be said of teachers currently serving in the school; they too lack visible recognition that they are part of the school community, yet without their presence the school community would be diminished.

Wise mentors understand the important role of honoring former teachers and highlighting the part each current teacher plays in making the school an exciting and caring setting. They understand that teachers want to feel they are making a significant contribution and want to be remembered for these contributions. With this in mind they use their mentoring role to establish visible connections between former and current teachers in the school, such as a memorial wall. When teachers walk through the hallways and see memorials to former teachers who labored on the front lines of the classrooms, they feel a sense of history, continuity, belonging to an ongoing community of teachers, and reassurance that they too will have an honored place when they move on. Mentors also help create a living memorial wall for current teachers and other members of the staff, a visible testament that it takes many different professionals and support staff to create a positive school community and an acknowledgement that each person counts, students included.

Matthew King speaks to the need for this kind of honoring and recognition system. He describes a project to erect a wall of recognition at Lincoln-Sudbury Regional High School in Sudbury, Massachusetts. The purpose is to "establish a tradition of recognizing and celebrating the lives of people who have made enduring contributions to Lincoln-Sudbury. This tradition should help students understand and value the lives of people whose commitment has made the school a special place. Those eligible will be faculty, administrators, staff, and school committee members who have provided vision, direction, and contributions to students, faculty and the life of the school."

Among those selected was Harriet Rogers (director of the drama department and English teacher, 1965–1978) who created the Lincoln-Sudbury drama program. An Emmy winner, "she was no prima donna. Sneaker-clad and chewing gum, she coached hundreds of students in a thirteen-year string of outstanding productions."

Also chosen was Paul Mitchell (history teacher, 1957–1990, department chairman, 1960–1979) who "lectured, led, and dazzled his students with the spectacular history of Russia. His course emphasized self-exploration as students kept journals and even graded themselves."

Another choice was former Superintendent C. Newton Heath (superintendent, 1957–1964), who guided the creation of Lincoln-Sudbury as a regional high school. "'Doc' interviewed every teacher, met with every committee, and knew every student. His confidence and determination created a nurturing atmosphere and his trust inspired loyalty."

King wisely notes that these kinds of programs help to build strong schools. As he suggests, "schools that get results are places where adults work hard, focus on improvement, and believe they make a difference in the lives of their students. . . . We also know that schools with strong, positive cultures are places where rituals and traditions celebrate innovation and commitment, where an informal network of heroes inspires colleagues and where a pervasive sense of shared purpose and an ethos of caring and concern exist."[23]

Honoring our past and present staff with recognition like the Lincoln-Sudbury Wall of Recognition sends a strong, positive message to students, parents, and staff, a message that says that something worthwhile has gone on and is going on here—produced by people like drama teacher Harriet Rogers, history teacher Paul Mitchell, and superintendent C. Newton Heath—caring and concerned people whose efforts make a difference in the daily lives of school-community members.

Developing a mentoring process for teachers at every career stage is a vital ingredient in helping our schools succeed. Simply put, most teachers do not improve if left on their own. They need an easily accessible and recognizable method such as mentoring to help them improve their skills. This list of mentoring characteristics hopefully helps future mentors become more aware of the complexity of the mentoring role and the skills that are necessary to do the job well.

In addition, there are also more subtle aspects of becoming a mentor that need illumination. Becoming an effective mentor has a lot to do with belief. An effective mentor, above all, has to believe in teachers and their capacity to learn and relearn. It is the same as teachers believing that each of the kids in their classrooms is capable of learning given the right intervention.

Mentors must believe that what they have to offer teachers matters and is of use to them. They must also believe that most teachers want sound advice, useful feedback that makes sense, and the opportunity to learn new skills if they are at ease and safe with their mentor. Teachers want to be successful.

It is necessary to understand that offering help and support to teachers is not always an easy task. In order for teachers to receive help and be open to acquiring new skills, they have to trust their mentor and be able to expose both their strengths and weaknesses, along the way discovering areas to build on, areas that need reworking, or areas that require a new beginning. It is a process of opening themselves up and saying, "This is me. What skills are working and what is dragging me down?"

Teachers, even the most successful ones, run into walls and experience failure at different points in their careers. Even the kindest and most caring teachers can get into the game of blaming the kids, the parents, society, or whatever else may be an easy scapegoat. In bad times, hostility and blame are never far away.

It is not easy to honestly look in the mirror and consider the possibility that one's own skills are not up to the task at hand and take responsibility for the failure. Ironically, taking responsibility for what is not working in the classroom is often more difficult for the most successful teachers. Dealing with a failed classroom experience can be crippling for every teacher, but it is doubly hard for those teachers who have been elevated to "teacher of the year" or the like—the best and brightest, the ones we should all emulate, the career .500 hitters who are now batting .150.

The well-prepared mentor also understands that a major reason for teacher failure is boredom and the line of thinking that fools oneself into believing that one understands all there is to know about kids and teaching. The teachers' work is over—paycheck, please! They get stale, stop learning, and begin playing the waiting game—waiting for their break, for 3:00 p.m. on Friday, for June, and for retirement.

When teachers play the waiting game, they are vulnerable to new challenges and the winds of change, like a sailboat drifting without a rudder. Kids sense when teachers are playing the waiting game, sitting and watching the clock, taking too many sick days. They are no fools. They often act out, demanding a response from the waiting teacher who may have forgotten how to respond.

The world of professional sports is filled with examples of failure on the part of star players who stopped working on developing their skills, thinking they would remain stars all the same. Skills and talent, they mistakenly thought, were givens. They, too, played the waiting game—in basketball not asking for the ball at crunch time, in baseball not wanting to be the man hitting with the game on the line, in football not being the "go to" guy on fourth down. They are, as Woody Allen says, reading their reviews.

The same goes for many teachers: thinking they understand kids and teaching and that things will never change. It allows boredom and waiting to enter their professional lives and do their destructive work. Good teachers must rage against this thinking. They have to fight sophistication. They have to fight knowing because once they know something, it's hard to be open and creative.

At the same time, failure also has the potential to be a professional life-saving experience. It can present the opportunity for new growth and learning. But all of this cannot happen without the intervention of a skilled and caring mentor who holds the belief that change is always possible, whether or not the teacher is going through a good time.

A wise mentor might say to a faltering teacher, "shift your weight. If you are willing, as a teacher, to put in the hard work to learn new skills, the sky is the limit. A part of the so-called hard work is giving up and letting go of what worked in the past and learning how to create a new teaching environment. You will no doubt be afraid and uneasy. Giving up tired skills, what used to work, for new and untested skills is risky. Should you? Shouldn't you? As Dr. Seuss suggests, 'You'll play lonely games. . . . Games you can't win 'cause you'll play against you.'"

Teachers need a wise and skilled partner to stay with them and support them on the journey. Can teachers reinvent themselves without intervention? There are miracles. Some teachers can hit bottom and, on their own, claw their way back up, acquiring new workable skills inch by inch. But most of them need a trusted mentor they can talk to and who has a nonjudgmental voice and heart that can help them get better. It reminds me of John Steinbeck's *East of Eden:* "Get your eyes set on where you are going and then look to your feet, lest ye stumble."[24]

The road to gaining and regaining effective teaching is filled with bumps and pitfalls. One of the biggest challenges of mentoring is creating conditions and pathways of success to overcome the isolation and sense of going it alone that almost every teacher experiences. Teachers seldom, if at all, get the opportunity to observe and engage in dialog with a master teacher at work.

Unfortunately, the window through which most teachers come in contact with other teachers is often limited to discussion in the faculty room of those colleagues and students who are not making it. These discussions of the failure of colleagues and students serve to fuel the fire of teachers' discontent.

These faculty-room conversations, reflecting a desperate need of teachers to make contact in their otherwise hurried and isolated days, are usually not helpful. Rather, these conversations often focus on gossip and ridicule of colleagues, parents, and students, representing, as Ann Carson suggests, examples of professionals trafficking in the inessentials of life. Teachers settle for less and become less so as not to be alone and lonely in their everyday work.

The stories and examples of how successful teachers work hard to develop their talent, art, and skill are rarely shared or heard and almost never observed in action. Schools have no forum or venue to go to watch successful teachers do their work. As a result, successful teachers usually go unheralded and underappreciated. The stories of how they got to the top of their game, how they stayed there, how they refined their skills over time, and how they dealt with failure are all locked inside. No one asks to hear about their journey and their secrets to success, and so others do not learn from their experience.

Effective mentors understand this negative and isolating process and work to create conditions that bring the work and skills of effective teachers into the full light of day, where colleagues can observe and learn the skills that truly make for professional competence. Mentors understand that in isolation it is easy for teachers to go down wrong roads and, like their failing students, reach a dead end. It is far too easy to lose the passion and spirit that may have brought them into teaching, especially with a daily dose of negative faculty-room talk.

As Antoine de Saint-Exupery reminds us, "old bureaucrat, my comrade, it's not you who are to blame. Nobody grasped you by the shoulder while there was still time. Now the clay of which you were shaped has dried and hardened, and naught in you will ever awaken the sleeping musician, poet, and the astronomer that inhabited you in the beginning."[25]

Finally, there are bumps and pitfalls for the mentors as well. They have to believe that their vision of investing in teachers' ongoing professional development is a doable undertaking. It is one thing to talk about change. We all get excited talking about change and reform, but the hard work, difficult decisions, and gut-wrenching reactions that are involved in change call for specific and knowledgeable action.

Mentors may have to reshuffle their priorities to meet the current needs of teachers. They may have to give up traditional practices, assumptions, and conventional wisdom about what a mentor's workday should look like. They may have to view the mentoring of teachers as the top priority, finding the most efficient way to intervene and help teachers and discarding practices that may look and feel good but do little to improve the overall effectiveness of the teaching staff.

Mentors may have to mentor teachers in small and large groups as well as individually and also train department heads and teacher leaders to be leaders and constituents, thereby enlarging the mentoring circle. Mentors may have to use so-called free periods for school-day mentoring opportunities. By doing so, mentors create a new landscape in the school for viewing teachers as learners and positive contributors to the growth of their colleagues and their students.

In baseball terms, this vision of a mentoring process involves using the whole field. Good hitters don't just look for their pitch and become labeled as left-field, right-field, fastball, or curveball hitters. Rather, they look for any pitch that is hittable to every section of the ballpark. They are not predictable. They use the whole field and are hard to defend against.

In teacher training terms, using the whole field means moving beyond the predictable staff development programs common to many schools, the hit-or-miss workshops and conferences often not based on the real needs of teachers and generously labeled as teacher training. Replace this out-of-date model with a full-service menu of learning and mentoring opportunities, making training so easily accessible and attractive that teachers want to say yes, not no, and use home-based mentors, administrators, and teachers as leaders in the process. Schools must fight the notion that their staff can't become prophets in their own land.

NOTES

1. John Lahr, "Making It Real . . . How Mike Nichols Recreated Comedy and Himself," *The New Yorker* (21 February 2000): 197.

2. Stephen Sondheim, "I'm Still Here," from *Follies*.

3. Alan Riding, "The Joy of a Comeback that Leaves the Past Behind," *New York Times*, 29 April 2001, AR3.

4. Alan Riding, "Looking at a France That's Seldom Seen," *New York Times*, 27 August 2000, AR17.

5. Jack Lemmon and Kevin Spacey, "A Couple of Winners Talk Awards and Acting," *New York Times*, 12 March 2000, sec. 2A, 2.

6. Melanie Rehak, "Things Fall Together," *New York Times*, 26 March 2000, sec. 6, 36.

7. John Lahr, "Been Here and Gone . . . How August Wilson Brought a Century of Black American Culture to the Stage," *The New Yorker* (16 April 2000): 49–65.

8. Amy Zipkin, "In Tight Labor Market Bosses Find Value in Being Nice," *New York Times*, 31 May 2000, C1.

9. Seymour Sarason, Creation of *Settings* (San Francisco: Jossey Bass, 1972), 115.

10. Jean Ciavonne, "Dandelions, Pine-Cone Turkey, and Abraham Lincoln," *Kappan* 66(2) (October 1984): 142–143.

11. John S. Holloway, "The Benefits of Mentoring," *Educational Leadership* 58(8) (May 2001): 85–86.

12. Caryn James, "Death, Mighty Thou Art: So Too, a Compassionate Heart," *New York Times*, 23 March 2001, E1, p. 27.

13. Susan Kieffer-Brown and Kathleen Ware, "Growing Great Teachers in Cincinnati," *Educational Leadership* 58(8) (May 2001): 56–58.

14. Holly Bartunek, "Classroom Teacher as Teacher Educator," ERIC, 1989, www.ericsp.org/pages/digests/classroom_teacher_edu_89–7.html (4 April 2001).

15. Elizabeth McCay, "The Learning Needs of Principals," *Educational Leadership* 58(8) (May 2001): 75–76.

16. Arthur Combs et al., *Helping Relationships: Basic Concepts for the Helping Profession* (Boston: Allyn & Bacon, 1971), 7–8.

17. Donald Cruickshank et al., *Preparing America's Teachers* (Bloomington, IN: Phi Delta Kappa Foundation, 1996), 63–64, 87–88.

18. Ibid.

19. George Thomas, "Jets Discover Their Coach's Joyful Energy," *New York Times*, 17 May 2001, D5.

20. Fred Andrews, "Learning to Celebrate Water-Cooler Gossip," *New York Times*, 25 February 2001, BU6.

21. Malcolm Gladwell, "Designs for Working," *The New Yorker* (11 December 2000): 60.

22. Emitai Etzioni, *The Spirit of Community* (New York: Crown Publishers, 1993), 128.

23. Matthew King, "If These Walls Could Talk," *Educational Leadership* 58(5) (February 2001): 64–65.

24. John Steinbeck, *East of Eden* (New York: Viking Press, 1952), 345.

25. Antoine de Saint-Exupery, *Wind, Sand, and Stars* (New York: Reynolds & Hitchcock, 1939).

Chapter Four

How Administrators Can Assess Their Mentoring Skills

How does a busy school administrator proceed to become an effective mentor? Mentor-leaders need to address the following issues before actually beginning the mentoring process. Failure to deal with each of these issues can lead to program failure.

- Assess personal mentoring skills: strengths and areas that need improvement and further training.
- Avoid the pitfall that every master teacher and education leader can become an effective mentor.
- Select a mentoring team.
- Train a mentoring team.
- Utilize the mentoring training described in Chapter 5 as a training guide for would-be mentors.
- Build an effective mentoring team by identifying possible mentoring conflicts.
- Analyze the change in role from administrator to a trainer of mentors and a mentor.
- Plan, with the team, the parameters and nuts and bolts of the program, such as how to hold one-on-one mentoring meetings.
- Sell the mentoring concept to the school, including administrators, teachers, and staff.
- Identify and overcome resistance from everyone involved in the mentoring process.
- Create antennae to identify and head off problems that will surely arise.

Chapter 4

This chapter focuses on the first issue—how a mentor can assess his or her own mentoring skills. Chapter 5 addresses the remaining issues that can lead to program failure if left unattended.

HOW TO ASSESS PERSONAL MENTORING SKILLS

Step 1: The Personal Experience Inventory

An important first step in assessing your mentoring skills is to reflect on the positive mentors you have encountered in your professional and personal life.

- What mentors helped guide you in your personal and professional life? Was it a coach, a teacher, a counselor, a minister, a college professor, a principal, a parent, an older sibling?
- What skills did these mentors have? Were they good listeners? Were they nonjudgmental? Encouraging? Capable of delivering criticism in a positive way that made sense? Were they intimate, knowable, and accessible? When you were involved with these mentors, did you feel comfortable and at home?
- What words of encouragement and support did these mentors use when talking with you? What words worked best to help you? Did they say something like, "You're doing really well coaching this team. One of the best coaching jobs I've seen in my career. Still, I have one small suggestion that may help you. You seem kind of hard on your second base player. How about sitting down and giving her some positive strokes? She gets easily discouraged. Build her up. It may be just the thing to help the team go all the way to the championship. You are good at this kind of thing."?
- Have you modeled your own professional life after these mentors? Many administrators and school leaders go into teaching because they have experienced positive mentors in their own school experience. Many teachers nourish the care and guidance mentors have given them. Becoming mentors themselves provides a way to pass on their own positive experience to other teachers and students.
- Do you employ some of the same skills you learned from your mentors in your role as administrator and school leader? Are you a good listener, nonjudgmental, encouraging, able to deliver criticism in a positive way that makes sense, intimate, knowable, and accessible?

It is also important to recall those would-be mentors who had a negative impact on you. Many professionals set out with good intentions to mentor colleagues, but in fact lack the skills, caring, compassion, and ability to work one-on-one in an intimate relationship. Consider the following points:

- What mentors set out to help and guide you but were unable to deliver in this role? We all get exposed to coaches, teachers, counselors, college professors, principals, parents, and older siblings who are unable to connect with us in a positive way. Was it your lack of ability, personality, appearance, color, or background that somehow made them set you apart? Or was their lack of intimacy and comfort with you really their issue or problem, somehow making you feel left out?
- What mentoring skills did they lack? Were they poor listeners, judgmental, not encouraging, critical, and not intimate, knowable, or accessible? When you were involved with these negative mentors, was something amiss or even threatening?
- What word did these mentors use that convinced you that you were in an unhelpful relationship? Was the conversation something like this: "Jim, I wanted to speak to you about yesterday's game. As athletic director it's my job to solve coaching problems. I felt you used poor judgment in leaving Mark Jennings in the game too long. He couldn't find the plate by the seventh inning. Then you chose to let Dwight Scott hit with bases loaded. Why? He's been hitless in the last four games. Sometimes I get the feeling you're just not the man we need in this position. I don't see much good. You may be a great teacher but I don't know about your coaching skill"?
- In developing your own professional persona, have you deliberately tried to avoid becoming like these negative mentors? Or have some of their negative behaviors and attitudes crept in silently and taken hold of your persona? As professionals, we enter the school setting priding ourselves on our ability to work effectively with every staff member and student. The reality of school life soon strikes with the awareness that we are not as open and inclusive as we thought. We do have communication and relationship problems with certain teachers and students.

  It is relatively easy to overlook this dilemma or even to say it doesn't exist. Over time, we become negative mentors for these teachers and students. Has this same excluding, denying process become part of your personal persona? Have you become a negative mentor for some? Are you a victim of settling and not willing to change, to be inclusive?
- What mentoring skills have you developed as an administrator and school leader to avoid the characteristics of the negative mentors in your life? Being an effective mentor takes ongoing discipline and work. It is easy to slip into a negative mentoring stance. Schools are hectic places in which relationships and communication are easily strained. There is a fine line between being helpful and being critical.

Mentors should take a personal inventory of the teachers they like to help and guide as an important part of assessing their own mentoring skills. Mentors need to identify which teachers they like and gravitate toward.

- What are the characteristics of the teachers you tend to want to help and guide? Do you feel more comfortable with female than male teachers? Younger teachers? Highly effective teachers? Teachers who present at conferences and help put your school, and your career, on display?
- What part do issues related to age, gender, color, personality, ethnicity, appearance, and subject or grade level play in determining whom you like to help and guide? Are you more comfortable helping teachers who have supported your vision and goals? Who teach in subject areas you have taught? Who came into the school with you and have remained close friends throughout the many changes in the school setting?
- What needs of yours are met through interactions with these favorite teachers? Are your needs for friendship, praise, affirmation, and support met by interacting with these teachers? We all come to our work setting with personal needs to be met. But is your overall efficiency and leadership style being diminished by focusing too much on teachers who are most like you?

It is also highly useful to assess the characteristics of teachers we tend to avoid and find difficult to help and guide:

- What are the characteristics of teachers you tend to avoid and find difficult to guide? It is important to reflect on those people you avoid. It happens to all school leaders and teachers. We arrive at the school door with our own biases, judgments, and prejudices. That is only human. The work is to try to figure out our own avoidance process and work at building our tolerance and inclusion level.
- What part do issues related to age, gender, color, ethnicity, personality, appearance, and grade level or subject play in determining what teachers you avoid helping and guiding? Do you have difficulty communicating with aging teachers who are resisting retirement? Those who teach subject areas and grades you are not familiar with? Teachers who are ineffective? Female teachers?
- What kinds of inner conflicts arise when you become involved in helping and guiding teachers who you sense are out of step with your image of an effective teacher? Resistance both within yourself and the teachers you have trouble relating to is a condition. Neither party welcomes the interaction. You have much to gain in coming to terms with the real you and overcoming your own resistance to helping others. Like teachers who have learned to overcome their inner conflict and resistance to help stu-

dents they have avoided, you can become a complete mentor. Acknowledge that you have a dark side that senses caution, threat, and the unknown aspects encountered with some teachers. You may feel that they are not on your side or that they are not worth the effort. In fact, they are worth the effort if you are to become the complete mentor. Mentoring only those you feel comfortable with is half the game; it's incomplete. It is important to become aware of your biases and acknowledge whom you push away.

The value of this inventory is that it helps administrators begin a conversation with themselves about the mentoring persona they develop based on their own professional and personal life experiences. The inventory also clarifies that administrators' own life experiences may in fact push them in the direction of wanting to mentor certain teachers whom they feel comfortable with and avoiding others with whom they feel out of sync. It reminds them that they are human and that more work needs to be done so they avoid this mentoring pitfall. Like teachers with their students, administrators are expected to connect with all of their protégés and avoid selective intervention.

In assessing their mentoring skills, it is also useful for mentors to reflect on their vision for the mentoring program. How is the mentoring program going to fit in with other ongoing programs? Will it be a comfortable fit or is there the possibility of jarring and upsetting resistance? Mentors might reflect on these questions in order to make the mentoring program run smoothly:

- What is your vision for the school?
- To what extent have you been successful in realizing your vision?
- What individuals and groups in the school and community have promoted your vision?
- What kind of ongoing support have you given these individuals and groups?
- What obstacles have arisen to block your vision?
- What individuals and groups in the school and community have resisted your vision?
- How have you handled these obstacles and setbacks in furthering your vision? Have you created communication barriers with these individuals and groups?
- New programs such as the mentoring program have two important requirements: a recognizable place and function in the school setting and wide-based support. How do you plan to achieve this goal?
- How will you promote your vision for mentoring?
- Who will be involved in your mentoring team?

- Who will be your allies?
- How will you win over your detractors?
- What kinds of problems can you expect?
- What kind of problem-control strategy will you have in place? Problems not addressed only get worse.
- The development of new programs can be risky at both professional and personal levels. The process usually requires an increase in emotional, intellectual, and physical energy. How do you rate your emotional, intellectual, and physical energy, your will to win, and your political savvy? What impact will this new program have on your professional and personal life?
- What new, different skills will be required in developing the mentoring program?

Step 2: Checklist for Understanding Mentoring Skills

In step 2, administrators take a hard look at their present mentoring skills and determine what areas need improvement. Not every would-be mentor possesses all of the characteristics identified in Chapter 3. Skill acquisition is incremental and ongoing.

This checklist helps administrators identify where they are, what skills are in line, and what work needs to be done. Like a teacher working with students, mentors should take the positive road first by identifying what they are doing well and then moving on to what needs fixing. This checklist is based on the mentoring characteristics described in detail in Chapter 3.

- Do I understand the dynamics of teaching and the real world of the classroom or have I been so involved in administrative duties that I have lost touch with the feel and texture of the classroom?
- Do I understand the notion that teaching is hard work and renewing oneself is not always easy or sought after?
- Do I understand that improving one's skills calls for risks and new directions?
- Do I understand that every teacher in my school arrives at the classroom door with their own set of biases, prejudices, and judgments?
- Do I understand that bad times, failure, and burnout can happen to every teacher, even the most successful ones?
- Do I value the loyalty and privacy of the protégés involved in the mentoring program?
- Do I understand that the personal and family problems of students can be very emotional and painful for teachers?

- Do I understand that problematic personal relationships of teachers—family, marriage, illness, divorce, death, addiction—affect the teachers' effectiveness and well-being?
- Do I understand that mentoring relationships change over time, often with newly skilled protégés gradually taking on a mentoring persona and stature of their own?
- Do I understand that resistance to mentoring takes place? Not every teacher embraces mentoring, and they have to be sold on the process.
- Do I know how to listen, be nonjudgmental, and provide useful feedback and modeling that can act as a guide for teacher improvement?
- Do I know how to administer self-care and how to be physically and emotionally fit and up to the mentoring task?
- Do I have knowledge about the aging process in career development so I can more effectively guide teachers?
- Do I have finely honed political skills so that I can effectively overcome resistance and sell the program?
- Do I understand that there will be mentoring relationships that don't work and will require new arrangements?
- Do I understand that there are huge personal and professional benefits for me in the mentoring process?
- Do I know how to help my protégés find and define their best teaching selves?
- Do I know how to help my protégés clarify the many complex roles they play in the classroom?
- Do I know how to bring a sense of joy, energy, humor, and lightness to the mentoring relationship?
- Do I understand that my lack of in-depth knowledge of every subject area and grade level need not reduce my effectiveness in mentoring teachers?
- Do I know how to teach my protégés to create ongoing sources of support, learning hubs, and ongoing opportunities for renewal?
- Do I have a sense of the history of my school setting, the good work that has gone on in the past by caring teachers, the creative responses to changing needs and times, and the good work that now goes on each day?

This self-assessment of the skills and understanding useful in effective mentoring should identify areas of strength and areas that need improvement. It should serve as an early sign for mentors who approach the task with good intentions but limited skills. Good intentions are not enough to help troubled and failing teachers. Skills matter and make the final difference.

We now move from an exploratory assessment and checklist into the everyday world of mentoring. The heat goes up and real issues begin to take center stage, often with no time for the mentor to think twice.

Step 3: Making Mentoring Skills Real: A Journey into Everyday School Life

Developing the ability to listen effectively, be nonjudgmental, and be capable of providing useful feedback requires the following skills:

- Effective listening and observational skills
- The ability to give constructive, nonjudgmental feedback
- The ability to help teachers overcome self-erected barriers between themselves, students, and colleagues
- The ability to confront teachers who seem headed in the wrong direction
- The ability to praise and support teachers who are doing well or poorly
- The ability to give teachers problem-solving techniques for the classroom
- Intimate knowledge of the teaching staff

Mastering these skills is not easy. At first glance, they may seem like a laundry list to be memorized for a class called Mentoring 101. How do we imbue real meaning into these words? The rush of school life—the smell, fast pace, and never-ending conflicts—needs to be added to get our blood rushing. It is useful for would-be mentors to ask themselves how they stack up as nonjudgmental listeners by reflecting on how this skill gets translated into mentoring relations in everyday school life. Let's fast-forward out of Mentoring 101.

DO YOU HAVE EFFECTIVE LISTENING AND OBSERVATIONAL SKILLS?

Listening to the other person and observing his or her nonverbal behaviors gives the mentor important clues for identifying those areas in which a teacher needs improvement. What is the teacher's tone of speech? Is it comfortable or does she appear under stress? What about her physical stance? Does she look at ease or is there tension in her movements? How about her appearance? Does she look composed and presentable or is she disheveled and loose at the ends? What are her fears and concerns?

Let's make these listening and observational skills more concrete. Here is a vignette describing a conversation between a mentor, Principal Brad Foley, and his protégé, social studies teacher Tom Murray. Their mentoring relationship has evolved over the school year. A strong sense of trust, loyalty, and friendship has developed between them. The mentoring conditions suggested in this book have been well established so that when a crisis emerges, Tom is in good hands.

Tom, as is the case with most teachers, begins the conversation by saying that things are fine. As the conversation unfolds, he begins talking about a near confrontation he had with a parent at a conference the previous evening. As he talks, his voice trembles and his hands shake.

Tom Murray: I don't know what happened. Mr. Moriarty, Jim's father, came at the end of the parent conference time. He had a 7:30 appointment but he didn't show up until 9:30. I was just on my way out after meeting with Mrs. Donato when he came down the hall. I could tell he had been drinking but I asked him in anyway. As soon as he sat down he began swearing at me, saying things like, "You son of a bitch, you don't give my kid a chance." And on and on. After a while I had enough. I said I wasn't going take that kind of abuse. I told him that Jim and I were working on things and they were getting better. But he wouldn't stop.

Finally I just got up and left. He followed me down the hall, still yelling and swearing. Just as we turned the corner at the office I caught a glimpse of Jim hiding in the corner. He was crying and upset. He said, "I'm sorry, Mr. Murray, I tried to talk him out of coming. But he's been drinking. He wouldn't let my mom come, pushed her around like he always does before we left the house. He doesn't even live at home any more. I'm so embarrassed. Please don't tell the other kids." I felt so bad for the kid and managed to tell him it was OK and I would keep it between us and we could talk tomorrow.

Then his father literally pushed me aside and grabbed Jim and said, "Don't talk to that creep. All he does is fail you." By the time I got home I was shaking all over and couldn't calm down. That's when I called you. I didn't know whether to call the police, and I was concerned about Jim. Who knows what this guy is capable of?

But I did meet with Jim this morning before school. He was outside smoking when I arrived so I asked him to come to my room. He seemed shaken, like me, but OK. I told him I had no idea how much stress he's been under since his parents' divorce and his father's violence. He just broke down and cried. I tried to comfort him as best I could. I'm wondering what to do next. I'm not a psychologist.

Brad Foley: Wow, what a night. No wonder you called me. I am so glad you did. It's no good to be alone with all that on your mind. Let me first applaud you for reaching out to Jim. I know you two have been at odds. Maybe this is the opportunity you've been looking for to start a real relationship with him. It sounds like he could use a positive role model like you. What to do?

Simple things first. Why don't you meet with Jim after your third period class and ask if it's OK with him if you set up an appointment with the school counselor, Gregg Barosa. I've spoken to Gregg already about the incident with Jim's father. He has an opening seventh period. If Jim is willing to get into counseling, why don't you bring him to Gregg's office seventh period and sit in on the session? That would make it more comfortable for Jim. I'll ask Gregg to call Jim's mother after the session and set up an appointment with her as well.

Jim should know that we are doing this so he's not in the dark. It sounds like she is going to need support, too. I hear she is out of work and her husband, or ex-husband, is not making any alimony payments. As for Jim's father, I'll ask Gregg to think about calling him and trying to steer him into rehab or counseling, as well.

Also, I know our team is meeting tomorrow. Be prepared to let the other teachers know what is happening. I want the entire team involved in making some concrete plans on how to help Jim. Again, maybe this is the opening we've been looking for. Good work, Tom. No one said teaching is easy. The job involves a little bit of everything, from being a father figure to parent educator to psychologist. I know they never prepared you for this but better now than later. You've just been baptized, Murray, in the real fire of school life and you've taken the hit and are using it to help one of your kids. That's being a professional. I'm proud of you. Someday you might be in my shoes and be doing the same thing for another teacher.

You know, Eva Nelson, the social studies teacher, has had similar problems with Jim and his family. Maybe you could fill her in and give her some advice on your way home. Get some rest.

Also, before I forget, what do you think about moving Jim's seat right up front near your desk? He would be away from his group and maybe now he's ready to become visible and part of the class. He's been invisible as a student since he came here three years ago. Let's milk this opportunity for everything we can.

I know you didn't catch the Knicks-Miami basketball playoff last night but I think it's useful to think about announcer Bill Walton's comment, "Everyone gets opportunities but not everyone knows how to use them." Let's use this one.

DO YOU KNOW HOW TO GIVE CONSTRUCTIVE AND NONJUDGMENTAL FEEDBACK?

As you can see, Brad Foley listens carefully without interrupting to give advice. Tom, as he says, has been baptized in the fire of school life. Things can get hot and out of control. One never knows what to expect when a student or parent walks through the door. As most experienced mentors understand, many teachers do not anticipate the pain and failure they will see on the faces of kids and parents who experience life's hurts when they enter the profession.

But kids bring their personal and nonacademic problems into the school each day and these affect their school life and lack of success in many ways—tardiness, truancy, acting out, and, sadly, a loss of hopes and dreams. They are deadened at an early age unless rescued by caring and skilled teachers.

Bad things also happen to so-called good kids who are born into families with resources and opportunity. Well-off kids, not just kids living in poverty, get hit by life's hard times. The only difference is that well-off kids are not supposed to have problems. All those vitamins, preschool training, tutoring, and test-prep courses are supposed to make them problem free and Harvard bound.

But they, surprisingly to some parents and educators, are human too and vulnerable to risks—the risk of being too good and too successful early on, more a productive machine than a kid. Being too good can rob them of learning the skills they need to make it in a hostile and competitive world.

As in the dialog above, Jim Moriarty may prove to be the lucky student because he is about to get the help he needs. His problem is out in the open for everyone to see. Embarrassed he may be, but he is attended to.

The silent, bright kids may not be so lucky. They don't cause problems. They show up on time, they do their homework, they join clubs. There are no noticeable holes in their achievements. To the untrained teacher's eye, they seem fine. Not as much attention needs to be given to them as to the Jim Moriartys, we sometimes think. Linking goodness and success to being problem free is not always a good approach.

Teachers observing the hurt and scarred children in their classes wonder, as Duke Ellington wrote, "Why anyone would tear the seam from anyone's dream." Teachers learn over time, as Tom is doing, that teaching is more often than not a painful business. They are never fully prepared for what the school day brings, no matter how many degrees, education courses, and years of experience they have under their belts. "I thought I'd seen it all but this situation is a new one," is a familiar teacher lament.

Tom seemed to have handled the situation well, but not perfectly. He might have called the principal earlier or called the police. Mr. Moriarty could have caused real damage to Tom, Jim, or himself. Tom might also have called Child Protective Services—Brad should make sure he has that number—and reported the incident and communicated that Jim might be in danger. This is all material for Tom and Brad to work on together. But for now, Brad rightly affirms Tom's responses, suggests that this is an opportunity to really get involved and help Jim, and sets up a plan for ongoing help and intervention for the Moriarty family. It's a step-by-step plan that shows Tom how to proceed.

Brad also wisely understands that it is important for mentors not to put too much on the teacher's plate, not give too much feedback and too many goals to be accomplished in the future. It's like working with anxious kids. You give them tasks and ideas that they can solve and handle so they can feel good about themselves; they must crawl before they can take baby steps.

Let's also keep in mind what Tom would have done if he did not have a solid, trusting, and caring relationship with Brad Foley. Would he have acted differently? Probably. Maybe he would not have called or involved Brad at all. He might have, like Jim, kept things to himself. Without their mentoring relationship, both Tom and Brad would have lost out on an opportunity to be helpful to and learn from one another.

Consider how many times similar kinds of incidents occur in schools in which teachers don't have a Brad Foley to turn to. Jim Moriarty and his family did not lose out on an opportunity for needed intervention, using the crisis as a springboard for help. Having a mentoring relationship is like money in the bank for the Toms of the teaching world. It's there when they need it.

DO YOU KNOW HOW TO HELP TEACHERS OVERCOME SELF-ERECTED BARRIERS?

Here again, Brad Foley shows us how to transform the way a teacher views his students. Until this crisis, Tom sees Jim Moriarty as a threat and a nuisance, a kid he would like to see jettisoned from the school's rolls. But the confrontation with Jim's father and Jim's cry for help touched Tom's heart and changed things between them.

Let's not forget Brad Foley's critical mentoring role in this process. If Brad Foley had taken a hard-line administrative approach, he might have pushed for a legal rather than a human response. But Brad Foley didn't take the hard line. He didn't make the wall impenetrable with a zero-tolerance approach. He also didn't use the incident to promote a political, legalistic agenda for his administration. He didn't ask police to do his work for him.

Rather, he reduced the barriers between Tom and Jim with a human, caring, family-centered approach. He understood that teachers are adults. They can handle adversity. They don't need an administrator who is a father figure telling them exactly what to do. They need an administrator who presents a caring, compassionate model that says, "Yes, we can help. Now go to it!"

DO YOU KNOW HOW TO CONFRONT TEACHERS WHO SEEM TO BE HEADED IN THE WRONG DIRECTION?

Not everyone listens. Let's suppose Tom Murray had reacted in another way to Mr. Moriarty's assault. Let's suppose that Tom arrives at school the next morning and makes a beeline for Brad Foley's office, demanding that Jim be removed from his class. Here is what he tells Brad Foley:

> Tom Murray: I am just a teacher and not a counselor or social worker. Jim has major problems. Sure, I would like to help him but I am a married man with a child on the way. I can't take the chance of Mr. Moriarty coming back, maybe this time with a gun, and making big trouble for me. Jim has to be removed from my class and put in

an environment in which he can get help. I know the district has an alternative school for troubled kids. Besides, if he left, it would be better for the other kids. Learning could go on again. I know he scares Janine and some of the other kids in the class. Janine's mother has come twice to complain about Jim. Listen, I feel bad but this is the last straw. I've done what I can. I'm no saver of souls. I am just a social studies teacher.

Brad Foley: Thanks for letting me know how you feel, Tom. It's been rough. And last night's incident was no plus. Those things can push you over the line. But Tom, hear me out. Sit down and have some coffee. Your adrenaline is running, as it should after that experience. I'll ask my secretary to get coverage for your first two classes. Let's talk. It's been a busy day and it's only 7:30. Tom, let's talk about your growth as a teacher first. When you first came here two years ago, I must admit you seemed a little shaky and unsure, especially with some of the tougher kids. But since we started the mentoring program this year, I've seen some good things happen with you and your kids. You are much more open, friendly, and at ease with them. You know their names, something about their backgrounds. Plus you're having some fun, which is great for both you and them.

I know your relationship with Jim has been strained. But let me stop right there, Tom. This is an opportunity for you to help a kid in real need. You don't have to get rid of him to save him or yourself. You are not too brittle or unskilled to handle the Jims of the world. Sure, you've had a frightening experience. But so what? You're not alone. We've all had them. Actually, I think you handled the situation with Mr. Moriarty and Jim very well, maybe not perfectly but I see no reason for you to throw up your hands and run for cover. You're not a wimp. I've heard you talk about your football days in high school and college. Linebacker, right? My guess is that you've been hit a lot harder in football than Mr. Moriarty could ever do.

Let me tell you something. If you keep Jim and continue to work with him, that's going to be a victory for you. A win. It shows your toughness and tenacity. But if you get rid of Jim—and I will move him if you insist—I think you are giving up too early on both yourself and Jim. You're letting a potential victory turn into a defeat. You are saying that you can't handle kids like Jim.

And do you know the message that the other kids will get? They will understand that you have run from a fight. You think you've seen some turbulent behavior? Wait until you see what the other kids do after Jim goes. I may be mistaken but I think they will be emboldened. Word travels fast, Tom. I want you to think seriously about this. You've got Jim in the palm of your hand right now. From what you've said, he believes you are in his corner. You aren't going to throw this kid into the alternative school where no one knows him and there are really troubled kids, are you? Go for your strength and power, Tom. Don't send the message to the kids and Jim that you are weak and not up to the battle. It's the wrong message at the wrong time.

As they say in baseball, "I've got the right man at the plate at the right time." And you are the right man, Tom. Be a contender, not a thirty-year-old guy who is giving up. You know it's been a painful learning experience for me with other teachers. Once you give up on that first kid, it's easier to give up on the next one who will confront you. You know teachers like that and so do I. They've lost the will to do battle with kids. Don't you, Tom.

DO YOU KNOW HOW TO PRAISE AND SUPPORT TEACHERS?

Praise is not always abundant for teachers in schools. Students by far receive the most praise. Usually it is showered on students who achieve academically, in sports, in music, or in theater. Teachers administer a lot of quiet, unnoticed praise for kids who make small breakthroughs after many setbacks. But praise for teachers who do good deeds and good works is limited. Sure, there is some, like the teacher of the year awards from unions, PTAs, and yearbook staffs, or being chosen for a summer workshop. But it's limited.

Why is this so? The good works and good deeds of teachers go unnoticed because they are carried out in isolation in the classroom. Usually no one observes the efforts by teachers to praise and support kids. Yes, I know, "no one" is a heavy indictment, but I believe it is mostly true. Maybe a few parents write letters of praise to the teacher or building principal, lauding the teacher's effort on behalf of their particular child. But most of the time, the good efforts and work of teachers occur in a vacuum, unnoticed and unappreciated.

Self-promotion—blowing your own horn and calling attention to your achievements—doesn't come easily for teachers. Being underappreciated and taken for granted are, unfortunately, hallmarks of the teaching profession. The lucky ones have enough pride in themselves to appreciate what skills they bring to the classroom, or better yet, they have a few colleagues and family who say when they walk by, "There goes a real teacher."

Effective mentoring, as Brad Foley demonstrates, can dramatically change this situation. Brad is clear in his praise and support of Tom Murray. The praise is an effort to clearly define skills that are working for Tom and to increase his awareness that, like a good musician or athlete, these skills are helping make him a successful professional. There is a method and a message to Brad's praise of Tom. He doesn't let him duck out of helping Jim Moriarty and take what appears to be the easy way out.

In fact, Brad knows that the easy way, farming Jim out to an alternative school, may be the tougher road because it helps make Tom easy prey for tough kids who need a tough but caring response. Brad's message to Tom is, "We are in this together. I won't cop out in tough times and I don't expect you to."

DO YOU KNOW HOW TO GIVE TEACHERS PROBLEM-SOLVING TECHNIQUES?

Fixing classroom problems is not rocket science. Sure, when teachers are in the midst of a classroom uproar, the answer and the way out of the dilemma are not easily at hand. Teachers do not readily see the solutions and the alternatives when they are failing and in retreat. Another voice and another brain to pick, a mentor with solid classroom experience, can quickly point out the problem areas and help develop a strategy to regroup. We know problems can create opportunity for change. The classroom after all, is a hectic and ever-changing environment. The lessons and kids teachers counted on one day backfire on them the next.

Tough kids make teachers sweat and feel confused and out of sync. They lose their way trying to figure out responses that will work. There are kids who, as the saying goes, "have our number." They smell teachers' weaknesses and vulnerability and zero in for the kill. But the difficult kids who taunt teachers and lead them down wrong roads also may be the bearers of gifts. The bottom line is that teachers often learn the most about the process of teaching, and about themselves and their kids, from students who rebuff their efforts and become confrontational.

Teachers have to work, sweat, try new approaches, fail, be soft, be tough, do what it takes—use the whole field—to win these kids over. It's good to remind ourselves, as Brad Foley reminds Tom Murray, that the classroom is not a civil, orderly, or nice place in spite of our efforts to make it so with the latest mediation, bully-proofing, and conflict resolution programs. Confrontation is always in the air or close at hand in a classroom.

It is easy for teachers to lose their way in trying to find solutions to classroom problems. They are too busy putting out fires and often lack the information and awareness they need. Sometimes very simple approaches can turn things around. It is not rocket science but just common sense when Brad Foley suggests that Tom move Jim's desk to the front of the room and get together with him to talk things out. For Brad, as a skilled observer, this situation is a no-brainer, as they say. Small moves can solve a big problem.

As Brad demonstrates, his mentoring sessions with Tom are really problem-solving sessions. What's going on? How can we change things around? Let's plan a simple intervention and see if it works. Tom is not left alone to solve his problems. As Brad suggests, they are in this together. It is amazing what a little support and problem-solving experience can do for a floundering teacher.

Cost effective? You bet! Ineffective teachers are costly. They often create ongoing problems with their students and parents, problems that have to be resolved by busy administrators and colleagues. Effective mentoring can help retrain failing teachers and provide them with the necessary skills to be successful with their students, parents, and colleagues. With effective mentoring, poorly skilled teachers can become valuable resources.

DO YOU KNOW YOUR TEACHING STAFF ON AN INTIMATE BASIS?

Developing an effective mentoring relationship with teachers requires establishing a level of comfort and trust with them. That means knowing them by name and knowing their backgrounds, their interests, their personal and family lives, their school relationships—how they fit in, whom they hang out with—their hobbies, hopes, goals, dreams, talents and strengths, the areas that may need improvement, and of course, their fears. Knowing and understanding a teacher's fears can open a dialog for further training.

Mentors must establish a relationship that has an easiness about it and in which each party is readily accessible for help. An example of this accessibility might be a late-night phone call from a teacher like Tom, wanting to talk about a confrontation he had with a parent and asking what he should do.

Developing this kind of trusting mentoring relationship requires a lot of legwork and prep work on the part of the administrator. It's much like the work an effective teacher must do to really understand each of his students or like a coach sizing up his players' assets and liabilities. The mentor has to go beyond the numbers rather than limit his understanding to facts: Tom Murray, seventh grade social studies teacher in his second year of teaching.

A mentor has to go further to understand and know the whole teacher just as teachers try to understand and know the whole child. Mentors must find out what makes teachers tick emotionally. They must realize that comfort, ease, and trust between them and the teacher develop slowly, just as in any other intimate relationship. These qualities are built on a series of interactions that work out well.

It will not be perfect. Issues and problems arise in building any relationship. One has to persist, which is easier when mentors know and understand the person they are trying to help and, of course, themselves. What makes us—mentors—tick emotionally? Where are our buttons that teachers can push, as kids do with teachers? What sets us off? In getting to know others, mentors soon find out that they had better understand and know themselves. Intervening, mentoring, helping, and being intimate all require more than a degree and good intentions. Mentoring is not therapy, but it does involve a process most therapists understand, that in helping others we learn about ourselves. This is an unexpected but valuable benefit of mentoring.

Chapter Five

Selecting and Training the Mentoring Team

In this chapter you take the next steps in developing an effective mentoring program. Your self-training and reflection in Chapter 4 has given you a better sense of your mentoring strengths and those areas that need improvement. Now it's time to select and train your mentoring team, with the caution that not every master teacher and education leader is well-suited for the mentoring role.

Not everyone can make the transition from being an effective teacher to being an effective mentor. Different skills are required, as suggested in the list of the issues administrators need to address before actually beginning the mentoring process identified at the beginning of Chapter 4. Let's move on to the second element of that list.

ISSUE 2: AVOIDING THE PITFALL THAT EVERY MASTER TEACHER CAN BE AN EFFECTIVE MENTOR WITHOUT TRAINING AND SUPPORT

One of the major arguments of this book is that would-be mentors need to be involved in some kind of readiness training so they can learn about the mentoring process and what is expected of them in this new role. The approach in this book is a self-training process for administrators, who can then use their newly acquired skills to train a mentoring team. The team is then available to each other to offer support, solve problems, and create new approaches to problems when needed.

This model program allows the administrator to be involved as a learner, trainer, and participant but not be totally responsible for the program. It allows for continuous support and oversight by each team member. No one team leader is alone, open and vulnerable to unforeseen circumstances and ongoing resistance.

Why are training and ongoing support and guidance vital to any mentor and mentoring program? Being unprepared can easily lead to resistance and setbacks. Failure comes easily, while success is hard to reach. Let's put a face, a persona, on what can happen when a master teacher such as Kentucky teacher Imgard Williams becomes a mentor for colleagues without acquiring mentoring skills, such as political savvy, and without receiving the ongoing support described in Chapter 3. Irmgard Williams as an example of the competent teachers we should be trying to develop and nurture. Clearly she has all the right stuff; while not perfect, she is a recognized leader in her classroom, school, school district, and state.

But does being the consummate teacher prepare a person to retrain subpar teachers to be more effective? Williams understands how much her colleagues need affirmation and "something to show people we're proud of them." She also understands that they need guidance from teachers like her if they are going to improve. So when the call came for her to become a Kentucky Education Reform Act (KERA) fellow and take a leadership role in retraining teachers in her school and schools throughout the state, she was willing to take this new step in her career. She was an accomplished teacher at the time, but clearly there were questions she and KERA officials should have considered before she took on this new role.

- In spite of her own success as a teacher, did she possess the right characteristics to become a successful mentor?
- Did KERA have a profile of a model mentor and the skills that were required for success in that role?
- Would KERA provide training for Williams that would teach her how to intervene with peers who need mentoring to become more effective teachers?
- Would the training provide her with methods of overcoming the resistance of peers to being retrained, especially by a colleague?
- Would the training role provide release time from her classroom in order to coach fellow teachers?
- Would her building administrator support this new role, now and over time?
- How would she handle the roles of being a classroom teacher and trainer of peers at the same time? How would she and her students handle this new role?

- How would she handle the jealousy of peers who would be envious of her new role and special place in the state's education hierarchy?

The central questions for Williams and KERA should have been: "Is Williams ready and set to take on this new role as trainer? Are we doing everything we can to prepare Williams and ensure that this is a successful experience for her? Or are we setting up this teacher-turned-mentor for failure by not providing her with the necessary training and support to do the job?" Williams may be a tough-minded teacher and able to handle anything in the classroom, but was she tough enough and skilled enough for this new role? Here is what happened.

Williams, with all of her talents and ability to work hard, develop skills, and change over the course of her career, typifies the simultaneous problem and opportunity involved in retraining teachers at the school level. The problem is, "How do administrators get other teachers to be more like Williams?" The opportunity is that Williams herself is a superb resource.

How do administrators showcase her talents as a successful, competent teacher so that fellow teachers can observe and learn from her and others like her? What happened to Williams when, as part of KERA, she began to serve as a model and guide for other teachers? Williams' experience provides us with some important guidelines on how we should proceed in training teachers to be mentors.

The following are some of the highlights and effects of KERA:

- KERA was an effort by the state of Kentucky to rebuild an entire school system from scratch.
- KERA placed great emphasis on teachers in the classroom. KERA stressed that teachers are directly responsible for making the reforms work and must improve their practice.
- State legislators increased the number of paid days available for staff training from four to nine and initially allowed school districts to absorb some of the extra days by replacing up to five of the required 175 instructional days with paid staff training. Legislators also boosted spending on staff training from $1 per student to $23 per student per year.
- The state held teachers accountable for making reform succeed and, ultimately, teachers could lose their jobs if their students didn't reach state goals on tests given to different groups of students in selected grades each year.
- While teachers were trying to learn how to do their jobs differently, they also had to field questions from parents, listen to complaints from colleagues, and deflect criticism from observers who claimed the teachers were not working hard enough.

- For many of Kentucky's 38,000 teachers, the cost of change was too high. They found themselves caught between the desire to do a better job and the impulse to stick with what they knew. A record number of Kentucky teachers retired in 1993 and 1994.

When KERA came along, Williams embraced its challenges. There was no limit to what she personally was willing to do. She became the leader of a team of teachers at South Heights and a KERA fellow, and trained other teachers in Henderson County.

But by 1995, the fifth year of reform, she was feeling more depleted than fulfilled. She believed strongly in what she was doing and wanted badly for the reforms to succeed. But she feared that hard-working teachers would stop trying to improve if people didn't acknowledge their efforts. When a record number of teachers retired in 1993 and 1994, Williams was concerned about the spirits of those who stayed on the job.

What Williams hadn't counted on were the demands that KERA placed on teachers as a group. The expectation was that teachers would work together to rise to a higher level collectively. But the state did not provide direction for accomplishing this goal. The new emphasis on collective responsibility forced Williams into an uncomfortable role.

For most of her life she had been content to stay in the background. She didn't like to draw attention to herself; she believed that others should mind their own business. Although she knew she was personally accountable for her own actions, she never considered it her place to judge anyone else. Now the state seemed to be suggesting that she should.

When she opened the door of her classroom after years of isolation to take on this new mentoring role, Williams couldn't help but notice the difference between herself and some other colleagues. They seemed to recognize the disparities, too, and often approached her for advice about teaching. When she became leader of one of the primary teams, the questions multiplied. Williams always seemed to know what to do.

Yet rarely did her guidance lead to improvements in other teachers' classrooms. Her colleagues had a tough time transferring her techniques and Williams did not have the luxury of mentoring them on the spot. The lack of progress among her colleagues troubled her. She preferred to influence others by example, not by dictating to them. They were professionals, too.

But despite her gentle reminders, some teachers hadn't heeded her message that they needed to make major changes in their methods, and fast. KERA expected all students to learn at high levels, but they would never succeed if teachers didn't give them the skills they needed.

What could Williams do about other teachers? What should she do? She was already busy trying to address her own students' needs. Wasn't that enough? Certainly, education reform required more of teachers, but did it mean that they must expect more from each other? Were they obligated to confront incompetence, even if it meant challenging a friend from across the hall? "How can you tell another teacher how to teach?" Williams wondered.

It is a question that many people in Kentucky and around the nation are beginning to ask, as well. Can you tell another teacher how to teach? Williams' case shows that you probably can't. She clearly cared about her colleagues and wanted to help them get better. But it was difficult for her to move out of her role as classroom teacher, a role she developed over twenty-seven years of teaching, and into the role of teacher/mentor and the political arena.

Over time, her role as mentor seemed to become less rewarding than teaching her children. She felt depleted, unrewarded, and confused about her role and how to proceed. It appeared she didn't have much support or guidance from KERA. She seemed on her own to wrestle with transferring long-held beliefs, values, and practices—they had worked for her for twenty-seven years—to her new role.

There were several aspects of the new role that Williams found troubling:

- Assuming that teachers would work together to achieve to a higher level of performance.
- Thinking that assessing the level of competency of fellow teachers and identifying areas they need to improve is "judging." For most of her professional life she had been content to stay in the background. Although she made certain she was personally accountable for her own actions, she never considered it her place to judge anyone else.
- Not seeing any major results using the training model in which teachers observe and the master teacher practices. Williams always seemed to know what to do when other teachers approached her for advice about teaching, yet rarely did her guidance of other teachers lead to improvement in their classrooms.
- Not having time to coach her fellow teachers. Her colleagues had a tough time transferring her techniques, and Williams didn't have the luxury of mentoring them on the spot. The lack of progress among her colleagues troubled her.

Williams preferred to influence other teachers by example, not by dictating to them. Her colleagues were professionals, too. But despite her gentle reminders, some teachers hadn't heeded the message that they needed to make major changes in instruction, fast.

How can you tell another teacher how to teach? Certainly, education reform required more of teachers, but did it mean they must expect more from each other? Were they obligated to confront incompetence even if it meant challenging a friend from across the hall?

Can we *tell* another teacher how to teach? Probably not. But in sound education reform we can *show* another teacher how to teach. We do know how to proceed to reach this goal. There is a profound difference between *telling*, influencing by example (as Williams did) and *demonstrating*, that is, showing and teaching how to improve.

Telling and influencing by example will not reach the large body of teachers who need intervention. They need demonstration—someone showing and teaching them how to improve. Mentors must give teachers the skills they need to confront incompetence in their subpar colleagues. Mentors and teachers need not so much to challenge a friend across the hall as to intervene when a friend across the hall is floundering and needs to acquire a new set of teaching skills that work—to be their brother's keeper.

We need to learn from KERA and the Williams case what not to do, or else we will end up with the same results—disgruntled teachers, unfilled expectations, and the energy of reformers being spent unsuccessfully trying to get resisters on board.

This case study of Williams' role as mentor of peers provides us with some important clues as to how we need to proceed to train future mentors so they will surely succeed. We should remind ourselves that enthusiasm and the willingness to mentor fellow teachers are admirable but not enough to get the job done. What is required is a new set of mentoring skills, similar to the ones described in Chapter 3, that get the Irmgard Williams of the future ready for the mentoring task.

Irmgard Williams is a courageous teacher who was willing to go out on a limb and do what she could to help other teachers. It appears she had precious little time and support to get the job done. She mentored by telling and example. What else could she do? It appears she had no release time for coaching her peers. Although she was troubled by incompetent teachers, she didn't want to intrude, judge, and interfere with their professional lives. She had always been content to keep to herself in the background. That was the education world she knew and felt comfortable and safe in. She was given too steep a challenge. She was asked to do too much with too little training and resources.

Implicit in the KERA training role was a subtle mandate to change her style, to move out of the background and initiate contact with fellow teachers who were less than able. She found it hard to develop a new style that to her appeared confrontational and intrusive. She saw it as being judgmental, not something she aspired to. She was asked to initiate mentoring with fellow teachers without being given release time to coach and provide follow-up support. Enthusiasm and willingness were her calling cards in the classroom, but they were not enough to carry her in the area of education reform.

Successful teachers like Williams can mentor their peers, but those in leadership positions need to make sure they have the training, resources, and support to get the job done. Who knows what Williams might have accomplished with release time from class for training and coaching, mentors who could have guided her through her confusion around fuzzy issues such as the difference between judging and intervening, and coaching in how to move out of the background and begin to showcase her talents? Chances are she would not have felt depleted and bereft of affirmation for her work. She might have helped some other teacher become a more competent teacher along the way.

We must remember that Irmgard Williams is not alone in her effort to translate a highly successful career as a teacher into a teaching–mentoring role. Let's examine another mentoring episode, as described by Abby Goodnough.[1]

New first-grade teacher Donna Moffett and her mentor Marie Buchanan worked at PS (public school) 92 in Brooklyn. The school used a highly organized approach to teaching, sometimes even expecting its staff to work according to a minute-by-minute script. Frustrated by these constraints, Moffett tried to squeeze in lessons of her own choosing: stories about New York City, for example, or writing assignments about "the funniest thing your mother ever did." But on this day, Marie Buchanan, a veteran teacher at the school and Moffett's official mentor, had come to observe the school's approach. Smiling stiffly, Moffett opened the textbook to Section 1, "Pets are Special Animals."

When she got to the line about a boy mischievously drawing on a table, she playfully noted that the boy was "just like some students in here." Buchanan frowned. "You don't have to say that," she admonished.

When Moffett turned to a page that suggested an art project related to the story and started passing out construction paper, Buchanan chided her again. "You're not going to have time to complete that. You'll have to prepare for these lessons and closely follow the teachers' guide," Buchanan told her afterwards. "We're going to do the same thing tomorrow and you're not going to wing it."

Despite her frequent criticisms of Moffett, Buchanan, her mentor, said she had learned a lot since September. Asked for examples, she said that Moffett had improved her classroom bulletin boards by putting up only the best work instead of work by every student and had become a better disciplinarian by not frolicking with the students as much as in the fall.

Moffett, who was among 350 people with no teaching experience recruited the previous fall to work in the most troubled schools in New York City, entered her new profession brimming with idealism and determined to put a unique style stamp on her classroom. But like others recruited to work in those schools, she had struggled to be creative within the highly specific guidelines set by the city and state.

Abby Goodnough's story of the education of Donna Moffett drew some critical responses in the Letters to the Editor section of the *New York Times*.[2] While some letters lamented the rigid curriculum Moffett had to adhere to in teaching to improve test scores, some of the criticism was directed at mentor Buchanan for encouraging Moffett to put only the best work on the bulletin boards instead of work by all the students.

In addition, Buchanan's verbal feedback during her observation of Moffett's class probably didn't do much for Moffett's self-esteem and confidence level, critical elements for all teachers but more so for first year novices with no prior teacher training.

Put yourself in Moffett's place. You're in front of your class, trying to bring an example in a story close to home. In the midst of the lesson you say playfully, and innocently it seems, that the boy in the story is "just like some students in here." This is a comment made by a teacher who cares for her students but knows her students are not perfect. They too can be mischievous like the boy in the story who draws on the table. But your mentor interrupts and says, "You don't have to say that."

Bang! The attention shifts away from you as teacher and from your students. The lesson and the point you are trying to make probably evaporate. Your students witness a superior openly challenging what you say. This is not the stuff that builds trust and respect between the students and teacher and certainly not the stuff that builds trust and respect between a teacher and her mentor.

But the verbal feedback didn't end there—or should we call them interruptions? As Moffett proceeded to begin an art project, Buchanan, as reported, said, "You're not going to have time to complete that." As the class and the observation wound down, Buchanan jumped in again and said, "We're going to do this again tomorrow and you're not going to wing it."

Many would say that seemingly critical feedback delivered to a novice teacher and witnessed by her class leaves much to be desired. Why weren't Buchanan's observations shared in a private, one-on-one conference? Why was there—at least as the *New York Times* article portrays it—little positive feedback for Moffett to build on?

This is not an indictment of Buchanan, a respected and veteran teacher. Rather, it is an indictment of a mentoring process that appears to ignore any of the characteristics of a wise mentor identified in this book. Was Buchanan's feedback helpful and useable? Was she making an effort to build up Moffett's confidence, worth, and belief in herself and her judgments? Was she as mentor developing trust, loyalty, and a sense of privacy with Moffett? Was she judging Moffett's practice in a negative way rather than accepting her style of teaching? Did she know how to bring a sense of joy, energy, humor, and lightness to the mentoring relationship?

The mentoring role here seems to have been more one of a supervisor, a person who oversees, directs, and manages. This is not our definition of a mentor: a wise, loyal advisor, friend, teacher, and coach.

In a sense, Irmgard Williams and Donna Moffett—at opposite ends of the spectrum in teaching experience—shared a similar fate. Williams gave up part of her highly successful classroom experience to mentor colleagues. The experience did not go well and she ran into barriers. It was difficult for her to move out of her teaching role, which she had developed over twenty-seven years, and into the role of mentor in the political arena. She felt depleted, unrewarded, and confused about her new mentoring role.

Moffett came into teaching brimming with idealism and determined to put a unique stamp on her classroom, but she too ran into barriers in trying to be creative within highly specific guidelines set by the city and state. As she said, "I feel like I am beaten down and I have to keep getting up over and over again."

Perhaps mentor Marie Buchanan was also a victim of her mentoring role of trying to help novice teachers adhere to a rigid curriculum with highly specific guidelines set by the city and state, a curriculum where creativity was often discouraged. She was, after all, at the flashpoint where there was growing political pressure to improve reading and math achievement in long-struggling schools. PS 92 had been classified by New York State as failing for more than a decade. There appeared to be great pressure to increase scores on the standardized reading and math tests in the third grade. Moffett's adherence to the rigid curriculum was a must or, as school officials suggested, a blessing for novice teachers like Moffett, who had only a month of training.

Given these conditions and the political pressures from the board of education, city hall, and the state education department, maybe Buchanan's overt and direct responses made to Moffett made sense to her in the setting in which she mentored.

There was pressure on everyone to raise test scores. Harold O. Levy, the New York City chancellor, is quoted in the article as saying, "You [teachers] are the cutting edge, the shock troops, the people who are going to make things happen." Maybe Buchanan didn't have time for positive feedback, building confidence, and one-on-one conferencing. As Buchanan suggested, "I just can't let her take off on her own and do things that aren't educationally sound. It's detrimental to the students and in the long run it's detrimental to her."

Teaching in urban schools is difficult at best. Teachers come and go. As cited earlier, in urban school districts, close to 50 percent of newcomers flee the profession during the first five years of teaching. As the National Center for Education Statistics' *Condition of Education 1998 Report* suggests, teachers in high-poverty urban districts are more likely to be underqualified.[3]

The mentoring role can have many pitfalls for mentors themselves. Not everyone is cut out for the work. Many times the conditions for mentoring lack support. The case of Irmgard Williams and KERA should remind us that hard-earned experience as a classroom teacher and the desire to help colleagues may not be enough to be successful at the task. Mentors need training, ongoing support, and time to do the job well. And as exemplified by Marie Buchanan, sometimes mentoring may become a political tool, trying to get novice teachers to adopt a teaching style determined by education leaders and bureaucrats outside the school setting.

Because of a lack of training and support and the politicization of the mentoring role, many teachers like Donna Moffett may find themselves hindered in finding their own teaching style and their best teaching self. Marie Buchanan suggests that Donna Moffett is "going to be a master teacher one day." But how is that going to happen in the context she works within and the ever-present demands to raise test scores?

As the article reports, her expectations for the job were different from the demands of the district, as summarized in an essay she included with her application to become a teacher through an alternative route program, New York City Teaching Fellows: "I want to manage a classroom where children experience the thrill of wonder, joy of creativity, and the rewards of working hard. My objective is to convey to children in the formative years the sheer pleasure of learning."

The work of would-be mentors is to keep Donna Moffett's vision of teaching close to their hearts. Her words and vision are a precious gift to be nurtured, her classroom a place we would all want our own children to be part of. Developing our own voice and persona as mentors should include not only the skills but also the philosophy to support such a vision for all children. Mentors' work is to make this happen.

We need to learn how to sell the notion of what effective mentoring is and how to bring it about. We also need to understand the political pressures that may try to lead us to mentor only for test improvement, and learn how to turn these pressures aside. We need to be about creating school settings in which effective mentoring is possible, places in which people like Irmgard Williams and Marie Buchanan, highly successful teachers, have the right kind of training and support to model and communicate their unique teaching style and experience.

We need mentors who can advise their protégés how to be master teachers, people who have been there, learned through trial and error, and still remain at the top of their games, creative and caring.

ISSUE 3: SELECTING A MENTORING TEAM

Administrators can't expect to accomplish the task of mentoring each teacher in the building by themselves, particularly if they are an administrator of a large secondary school, many of which have student populations of 2,500 students and more. They need a team made up of other educational leaders in the school, a team that represents a cross-section of staff such as an assistant principal, department chairperson, teacher leader, and counselor leader. Mentor-leaders need to look for people who have the following important attributes:

- They are known as trusted, loyal leaders.
- They are respected by various groups—veteran teachers to newcomers—in the school. They haven't built walls and isolated certain groups.
- They are highly skilled in more basic mentoring skills such as listening, leading one-on-one discussion groups, providing nonjudgmental feedback, and delivering criticism in a positive framework.
- They have political and selling skills that can be vital to promoting the mentoring program. They know how to work the room and get people to make a commitment.
- They share the mentoring vision that teachers at every developmental stage in their careers need support and renewal opportunities.
- They share the belief that teachers need opportunities for career alternatives such as becoming mentors themselves.
- They are committed to the definition of a mentor: a wise and loyal advisor, friend, teacher, and coach. They are not interested in a "supervisory" mentor role in which they would oversee, direct, and manage teachers' work.
- They are emotionally tough and physically up to the mentoring task. Some teachers will resist mentoring. Mentors will be attacked at both the professional and personal levels. Names will be called and rumors will spread: "What is he after now with this mentor role? A new job in administration?"

Feelings of jealousy go with the territory. Schools, after all, are fertile places for jealousy, envy, and even retaliation toward anyone who tries to get out from the four walls of the classroom. The lack of novelty and change in teaching can fuel anger and resentment toward any colleague who tries to be different, start a new program, or take on a new role. New programs, new roles, and new arrangements often cause threat and unease.

People like the status quo even if it's not working. They know it, like the threadbare, worn sweater that should be sold at a yard sale but remains snugly in the bottom drawer. When the status quo changes some teachers fight back. Mentors need a tough skin and fire in their belly to continue. And they need to be in good physical shape to take the punishment of resistance.

Not everyone can make the transition from being an effective teacher to being an effective mentor. Different skills are required. Does every mentor possess all the right attributes? No, of course not. But these are the attributes of a mentor that you are looking for. The key is selecting people who have the potential to grow into these important aspects of the mentoring role. Your modeling and training of these would-be mentors should enhance their skills and in the process make them more effective education leaders.

ISSUE 4: TRAINING A MENTORING TEAM

Training mentors places administrators in a new and exciting role. You are moving from managing curriculum and budgets to a training role. The training process should be very similar to your own self-training model described in Chapter 4. Here is a nine-step plan of approach:

1. *Guide your trainees through the personal experience inventory (see Chapter 4) and encourage them to reflect on the following points.*

• The positive mentors in their personal and professional lives
• The negative mentors in their personal and professional lives
• The characteristics of teachers they tend to gravitate toward and help
• The characteristics of teachers they tend to avoid and not help

2. *Suggest that they explore their vision for the school and past efforts, successes, and failures that would help or hinder the creation of this vision.*

3. *Have them compare their skills to the mentoring skills and understanding checklist, taking a hard look at their current mentoring skills and what skills need improvement (refer to Chapter 3).*

4. *Next, trainees should undergo training to be team members and assessment of their overall team strengths and non-strengths.* This is a critical part of the training program. Skill acquisition is the critical element in the preparation of mentors. But skill acquisition doesn't get far without the ability of the mentoring team to function as a cohesive, democratic unit. Here is one approach you can use to build your team before they go into action.

- Have each member identify his or her mentoring strengths and skills and what resources they bring to the team. Use this data to identify the overall strengths and skills of the team.
- Have each member identify his or her mentoring skills that are not strong and need improvement.
- Have each member reflect on his or her communication skills and ability to interact with others. Teaming with others can be difficult. Fellow team members can differ in terms of philosophy, values, and educational vision. It is critical for would-be mentors to identify which team members they feel more comfortable with and those with whom they feel some dissonance. It is good preparation for getting ready to mentor teachers who may be different and, as such, more difficult for mentors to connect with. Also, it identifies early on potential conflict and communication problems, serving as an important reminder to the team that differentness need not lead to conflict and distrust.
- Have each would-be mentor reflect on his or her individual role in group planning: how does he assess his ability to be heard, offer ideas, listen, and promote effective group decision-making?
- Have each team member reflect on how he or she plans to support and empower each team member and the entire team. Teams are like families. They can be an effective mechanism to help all members be all they can be. Team members can be available to listen to other members' concerns about not being able to mentor a certain teacher or be available to hear about a major breakthrough in helping a resisting teacher become more effective. But teams, like all families, can work the other way and stifle individual and group success. Self-interest can and will take over if the goals shift from collegiality to individual stardom. Mentors, like newly acclaimed star teachers, can quickly become famous, coveted as conference speakers and presenters, and may begin talking more about the process of mentoring and doing it less.
- Have each team member reflect on how he or she intends to go about seeking out the assistance of the team when she runs into problems in the mentoring process. Here are some examples of mentoring conflicts that have a good chance of occurring.
- Remember that not every teacher will want to be mentored. Some will resist quietly ("Oh, I'm sorry I missed our mentoring conference again. I've been so busy with my kids I just forgot."). Teachers who fit into this category are hard to pin down. Mentors are in a position, based on collegiality, requiring quiet persistence, a not-letting-you-off-the-hook attitude delivered with force, and kindness. However, would-be mentors are not in a supervisory role.
- Other teachers will resist more overtly ("Look, Brad, I know your intentions are good. But I've got five years and three months before I retire. I'm

out of here. Sure we can meet and you can observe my class, but don't expect any enthusiasm from me. You have a job to do but it's over for me."). For some mentors this kind of quick shot is hard to take. It may shake their confidence. Yet knowing exactly where you stand in a mentoring relationship does cause you to reassess and mount a new approach. Overt resistance may be viewed as a gift.

- Some protégés will want more out of a mentoring relationship. Effective mentoring is an intimate and caring relationship. Some teachers, because of their own loneliness and separateness, may seek a deeper relationship beyond mentoring, a deeper friendship, intimacy, even a romantic relationship. This is not an unusual or unforeseen part of any helping relationship. Professionals in the helping professions—mental health counselors, psychologists, medical doctors—often find they have to set clear boundaries of what the relationship is about and what it is not. Maintaining professionalism is critical to the mentoring relationship. One-on-one conferencing is held in the school, not in a social setting. While issues brought up in conferencing may involve personal concerns, they should not dominate the discussion.

- Some mentors may want more out of a relationship. Being human, mentors may find themselves at risk in some mentoring relationships, finding themselves seeking more in a relationship—a deeper friendship or connection. They need to be able to talk to team members about their feelings. Mentors also need to be sensitive to their own needs and behaviors that may signal a red light and seek out the advice of a teammate. Team members can be helpful in observing a mentoring relationship that may be crossing the line from a professional to a more personal, even romantic, relationship. Too much intimacy can be a warning sign. Having a clear definition of professional boundaries helps.

5. Discuss your changing relationships with the team and theirs with you. As administrator, you are the boss, so to speak. Yes, you operate democratically, and collegiality is a hallmark of your administration. But still you are a supervisor who oversees and manages people. Here, as a trainer of mentors and a mentor yourself, your role changes dramatically. You are now operating more as a peer and colleague.

This can be unsettling for you. The trappings of your administrator role are not necessary or even wanted in this new role. You are there based on one prerequisite—skill as a trainer and mentor. It takes getting used to, and it may take some getting used to for your mentoring team. To them, you've been in charge until now. You still are, but this new role as trainer, mentor, and team member is different. In fact, one of the team may emerge, based on skill and successful experience, as the leader of the mentoring program. How much freedom and equality do you allow? These issues need to be addressed with your team by asking the following questions.

- How do they perceive your new role as trainer of mentors and a mentor?
- Do they plan to interact with you as a peer and colleague rather than as an administrator?
- How will these interactions be different? What has changed?
- Suppose they observe you having a problem as a mentor. Do they plan to give you the necessary feedback to improve? Can you count on them to be trusted critics?

6. Plan, with the team, the parameters and nuts and bolts of the mentoring program. Now you are moving into an action plan. Here are some practical issues you and your team need to deal with.

You should clarify the three major parts of your intervention. The following activities should provide the cornerstone of the mentoring process.

- Classroom observation of the protégés
- One-on-one follow-up conferencing
- Team meetings to review interventions, resolve problems, offer support, provide ongoing training, and create ongoing hubs of learning such as workshops on effective discipline

Next, identify time allotments for mentors. Mentors now have a full-time position. They need release time for mentoring and tools to keep a close check on how they are balancing the role of mentor with their other position. It is easy to spend too much time on mentoring and neglect other duties. This can create problems and cause other educators to question the program. Encourage your mentors, and yourself, not to neglect regular duties and leave work for others to pick up. Things need to function as smoothly as they did before the mentoring program was introduced. There are issues that can arise for teachers, counselors, department chairs, assistant principals, and principals who become mentors.

- *Teacher as mentor*: The optimum arrangement is for the teacher to have a permanent substitute, a person known to the students and ready for the daily tasks required. Hiring a substitute who is ill-prepared creates problems for the program and the students. Hiring a number of subs to fill the teacher slot can also cause chaos for the program and the students because the classroom does not have enough consistency and normalcy. Parents also have to understand and support this new role of the teacher. Left out of the loop, they can—and rightfully so—cause great resistance.

- *Counselor as mentor:* The optimum arrangement is for the counselor to have a reduced load, which does not mean dumping some of his or her counselees on other counselors—a surefire way to incite resistance. As with the teacher as mentor, the best approach is to hire a permanent sub.
- *Department chairperson as mentor:* Department chairs usually have a teaching duty in addition to their supervisory role. They may be the best-positioned members of the team to do mentoring as they already have available a block of time in their schedule. The key here is moving from an oversight and management role to a mentoring role. This dual role can cause conflict if not thought through. Department chairs are expected to perform such duties as managing book orders, budgets, testing arrangements, and so on. These tasks are not part of the mentoring process. Department chairs have to leave their management tasks at the door when they begin mentoring or mischief and confusion—for them and their protégés—can arise.
- *Assistant principals as mentors:* This can be a difficult role. Usually assistant principals are in a reactive and negative role—on the front lines, handling crisis and discipline situations. It is. It may be tough to try to fit mentoring into such a chaotic schedule. Yet having some mentoring opportunities may prove to be a big boost for these educators. Helping and guiding protégés can open up a positive career alternative for creative educators mired in problem-solving roles. Assistant principals too need novelty, change, and opportunity for renewal. Their daily work can be draining and have few positive moments. Again, it is a matter of trying to achieve the right mix, still maintaining their work schedule but creating time for mentoring.
- *Principals as mentors:* Again, there is no easy arrangement for principals to become mentors. It requires determination, commitment, and discipline. They have to want this new role and create the conditions for it to happen. Many teachers, central office, and middle management personnel may want to retain the status quo and keep the principal in the office.

But principals, too, need novelty and change. Much of their daily work involves solving problems and dealing with the negative side of school life—students acting out, angry parents, problematic teachers, and so on. This is an opportunity for the principal to take on a training and teaching role. It is no secret that administration jobs are hard to fill. Forty percent of all U.S. principals will probably retire within the decade.[4]

A 1998 survey by the Educational Research Service found that many schools are having difficulty filling administrative positions that opened up because of resignations, promotions, and retirement.[5] This should come as no surprise to working administrators. Who wants a job that focuses mainly on solving problems?

Becoming a mentor can change a principal's work in drastic ways. It creates an opportunity to help and guide teachers, train new mentors, and learn new skills. The mentoring role gets principals out of the office, temporarily away from the business, marketing, law enforcement, and political aspects of the role. It is a rewarding part of the daily schedule when principals can focus on real instructional leadership and address the problems of ill-trained teachers, and teachers and students can have more positive contact with them. Principals' needs for novelty, change, learning, and positive relationships may be answered in mentoring, and it might give them new energy to deal with the more mundane and isolating part of their regular principal duties.

7. Along with the full mentoring team, plan how to sell the program to the teaching staff. Good ideas and good intentions don't make a new program successful. It is very important for the team to understand that they have to go out among the teaching staff and get people involved in the program. Memos, written reports, and speeches at faculty meetings may be useful, but the real work is one-on-one involvement with teachers that helps them see that the program has something in it for them, something worthwhile, useful, and yes, even fun. How is this accomplished? Here are some suggestions.

- Make time available to query each teacher in the building personally before the team formulates any start date for the program. Teachers need to understand what's in it for them and how the program will impact them and their students.
- Assign each mentor a list of teachers with whom to have informative meetings. Every mentor should have certain teachers with whom to communicate initial ideas. Allow teachers to air resistance and negative comments. Acceptance is the key word.
- Have mentors prepare a list of positive aspects of the program (e.g., the possibility of becoming a mentor in the future) and how teachers will benefit.
- Enlist teacher leaders to serve on an advisory board for the project that meets periodically with the mentoring team. Get teachers involved.

8. With the team, discuss how to identify and overcome resistance to the program. The team needs time to discuss resistance to the program and how they will handle it. Any change has its critics, and the burden of swaying these resistors is on the mentoring team. It is their idea, so if they want to make it fly, they must show everyone why it is an excellent idea. If they can't, they will have to bury the failed mentoring program in the school's graveyard replete with failed programs.

Overlooking resistance and mistaking a lack of comments for support are secret killers of any new program. How does the team proceed to let resistance emerge so that it is identifiable, welcomed, and confronted in a positive way? Here is one approach.

First, have the team list the teachers who they think will welcome and support the program. This is the allies list, a critical constituency. These are the people mentors need to cultivate and encourage to speak up in support of the mentoring program. The team needs to make sure that this group is given ongoing attention. Don't assume that because they are initially in favor of mentoring their support will continue once the project gets into the reality stage. The team needs to continuously shore up these allies.

Then have the team list teachers who they think will oppose or even try to divert the mentoring program. These are the naysayers capable of blowing up the project—another critical constituency in a different way. They are critical in the sense that if their concerns are not heard and responded to, they are not going to go away. They are going to come back and haunt the project, continuously raising questions about its efficacy.

Resisters can be cruel. How can their concerns be heard without giving them a platform to destroy the project? Large-scale meetings to review the project can be taken over by resisters with their own agenda. Well-intentioned teachers can easily be swayed to abandon their support of the project when they are faced with disagreeing with their peers.

Your best approach is for team members to sit down one-on-one with each critic, hear them out, and try to get them on board at some level. One meeting may not be enough; it may take several meetings to establish a level of trust. Can every resister be turned around? Probably not. The goal is to incrementally reduce the number of resisters, one by one, so that only a small group remains, no longer in a position to torpedo the project.

It is important that the team not isolate or make enemies of this group. Keep communication lines open and keep working with them. Times change, and when the project runs into foul weather, the team doesn't want these resisters to begin their assault again.

9. Have the team reflect on how they can remain sensitive to problems and how to create a safety antenna. It is important for the team to reflect on how they plan to address problems that may destroy or alter the mentoring process in the future. Often, we assume that what is working well will continue to work that way, without adjustments or setbacks. Time can bring many changes, however, as new projects evolve, grow, and change. The original leaders of the project may move on to new positions or turn over the reins to new mentors. Although a mentoring team may not be conscious of it, change is always taking place within the project and everyone involved.

With change, there is always the possibility of extinction. How does a mentoring team identify problems and make the necessary adjustments? Problems are signals that something is amiss, and as such they can be seen as friendly reminders, shaking our complacency and alerting us that adjustment is necessary. Here are some ways the team can remain sensitive and be proactive problem solvers.

- Anticipate changes in the teaching staff. Staff changes can rearrange the teaching staff in dramatic ways. Teaching staff are often graying, ready for many veteran teachers to retire over the next several years. There may be an influx of novice teachers, some without preparation. This may result in increased demand for mentoring.
- Be vigilant. Don't become set in your ways. Complacency is always near-by in any successful project. It is the quiet enemy, lurking, waiting for the opportunity to take over. The team will probably get tired. The initial push for a new program requires a great deal of emotional, physical, and intellectual energy. There comes a time when we want to rest and turn on the automatic pilot. That's when complacency rears its head in unusual ways. If the program becomes very successful, participants begin spending time presenting at conferences and away from the real world of kids and mentoring.

  The mentors become stars and instead of the focus being on mentoring teachers, it is now on accommodating visiting educators and researchers and on self-promotion. What took years to build falls apart quickly when no one takes care of business, and the great goals of the project slip away. The team needs to be vigilant for such a process and understand that it can happen to them. Be wary of success and self-promotion.
- Anticipate changes in support. Administrators come and go. Budgets get reduced. Supporters retire or withdraw to other interests. It is important for the team to continually reassess their level of support. What was initially strong support can easily change with the arrival of a new superintendent or principal with different agendas. The resources for release time for mentors can easily be wiped out in a failed budget.

  Being political, the program needs to try to develop a variety of resources that can keep the project afloat during bad and changing times. The team might connect with a university or the state education department to fund the mentoring program as a professional development lab. Knowing and understanding local politics and the funding and program opportunities available from external sources are critical tasks for an alert mentoring team.

At this point, you have assessed your own mentoring skills, done some reflection and self-training on how to improve your skills, and trained your mentoring team. Now you are ready to take a more comprehensive look at mentoring relationships.

NOTES

1. Abby Goodnough, "Teaching By the Book, No Asides Allowed," *New York Times,* 23 May 2000, A1, B7.
2. Letters to the Editor, "The Education of Donna Moffett," *New York Times,* 29 May 2001, A14
3. NEA Teacher Quality Fact Sheet, "Ready or Not: A National Teacher Shortage Looms," NEA, 2001, www.nea.org/teaching/shortage.html (19 April 2001).
4. Vincent L. Ferrandino and Gerald N. Tirozzi, "Our Time Has Come," NAESP(National Association of Elementary School Principals) Online, www.naesp.org/ misc/ed-week_article_2–23-00.htm (23 February 2000).
5. Education Research Service, "Is There a Shortage of Qualified Candidates for Opening in the Principalship? An Exploratory Study," NAESP Online, www.naesp.org/misc/short-age.htm (20 April 2001).

Chapter Six

The Mentoring Team in Action

TAKING STEPS TOWARD BUILDING A WHOLE-SCHOOL MENTORING PROCESS

This chapter's focus is on a series of vignettes that highlight different team members' unique mentoring roles. Hopefully, these vignettes will reinforce the mentoring skills you and your team need to be effective and will point out the subtle differences involved in differing, unique mentoring roles.

These vignettes are based on successful mentors I observed in action in my capacity as director of the Bay Shore Public Schools–Stony Brook University Teacher Center, an innovative school-day training program facilitated by classroom teachers, and as director of teacher training at the Louis Armstrong Intermediate School, a project jointly sponsored by Queens College, the United States Department of Education, and the New York City Board of Education. These mentors were able to make a difference in the lives of many teachers and spark lagging school renewal projects.

Are there mentors like this in every school? Probably not. But I believe many schools have administrators, teachers, counselors, department chairs, and assistant principals who have the potential to fill a mentoring role. The key is recognizing that the skills educators use in helping kids—nonjudgmental listening, positive feedback, affirmation, positive role modeling—can also be applied to helping teachers renew themselves.

It's no mystery but it does take a redoing of the way help is delivered to teachers. It is not a "you should be" or "you shouldn't be" message but rather a message based on accepting and recognizing where teachers are and helping them make the changes that are required for success.

Will every effort to renew and guide teachers be successful? Of course not. But we can lay the foundation so teachers don't fall through the cracks.

99

We can invite them into a process of renewal and gently, or sometimes forcefully, inch them forward to being master teachers. To do otherwise is to abandon our work of helping make every teacher the best teacher our kids can have.

This chapter also highlights the kinds of issues that might be discussed at team meetings with mentors, bringing to the team issues and themes that teachers are dealing with in the school. This is not a process that invades the privacy of the mentor–protégé relationship but is a compiling of the areas in which teachers need support and further training.

For example, a need expressed by many protégés is that they need to acquire better discipline skills. This data can then be translated into hubs of learning such as teacher-led workshops and networking with needed university resources. In a sense, the issues and themes raised by protégés become the curriculum for ongoing learning, a vehicle to respond to the immediate and long-term needs of teachers.

Finally, while these vignettes focus on secondary educators, the basic core of the intervention, follow-up support, and creating of ongoing learning hubs can easily be applied to the elementary level as well.

THE PRINCIPAL AS MENTOR

This vignette focuses on the role of the principal as mentor. Here we see in action some specific mentoring characteristics identified in Chapter 3:

- Mentors understand the dynamics of teaching and the real world of the classroom.
- Mentors understand that every teacher arrives at the classroom door with his or her own set of biases, judgments, and prejudices.
- Mentors understand that the personal and family problems of students can be very emotional and painful for caring teachers.
- Mentors understand that there are huge professional and personal benefits in the mentoring process.
- Mentors know how to help their protégé find and define his or her best teaching self.
- Mentors know how to teach their protégés to become involved in ongoing sources of support, learning hubs, and opportunities to enhance renewal.
- Mentors understand that the mentoring relationship will change over time, often with the newly skilled protégé gradually taking on a mentoring persona and stature of his or her own.

This vignette further expands the mentoring role of Brad Foley and his protégé, social studies teacher Tom Murray, described in Chapter 4. One of the key figures in Tom Murray's search to become a more effective teacher is a student who is acting out, Jim Moriarty. Jim first challenges Tom but as their relationship evolves he begins to see Tom as a caring and helpful mentor.

Brad Foley uses Tom's conflict with Jim as a catalyst in getting Tom to learn new skills. Hopefully this vignette helps pinpoint Brad's mentoring skills and in the process demonstrates how Tom integrates these same skills into his own teaching persona to help Jim Moriarty become a successful role model and leader.

Our First View of Tom's Class

Picture a social studies classroom in a junior high school. The bell rings. Students come into the classroom. Some arrive in groups, pushing and laughing: they are the in-crowd. Others walk in alone: the loners who are part of the out-crowd.

The teacher, Mr. Murray, stands behind his desk. He asks for quiet. "Take out your textbooks and notebooks. Our topic today is the Depression years in America. Also take out your homework and pass it forward. Moriarty, I don't expect a repeat of your behavior yesterday. You've got two strikes against you. Your next move is out the door. Got it? I've spoken to the administrator about you. Am I being clear? Let's begin. Janine, what's your answer to question one?"

An unskilled mentor's view of this class sees order and control. But he misses the opportunity to help Tom Murray become a more effective teacher. Tom is lucky he doesn't have this administrator as his mentor. An administrator unskilled in mentoring observing this class would say this is a standard junior high school classroom. Students walk in and get settled down. The teacher gives directions, throws in some needed reprimands to student Jim Moriarty, and proceeds with the lesson. Things are under control and the lesson is proceeding.

Janine, one of the brightest students in the class, sets a positive tone with her usual insightful and correct answer. Even though Tom Murray is a beginning teacher, he has things under control. We need more Murrays in our profession.

Fortunately, Tom has Dr. Brad Foley, a skilled mentor, as his administrator. Foley quickly identifies the problem areas that Tom needs to address. A skilled administrator as a mentor observing the class sees and hears much more. He notes that the teacher is not at the door to greet his students. He remains behind his desk.

He also notes that Tom doesn't greet any of the students by name or get involved in welcoming conversations: "We missed you yesterday. I heard your dad's been sick. Is everything all right? Let me know if I can help out," or "Hey, you played great yesterday. Is the soccer team really in the playoffs? When is the next game? I'll be there."

Nor does Tom make any effort to involve the loners with invitations to get involved: "Frank, the social studies club is meeting today. How about joining us in Room 317 after school? I think you could be a big help to us with your interest in history. Your report on World War I was great."

Dr. Foley observes that Tom Murray remains behind his desk throughout the class. He doesn't move around the room and make contact with students who are clearly not involved in his presentation. It's as if he is talking and interacting with only a small percentage of the students, those who seem bright and constantly raise their hands to answer questions.

Out of the twenty-eight students in the class, Dr. Foley notes that only ten are participating on a regular basis. The remaining eighteen students, mostly boys, are sitting quietly, many with their heads down, or whispering and acting out. Many are minorities.

Among them is Rachael, a new student from Puerto Rico, and Christian, who just moved from Texas with his mother after his parents divorced. Jim Moriarty is desperately trying to get Tom Murray's attention with his laughter and joking. Dr. Foley notes that he needs to ask Tom why he calls Jim by his last name and seems to let him remain isolated and uninvolved. He seems afraid of Jim and threatened by his behavior.

Finally Dr. Foley notes that Tom Murray's focus on only a small percentage of his students has another element to it. He often focuses on girls who are known as high achievers in the school. He seems to feel safe and unthreatened with this group, a class within a class. Dr. Foley wonders if Tom is aware of this dynamic. It's only October and the class is clearly divided into those with the answers and those who choose to opt out of participation. The class is also divided along gender and racial lines.

As Dr. Foley notes, "Things seem quiet, but as the year progresses these issues may become more combustible if they are not addressed and resolved by Tom. He may not sense he is in trouble, but he is. I plan to address these issues with Tom at our next mentoring session."

After class Dr. Foley asks Tom if they can meet during third period. He says, "Let's meet in our new conference room, Tom. It's more comfortable than my office. I think we are off to a good start but there is work to be done on both our parts. See you then. I'll bring the coffee. Two sugars, right, Tom?"

Dr. Foley uses his mentoring skills to help Tom become aware of areas where he needs to become more effective. As promised, Dr. Foley arrives at the mentoring session with coffee. He understands that Tom is a relatively new teacher, in his second year, and he is apprehensive about his first mentoring session. So is Dr. Foley.

The mentoring program is new this year and Foley has had to delegate more of his responsibilities to his assistants. Being out of the office, away from the rush of daily crises, is a new world for him. But he believes he can have his biggest impact helping each of his teachers raise their level of competence.

His boss, superintendent Mary Lewis, is behind him as long as "you keep the lid on the school. Not everyone is going to understand, but if the mentoring program works out, maybe the other administrators will come on board. I'll give you two years." In a way both Tom Murray and Brad Foley are in the same boat. Both are starting anew.

Brad Foley sets the stage for the mentoring session by inquiring about Tom's personal life and interests. Brad knows that Tom is interested in sports and is a Civil War buff. He also knows that Tom is recently married and has a baby on the way. His wife, Mary, is a pediatric nurse at the local hospital. Tom is a New Yorker who migrated to the Midwest to go to college and stayed because, as he says, "I like the slower pace."

They talk quietly and in the conversation Brad lets Tom know that while he is still finding his way through the new mentoring program, he is enjoying the face-to-face interactions with teachers. He is having much more contact with real teaching situations and is learning a lot about classroom dynamics and how good his teaching staff is.

No, they are not perfect. There is work to be done if they are all going to grow professionally. His paperwork and problems are still there when he gets back to the office but it's been worth it. The first few minutes of the mentoring session are designed to create a sense of ease and safety for both the teacher and the mentor. No, Tom and Brad are not friends, but so far they are trusting of each other and believe that they will be able to learn from each other.

Once the coffee is gone and the opening conversation has established a sense of ease and trust, Brad begins his work as mentor. First he offers Tom some praise: "Tom, your classroom control is excellent and you are ready to go when the students come into class. The lesson proceeds fine. All in all it's good stuff."

"But," he adds, "I have some questions for you that may help us pinpoint some areas that you might want to consider as you work toward being more effective with every student in the class. And let me emphasize the words *every student* because I think you are making good contact with some students but more can be involved with some simple steps on your part.

"First, I notice that you're standing behind your desk when the students come in. Have you thought about standing at the door or in the hallway and greeting each student with a hello and sharing something personal with them, such as that you missed them when they were absent or you saw them play a great soccer game?

"Second, I notice some kids, like Larry Donato, come into class pretty much alone. You probably know that Larry's parents recently split up and he is having a rough time. Have you thought of ways to get him involved? I've observed that he does pretty much the same thing in every class, just sits by himself. I've asked your team leader, Frank Munson, to bring his name up at our next meeting. We need to get him off his duff and into some ego-building activities. How about the Social Studies Club? I know he loves the Civil War.

"The same goes for the new kids, Rachael and Christian. This is a huge move for them. Imagine coming from Puerto Rico and Texas. This is a well-to-do suburb. I don't think we really understand what they are going through. Maybe for our next meeting you can think of some things we can do to help them get settled. Hank Mobley, the gym teacher, tells me they are both good athletes.

"Another area that I notice, and I know it is a difficult one, is that you are really interacting with only ten or so students. They seem to be very bright kids, like Janine, and pretty much dominate the class. I know myself, when I was a teacher, I often went with the kids who had the answers and kept things moving. In fact, I was hesitant to ask the other kids because I knew they either didn't have the answer or would take forever to say what they had to say. I was afraid of losing the momentum, of the silence. I was impatient, rushing. That was not good for me or for the kids. And to be honest, some of the other kids, like Jim Moriarty, who sat in back of the class and carried on, made me shake. I didn't know how to get across to them and get them involved.

"So what did I do? I went with letting the quick and well-prepared kids answer. It was easier. It took me a while to figure out how to get the other kids involved. But you know, the answer was simple. I had to spend time with them, get to know them, not address them, as you do with Jim Moriarty, by their last names. And believe me, I did the same thing as you.

"I had to come to believe that every kid wants to be involved, be successful, fit in, be someone special. You know, it comes down to this. It's up to us as teachers to find the way. That's why they pay us the big bucks, right? How about inviting Jim in for a conference and having lunch on a regular basis? He's a very good drummer, by the way. He plays in a rock band and hangs out at the mall. No, he's not much into school but he has something to offer. It's something to think about.

"And finally, I think that, while things are going well now, you may be setting yourself up for some trouble as the year goes along. Here is one area that could get to be a real thorn in your side. It's not something to be threatened by or to be avoided. We can work on these issues together. I notice that most of the interaction in your class is with the girls. Most of the ten students participating actively are girls. Most of the eighteen others are boys or minorities.

"I am not saying there is any maliciousness here; you may not even be aware of it. But the good news is that it is an area that you can address now that I am making you aware of it. Be consciously aware of this dynamic and try not to be afraid of it. It's there. It's an area in which you need to develop some new skills.

"In order to get better at the teaching process, we all have to look at the dark side, those kids and issues we tend to avoid. Let's put it another way. I know you are a New York Yankees fan. David Cone did not get to win twenty-five games a year throwing only fastballs. He has had arm injuries; he has had to adjust, change, learn new approaches, develop a change-up, throw sidearm sometimes.

"That's also true for you. Tom Murray needs more pitches, if you will, to be a more effective teacher. You have to open up your vision and see the whole field. That means involving yourself with the whole class. Make sure you are connecting with each student, each day, in every way possible.

"As I said, we can work together on these things. I am learning new things about this job and so are you, so we're both in the same boat. By the way, I've invited one of my associates at Spring College in for a coffee klatch to talk to teachers about how we can all better understand minority students. His name is Frank Able; he's a talented and helpful guy. He is coming over next Monday at 7:30, before school. How about joining us?

"I am thinking that down the road maybe you and some other teachers could team up with Frank to run a workshop on how to overcome the barriers of working with some students who come from different backgrounds and cultures. It's food for thought."

Brad Foley then asks Tom to try out some new behaviors. He gives Tom the following list of suggestions to work on during the coming week:

- Change your behavior at the beginning of the class. Be more welcoming and inviting as the students enter the classroom. Let them know you are glad they are there. Make a big deal of saying hello and making meaningful small talk. Think of yourself as the maitre d'.
- Get to know your students more intimately—what they like, what they do for fun, their personal issues.
- Invite students like Jim Moriarty in for a lunchtime conversation. Break down some of the barriers that exist.
- Be assertive about asking everyone in the classroom questions. Move around the room. Get them involved. Try not to go for the right answer every time. That will help the Janines in the class be aware of others who struggle to get it right and take some of the pressure off her.

- Use Janine and her able classmates to help tutor the other students. Instead of lecturing, break the class into small groups and bring different parts of the class together to work on projects. Use the bright kids as mentors.
- Remember the resources we have that you can tap into, such as Frank Able from Spring College.
- Begin thinking of yourself as a resource, a mentor, for fellow teachers by becoming involved in workshops on issues that you are trying to work through.

Now it is Brad Foley's time to ask for feedback. He is direct and he asks Tom to rate his performance in this mentoring session. Tom, of course, is hesitant. Brad accepts this behavior. It is a new area for both of them. But Brad persists by saying that in order for him to be a more effective mentor, he needs to know how he is coming across. Is he helping, supporting, pointing out the necessary work that both he and Tom have to do to help Tom be a more effective teacher, or are his comments too intrusive, aggressive, or off the mark? Tom's answer says it all.

"I am so glad that we talked. I was very apprehensive about this mentoring program. I knew you would be coming into my class on a regular basis and we would be having these one-on-one sessions. I didn't know you very well. You were always in the office and busy my first year here. I know a lot of the other teachers, even the most experienced ones, were apprehensive too. And our union rep told us to be very careful about what we said, although he said you were very pro-teacher.

"But this seems to be working out well for me. I like your casual approach, the coffee, and our easy talk in the beginning of the session. I am surprised you knew so much about my personal life. It made me feel good. As for your observations, I think they are right on target. I've always tried to keep myself a little distant from the kids, not get too involved with them by sticking to my subject area.

"My graduate school professors stressed that getting too close to them can lead to losing control. I remember them saying, 'Don't be friends with your students. Be an authority figure and things will go your way.' But I think that's not been good. I've isolated myself and I am surely not enjoying the kids. Even Jim Moriarty—I was just like him as a kid. But I made him an enemy, an outsider.

"As for the girls/boys/minorities thing, I frankly wasn't aware of that but now that you bring it up, I can see it could be a time bomb. I've been pretty tight just trying to get the right answers out and have the kids be ready for the state tests. Plus I've been worried about my wife having the baby. She's been having problems. I guess things will be all right. I don't want to burden you with my personal problems.

"Your ideas for inviting the kids for lunch and breaking kids into groups sound good. Maybe the next time you could help me set up the groups and sort of co-teach with me so I get the hang of it. I've never worked in groups before but I see that it could help the kids who are not so involved.

"You made me think about a lot of things today that will help me improve as a teacher. I like your easy conversation and your making critical observations that seem very helpful and doable. I never felt you were putting me down or demeaning my work. You are a good listener. You're not afraid to say what needs to be said. You give good, workable suggestions and you are not in a hurry.

"My last principal, in Indiana, was in and out in a flash. All I got from his visit was a written checklist that contained mostly plusses on work. Not one word was spoken. It didn't help me learn much. I don't know how to describe our relationship. It's different. It's both personal and professional. You are opening up to me about your work and asking, imagine that, my advice. I never had a principal do that before.

"And thanks for the information on Frank Able. It would be great to discuss some of these things with colleagues. These topics, you know, don't come up in the faculty room. Are you really serious about my being involved in offering a workshop with Able and other teachers? That would be great stuff. Wait until I tell my union rep about this meeting. He'll be knocked out. Teachers giving feedback to administrators on their performance? Wow!"

This story suggests the positive power and possibilities for both the teacher and administrator involved in an effective mentoring relationship. It also clearly describes the loss of opportunity for Tom to grow professionally if his mentoring is carried out by an unskilled mentor who sees only issues to control. Fortunately, Tom now has the data necessary to begin to acquire new skills and behaviors and he has the support and the guidance of a good mentor in Brad Foley. Most important to our work is identifying the skills that Brad Foley brings to the table, skills noticeably lacking in our first mentor's observations. Here is a list of the skills Brad Foley brings to the mentoring sessions:

- He has informed himself about the personal life and interests of his teachers.
- He is not a threatening figure. He creates the conditions in which a two-way helping conversation can take place and grow. There is safety and ease in his intervention.
- He understands classroom dynamics and knows what works and what doesn't. He has been there as a teacher and is not afraid to share his mistakes.
- He is a good listener and observer.

- He is aware of the barriers that both teachers and students put up to remain uninvolved and isolated.
- He is nonjudgmental in his view of Tom's classroom performance. His focus is solely on the skills and new practices Tom has to learn to be more effective.
- He is not interested in blaming or being the guy with all the answers to Tom's problems. He is not blaming Tom for the behavior of some of his students. Rather, he is saying, "Let's address it with a set of new skills and interventions before it clouds your other areas of successful teaching."
- He knows how to praise, reward, and shore up good teaching practices.
- He knows how to give teachers classroom problem-solving techniques that can help them avoid practices that produce failure.
- He introduces his teachers to school and community resources. He knows he can't do all the mentoring by himself. He is always on the lookout for credible resources both in the school and in the community who can share the leadership.
- He encourages teachers to view themselves as potential mentors for colleagues and students by becoming involved as workshop leaders. Again, this is another way to build his mentoring constituency and expand his leadership team.
- He encourages teachers to use successful students as mentors to help other students.
- He is having some fun and enjoying his staff. He is not locked in an office reacting to the phobias of poorly trained teachers; he is doing something about it.
- Brad Foley has a vision of where he wants to go. His plan is to involve all his teachers in the mentoring process but he doesn't plan to stop there. He wants the Jim Moriartys and the Janines involved as a team, putting together the brightest and the neediest, to be mentors for other students. Brad understands that's how kids learn tolerance and acceptance of each other, by being involved in projects that build community, awareness, and trust.

Brad Foley's skills are attainable by administrators who set out to be effective mentors. It is sound, effective communication and coaching skill. Many administrators would like to have Brad Foley's skills and many teachers would welcome and need his intervention. Administrators are eager to learn how to embrace this new mentoring role. Teachers want to get better at their craft and be more effective. Like at-risk students, teachers don't want to fail or to be viewed as less than competent. Administrators, armed with Brad Foley's mentoring and intervention skills, hold the key to their teachers' success or failure.

Teachers who are failing their job know it, and often their plight and story are known by everyone else in the school and sadly become a topic for faculty room and PTA talk. Administrators who are skilled mentors can intervene and change the lives of failing teachers and in the process bring life, energy, and hope back to the students in the classroom and set an example for other teachers, wherever in their careers they may be. The teachers can learn that things can change and new skills can be acquired, but it does take hope, work, commitment, and practice on the part of the teacher and also the mentor involved.

As Tom Stoppard, the playwright, suggests, happiness and change involve equilibrium and shifting one's weight. It often means giving up outmoded skills, jumping from the ledge, and creating new classroom dynamics based on the present.

Finally, early intervention to help teachers like Tom Murray identify and learn new skills is surely a clear-cut way to save taxpayer money by cutting down job-induced illnesses and sick days related to lack of success, and by improving skills so students can have the academic gains they may have missed with a failing teacher. It is also a clear-cut way to save and improve the lives of professionals who, without intervention, deteriorate over time because nothing seems to work right in their classrooms.

THE TEACHER AS MENTOR

This vignette focuses on the role of the teacher as mentor. Here we see some specific mentoring characteristics identified in Chapter 3:

- Mentors understand that a teacher's personal problems, such as divorce or a growing addiction, affect the teacher's effectiveness and well-being.
- Mentors know how to listen, be nonjudgmental, and provide useful feedback and modeling.
- Mentors have knowledge about aging and barriers to career development.
- Mentors understand that renewing oneself is hard work; it's often not simple or even sought after.
- Mentors know how to take care of themselves and be physically and emotionally up to the mentoring task.
- Mentors value the loyalty and privacy of the protégé.
- Mentors know how to bring a sense of joy, energy, humor, and lightness to the mentoring relationship.

This vignette describes a relationship between mentor and teacher Frank Bronkowski and his protégé, math teacher Ellen Turner. Frank, a veteran twenty-year English teacher, is in his first year as a mentor. He has been a very successful teacher and coach.

Coming to the school fresh out of college, he quickly established himself as a class act, an effective classroom teacher who was great with kids, a colleague others sought out for advice, and a teacher committed to working with kids after school as a basketball coach and faculty advisor.

He also continued his own learning experience, acquiring a master's degree and more. He now serves as adjunct professor in a local university's education department and recently coauthored a book on how teachers can help teens solve personal problems.

Frank was clearly an easy choice for the mentoring program. Still, the mentoring position is a new and challenging one for him. He has two periods each day for mentoring. While he has a gifted permanent sub, he continues to oversee her work, teaches two classes himself, coaches, and participates in weekly mentoring team meetings. He thanks God that he has a stable, caring home life that offers him support. And he is in excellent physical shape, running five miles a day.

Ellen, his protégé, has had a rockier career. She is in her thirtieth year of teaching, coming to the school fresh out of a master's program in 1972. For the first twenty-five years she was a school leader, teaching the more difficult math classes, administering the tutoring center after school, and working on a Ph.D.

But for the past five years she has seemed to withdraw from all activities except her classroom teaching; she has given up on her long-sought Ph.D. and turned the tutoring service over to younger teachers. Consequently, her teaching has suffered. Her department chair assigns only the most basic classes. She has started to miss school, calling in sick at least once every few weeks. The administration is considering requiring her to bring a doctor's note to verify her so-called illnesses. She doesn't look well and rumors say she is drinking heavily and is seen at a local liquor store each evening.

What happened to this once energetic, gifted teacher? The faculty room gossip says she's turned into a nightmare teacher, poorly prepared and unable to be an effective disciplinarian. Gossip also suggests that she has home problems. For the past three years she has been involved in a hostile divorce. Close friends say her marriage has been on the rocks for years. She increasingly isolates herself, arriving at school at the last possible moment, eating lunch in her room, and as one administrator puts it, "is out of the parking lot before the buses leave."

The school's administration and some of her colleagues are very concerned for her well-being, but they seem unable to help her, somehow not able to find the right words. It is sometimes easier for teachers to help troubled kids than colleagues. There are other teachers who are not so kind.

They mock her behavior in the faculty room and even have placed bets on how long she will be able to survive.

Some teachers are not kind when they see a colleague in trouble. Does it create uneasiness in them, an uneasiness that suggests that this could happen to them someday? To them it is better to make a mockery of it, to make the failing teacher the victim, rather than internalize their own fears and vulnerability.

Does the mentoring program offer some hope for Ellen? Clearly, Frank has a big challenge trying to help Ellen get back on the right track and fight for her professional and perhaps her personal life. She seems to have given up.

But how should a mentor give someone life? How does a teacher break through the depression and wake up to the reality that she is failing and failing fast? We all know teachers like Ellen who are in flight; they are not strangers to us. Yet, like Frank, we ask ourselves, "How do I help?" Like Frank, we are not counselors or therapists. Teachers are not certified as helpers.

But that doesn't have to matter. Everyone has helping skills. We know how to listen, be nonjudgmental, and provide feedback that can help shake and shape our colleagues in need. We can be helpful in our own unique way if we are willing to take the risks to intervene and be a loyal friend. We understand that problematic personal relationships of colleagues affect the teacher's effectiveness and well-being. And we understand, because we have been there ourselves.

Maybe the words a mentor uses to connect with someone like Ellen are not terribly significant. Maybe what is important is the effort, a willingness to try and in trying to be willing to accept the rebuffs and refusals. In trying, we learn by doing and hopefully find the right words that have meaning to someone like Ellen.

Mentors need to remember that there are few instant successes in connecting with teachers headed for trouble. The red light of danger may be on but they don't see it or they choose not to see it. It is the job of mentors like Frank Bronkowski to have them see the warning lights and advise and direct them to sources of help. Let's see how Frank proceeds.

Frank is a master teacher and he has been trained as a mentor. He knows the drill. But being well trained and knowing the drill doesn't always prepare him for mentoring real people with real problems. Frank's first task in helping Ellen is to understand what is wrong and right in her classroom. Once he has this data he can make an accurate assessment and plan for intervention. Ellen's is a classroom that was once alive, with an energetic, caring teacher and students at ease, knowing they were in a safe place but yet challenged. There were no negative criticisms, no accusations, no screaming; it was a class students looked forward to each day.

But now, as Frank is to see, it is a classroom in despair, a teacher scream-ing and name-calling, a classroom inhabited only by students who have no way out, no parent to rescue them by complaining to the principal or counse-lor and demanding another teacher. It is a classroom in which the teacher—Ellen Turner, who almost has a Ph.D.—and her students have no way out. The only escape is for the teacher to call in sick and the students to cut class. Who will care if they do?

A View of Ellen's Class

Picture a classroom in despair: the bulletin board holds pictures yellowed with age describing events long past; a blank chalkboard looks strangely unused for a ninth-grade consumer math class; desks are spread out around the back of the room with no order, no rows, pushed as far away from the teacher's desk as possible. Ellen's desk seems isolated, not part of the class-room at all. The students slowly drift into class, many of them late, minutes after the final bell.

Although the class enrollment is twenty-two students, only fourteen are present. Ellen, sitting at her desk, seems to ignore what is going on, waiting for the kids to sit down. Five minutes into the class she takes attendance. When she calls out the names of absent students, the response of other students is often, "She cut."

Sometimes the students deliver quick, insulting remarks such as, "I don't know why I'm here. This class sucks," or, "How come Fred got transferred to Ms. Eglin's class? Probably his parents got him out. I wish my parents would do that. I agree with Sandra. This class sucks. We're not learning anything."

Ellen is unresponsive to the insults and challenges to her authority. She doesn't even seem to mind that her mentor, Frank, is observing this fiasco. It's almost as if she is saying, "Who cares what these kids do or what I do? I certainly don't any more. These kids are the bottom of the barrel. Teaching consumer math is the lowest of the low. I can't get much lower." She passes out a worksheet and says, "Do problems one through six in class and finish the rest for homework. If you fail to turn in the worksheet tomorrow it's an automatic failure."

One student, named Mike, interrupts: "What if you're not here? You're always out on Fridays. You sure get sick a lot. It's a wonder they still pay you."

Ellen, seemingly oblivious, returns to her desk. The students quickly be-gin fooling around, throwing papers out the window. They look at Frank in a somewhat embarrassed way as if to say, "We know we shouldn't be doing this but Ms. Turner doesn't care so why should we?"

Minutes before the bell the students get up and leave. Ellen doesn't chal-lenge them, telling them to stay in their seats until the bell. Frank thinks it's a miracle that the students hadn't acted out even more. Ellen established no control or boundaries and demonstrated no preparation or interest.

Was Ellen really that oblivious to all the chaos in her classroom? Clearly she knows the difference between good and bad teaching. She was an effective teacher at one time. Frank wondered how she had arrived at this point. What happened to her pride? Her skills? Her craft? How did she develop such a tolerance for pain?

An unskilled mentor's view of this class rightfully sees disorder and chaos. But he misses the opportunity to help Ellen Turner become a more effective teacher. Ellen is lucky she doesn't have someone unskilled as her mentor; she might be out the door. An unskilled mentor might say, "Some way has to be found to get rid of Ms. Turner. Medical leave, whatever. Let's find a way and quickly. This lady is in trouble and we are not a clinic or rehab. We don't have the time or resources to coddle her. Let's call her in and encourage her to resign or apply for medical leave. I don't care that she was once a great teacher. The past doesn't matter. She's killing the kids. I know the union will go along with us."

Fortunately, Ellen has Frank Bronkowski as her mentor. Frank has a plan to help. He knows that there has to be a good reason for this decline in Ellen's performance. He feels that the best approach is to go to Ellen in the one-on-one conference with what he has observed as problems and get her to react. He'll do it gently, of course, but will accept no avoidance of issues.

He thinks, "Let's stop treating her as a patient. Let's forget about her divorce, isolation, even the drinking—if that rumor is true—and focus on classroom issues." He will leave Ellen plenty of room to bring up personal issues that may be draining her enthusiasm and energy, but the first step is to identify the classroom problem areas she needs to address.

Ellen is no dummy; she knows good teaching. He will remind her what that is and what it would take for her to get back there. Frank begins to wonder who is isolating whom. Has the school been isolating her, avoiding her? Was her seeming incompetence a cry for help? Frank sees opportunity here. He does not allow his students to become isolated and uncared for, and Ellen will get the same treatment from him.

It is not hard for Frank to identify the problem areas that Ellen needs to work on. He lists his reflections on the problems and how he might address them in the conference:

- Get some life into the classroom. Fix the bulletin boards. Bring in some flowers or pictures of your daughters and grandchildren.
- Let your students know something personal about you, not your personal problems but something you're involved in. Do they know you started the tutoring program here? Many of your students get the help they need

there. Think about going back to work there. It would be an ideal spot to help your students.

- Find out something personal about your students. Sandra has just completed a great season with the soccer team. Mike has been doing some good stuff with the peer-counseling program. His dad passed away last summer and he is working with a group of elementary kids who have lost a parent. You have some interesting students. Many of them don't have much parental support but they're survivors, like you.

- Let the students know you want them in class on time and they are not allowed to leave early. First appeal to their good judgment. Say it looks bad for you and them if they are in the hall after the bell. If that doesn't work, give out detentions. Be tough. They'll respond.

- Get rid of the worksheets and do some real teaching. You're putting the kids and yourself to sleep with the worksheets. You don't seem to care, so why should they? You've been there. Use what you know.

- Rearrange the desks so there is an emphasis on discussion. Give each student an assigned seat. No more back-of-the-room isolation for them or you.

- Create an atmosphere of self-respect and caring. Stop letting the students take pot shots at you. Stop the insults. Tell them you won't tolerate it any more. In turn you will respect them and treat them the same way. It will take a while because you've let it go on.

- Get out of your room and start mingling with the staff. You've isolated yourself. I know some of our colleagues can be cruel and criticize others to keep the heat off themselves. But keeping to yourself doesn't help you, and it sparks unkind and malicious rumors. If you make yourself known people will talk less behind your back. Show your face.

- What I am saying is to take back your classroom and your self-respect. We are going to work on this together. I know rebuilding pride isn't easy. You're going to have to make some changes but that's OK. I'll be there as a loyal friend. What goes on between you and me stays here. I'll be loyal and respect your trust in me—if you'll give it to me. This will help me learn as a mentor. And who knows? Maybe this is a way for you to become a mentor someday. You're not the only struggling teacher in the building. You know that.

One-on-one conferencing following classroom observation is the heart and soul of the mentoring process. What kinds of conditions does Frank have to create? Consider the following suggestions.

If possible the meetings should be held in an attractive and comfortable environment, in an atmosphere of safety, trust, and professional respect. Protégés need to feel welcomed and affirmed and have a sense that this is a good place to be. Simple things can help humanize the mentoring setting: a pot of coffee, snacks, flowers on the table, comfortable seats. It should be a setting that encourages conversation. Ironically, these kinds of setting are rarely found in schools.

The environments in which we work often lack comfortable, professional spaces that allow for privacy, as educators often place all of their emphasis on the students and their needs. Professional comfort zones that can enhance conversation and professional dialog hardly exist. What we often have in schools are faculty rooms, often unkempt, with outdated, yard-sale furniture brought in by teachers.

Teachers settle for the minimum, as if they as educators aren't worthy of better conditions. This is a glaring example of teachers' inability to take care of themselves professionally, to demand more. Effective mentoring requires different, comfortable settings. Mentors need to create these kinds of comfort zones and learning hubs if they want their protégés to reflect on their teaching issues. Trying to carry on mentoring conversations in the anomie of the faculty room doesn't foster a feeling of privacy and safety.

In addition to creating an attractive setting, Frank needs to be ready to greet Ellen, raise critical issues, encourage her to respond, and develop an informal contract on how they will proceed as a team. Consider the following suggestions.

Frank should bring some joy, energy, humor, and lightness to the meeting. He should greet Ellen with some positive feedback even if it's hard to find. His physical stance should be welcoming. He should smile, appear relaxed, and seem to be looking forward to the meeting.

Frank is good at asking questions that lead to reflection on Ellen's teaching process. He uses expressions like, "What is your take on what is happening? Here is what I see. Have you ever thought about . . . ? Here is how we might proceed. How does that sit with you?"

Frank gives homework assignments to both Ellen and himself. He might ask Ellen to write a reflection on how she views her teaching style, the positives and negatives, and how she views what work has to be done to improve. Frank suggests that he will do the same and take a look at his own teaching style. He also suggests to Ellen that she do a daily reflection on her teaching day, a reflection she can share with Frank if she chooses.

Using these hints, Frank does not arrive at the meeting clueless. He has set the right conditions, he knows the right words to use to encourage communication, and he has a plan to help Ellen based on his classroom observations. This is how their conversation goes.

Frank: Hi, Ellen. Thanks for coming. Coffee? I got some great donuts at Hilda's bakery. Try one. Look, I am glad we could get together. As you know, this mentoring role is new for me. I want to be helpful if I can but I am not an expert by any means. I know every teacher has to be involved in the program but I want to keep this as simple and low-key as we can.

With that in mind, let me say that what we talk about and work on together stays between us. Brad Foley made it clear that this is not a supervisory situation. I am here to help . . . period. Maybe we could begin by my asking you how you view the program.

Ellen: Frankly, it's not something I want to be involved in. I've got other things to do. I also haven't been feeling too well lately so this is another burden. I am here because I have to be. I can't afford to jeopardize my job, especially right now. Frank, I like and respect you. You are a person I know I can trust, not like some other people in the building. But don't expect too much from me.

Frank: Sounds fair to me. I appreciate your honesty. Let me ask you how you think things are going in your classes. I've observed you three times and I've got some suggestions. But first I'd like to get your take on things.

Ellen: Whew, that's a tough one, particularly since I just told you that I'm not into this mentoring thing. Well, you're no fool, Frank. You see what's going on. I've just sort of caved in. I'm there. That's about it. Kind of weary of it all, I guess. And you're too nice a guy to bring it up but it's all over school that Rob and I have finally split up. Twenty-two years and the last few hell on wheels. I am just worn out. But money is tight and I can't afford to leave. Everyone's upset—me, my kids, my grandkids. I've got to sell my house and get an apartment. Jesus, I've lived there for twenty years. It's all I have and now that's gone too. But no one here seems to care. It's a mess and I'm a mess. You see it, the kids see it. I used to teach calculus and now they've stuck me with consumer math. I've become a nothing. Am I a burnout? I don't know. What a comedown.

Frank: I'm glad you're sharing this with me. Yes, it does look like you're struggling in the classroom and at home. It's a tough time. I'm glad I'm going to be around to support you. Part of mentoring is getting to talk about real life problems that may be affecting your teaching. And you are experiencing some tough ones. But, as you say, you also seem to be experiencing feelings that you've landed in a bad spot, dropped from calculus to consumer math, and your home problems may indeed be making you weary, burned out maybe. I'm not a counselor or a therapist but it's easy to figure out why you're struggling in the classroom. There's not much joy around right now.

Ellen: You've seen it. I'm just letting things go in my classroom and that's not really helping me. It's making things worse, really. You can't imagine how ashamed I am when I go home each day. It's so painful to see me as I am now. My poor performance only adds to my woes. I think if I enjoyed teaching and the kids once again, I would be a lot happier, but I can't seem to get started in that direction. I've got no one to talk to, except maybe you. I don't know. I'm open to any suggestions. This is killing me.

Frank: I think you're right. Working on some ways to improve your teaching may be the way to go. It may give you some uplifting success and increase your feeling of self-worth, which I sense has taken a beating. My sense is that it will probably take a while for your home issues to work out. Getting some counseling might help but I'm sure you've thought of that. It might take some of the burden off your shoulders. Having someone to talk to does help. But I think there are some things you can work on right now to begin to get back to your best teaching self. You've been there. You know what good teaching is.

I have some suggestions that might help you. Let me share them with you and see if you agree. Am I on target? Some of the suggestions are quite simple and I don't think you have to make a lot of major changes. Try brightening up your classroom with pictures and flowers. It'll help you and the kids. Let the kids know you have been having a tough time—you don't have to get into the details—and you're trying to change things. Think about rejoining the tutoring service or some other activity so you can get out and see people.

The peer-counseling program is looking for facilitators to help lead a divorce group. It may be just what you, and kids experiencing divorce, need. You're there; you know how hard it is. Get to know your students on a more personal level. Ask about their lives outside of school. Who knows? Some of them may be experiencing a divorce, too.

Also, set some rules and boundaries in the classroom. Expect the students to arrive and leave on time. Get a little angry and demand respect. You don't need to be talked down to. You may be weary but that doesn't mean you have to take crap, excuse my English. Rearrange the desks for discussion. Get back to questioning. Using worksheets, in my opinion, is not adding zest or creativity.

Think about how else you can reach these kids. You're a pro. You've been there. Get that bright and experienced mind of yours going. Think about getting out of your room for lunch. Stop letting people think you're troubled. Don't let them label you. The more you're out talking with others, the better it will be for you. Sure, you're having a rough time, but so are a lot of other teachers and administrators. Life hits us all.

Also think about writing a reflection on your teaching every day. It might help you focus on what's going on and how you're doing. And finally, think about counseling. It might help shore things up as you make changes. It might also help you find the words to talk about what's going on with your kids, grandkids, and colleagues. Finally, I wrote these things out for you. If you want to take them with you, great. It's a list of things we might both work on. What do you think?

Ellen: You're right. A lot of these things are very simple but it does feel like too much to do all at once. Maybe I could just start with the room. I've got some great pictures of my kids and grandkids. Funny, I don't think I've ever shared anything about them with my class. I also have a great garden with lots of flowers. Gardening is a passion and hobby with me. It makes me feel at peace. I'll bring some flowers in, maybe even try to tell my students about my garden and what it means to me. Maybe I'll even make a lesson out of it, the profitability in professional gardening.

Look, Frank, this has been very helpful. I dreaded coming here. Even thought about calling in sick. But thank God I am here. Let me take the list and see what I can do before we meet again. I appreciate your concern for me and your offer to help. You really listened to me, got me to think, and your suggestions make sense. It's the first time in a long time that I've felt a little energy and hope that things can change. I just got through reading an article last night called "The Kindness of Friends." You certainly are one. Thanks.

Perfect ending? Who knows? Time will tell. But for this day, this moment, Ellen has some hope that things can improve. She has a little energy and a pulse. Without the well-thought-out and skilled intervention of Frank, chances are that things would have only gotten worse for Ellen. But now she has a trusted, loyal friend and some concrete issues to work on. She is not left to deal with her demons alone.

And Frank has the positive feedback he needs to reinforce his self-worth and mentoring skills. He sees that his effective questioning can result in reflections that make his protégé more aware of her teaching self, the good and the bad, and the work that needs to be done.

Where does someone like Ellen go if her school does not support mentoring? Some lucky ones find angels and saviors, or they save themselves. But most slip away, some silently—"She just called in and said she wasn't coming back. I knew she had problems but this is so sudden. Who do we have to fill her spot?"

Others, though, exit their school with a bang: "I knew it was going to happen. I could see it coming, that one day she was going to lose it. It was that seventh period class with all the difficult kids. She just exploded, started screaming and cursing and then she ran out of the building. Everyone—the kids, the teachers, the aides—was watching. Her ex-husband called last night and said she wasn't coming back. I wish we could have done something but we're no miracle workers."

THE DEPARTMENT CHAIR AS MENTOR

While both Tom Murray and Ellen Turner had personal issues, the focus of mentoring support was on improving classroom performance: different teachers with different issues but the same goal. Every teacher needs help at some stage. In Ellen's case help came fast. She just had to be asked how things were going. She knew things were falling apart and she was ready when Frank arrived to help.

Both vignettes describe an important part of an effective teacher's work—setting clear boundaries. Tom is a new teacher searching for and creating, with Brad Foley's help, a set of rules to govern what student behavior should be like in his classroom. He is also creating a teaching persona that defines his role. He will be available to help students like Jim Moriarty but he avoids taking on a parenting role. He realizes that he can't take Jim home with him and give him the care and love he needs, but he can, within the classroom limits, be a mentor and advisor for him.

Setting clear and reasonable boundaries is also an important goal for Ellen. Somewhere along the way she has lost the ability for, and maybe interest in, making very clear what is acceptable for her students. She has also lost the ability for and interest in setting clear boundaries for her personal and professional behavior. She arrives at school at the bell, leaves early, calls in sick regularly, and allows her classroom environment to deteriorate. She has also lost important personal boundaries, her marriage, and soon her home. But with Frank's intervention, she has a guide and a plan to restore order.

Sometimes important issues about setting boundaries occur outside the classroom. Some involve quiet, little-spoken-about relationships between teachers and their students, the kinds of issues that "aren't supposed to happen here." These are certainly not simple issues that can be easily addressed, as in the case of relationships that cross over the teacher–student boundary into friendship or even romantic involvement.

Sometimes teachers involved in helping their students work through painful personal experiences take on Messiah, savior, friend, or parenting roles, spending more time with certain students, sometimes in evening meetings outside of school. These teachers, some inexperienced in setting boundaries, don't heed the red light of caution and cross over their professional boundaries. Their behavior is often observed by colleagues and administrators who fail to intervene. They can't seem to find the right way to help, the right words of caution, the right skills to bring sense to the situation.

In this vignette we focus on such a teacher, Shawn Mallory, and his mentor, department chair Randy Edwards. The difference here is that Randy Edwards does try to intervene and advise Shawn Mallory to be careful. He realizes that Shawn is a novice teacher. Shawn may think he knows what teaching is all about, but he has many lessons to learn.

He is well liked by his students, even adored some might say. As a new teacher he has brought excitement and zest to his department and the aging school faculty. He's loving his job, but he may be headed for trouble. Being too involved with needy teens can be risky business, for them and for the teacher. Highly successful careers can easily be detoured when boundaries get blurred. Interventions don't always work.

With the current rash of school violence, aren't we all looking for teachers who care for at-risk students and reach out to them? Aren't our schools calling for more teachers to be mentors and advisors, to see that their teaching role should now include helping students solve nonacademic personal problems as well as academic problems? Doesn't helping students resolve personal problems free them to be better academically?

Before we search out teachers to be mentors and advocates for students, we need to have a support system in place, such as mentoring, that can give off an early warning sign when a teacher's own personal feelings and need for relationships spill over into an intimate relationship with a needy teen. Our emphasis is on reflecting on some specific mentoring characteristics identified in Chapter 3:

- Mentors know how to help their protégés clarify the many complex roles they play in the classroom.
- Mentors understand that the personal and family problems of students can be very emotional and painful for teachers.
- Mentors have finely honed political skills, skills that may be put to good use in protecting their protégés from external and internal threats.

This mentoring relationship involves the health and physical education department chair, Randy Edwards, and first year teacher Shawn Mallory. Randy followed and found his dream. He was a local boy who graduated in the top of his class and starred in three sports—football, basketball, and baseball—deciding early on to be a coach and physical education teacher. He was awarded a scholarship to Springfield College, where he was named All-East Coast in both football and basketball.

He returned to the district, where he became an innovative teacher and coach, a new kind of physical education teacher who moved a stale program. Randy introduced a number of new programs to address the health and well-being needs of students, such as a weight training room, Project Adventure, peer support for athletes, and workshops on eating disorders and substance abuse problems.

He also developed a wellness program for staff and parents. At least half the staff made use of the training room and participated in faculty workshops to address health and aging issues. When the department chair slot opened up he was the front-runner. He vowed to continue building a model health and physical education program by bringing in teachers who represented new thinking in the field. Shawn Mallory was his first hire. Randy was a natural selection for the mentoring program. His interest and expertise in wellness added an important resource to the team.

Randy also brought an additional resource to the team. He had developed a network with a local university's education department and medical school. He periodically brought in experts to offer a wide range of wellness programs to students, staff, and parents. In turn he served as an adjunct professor at the university wellness lab. As part of his training he participated in a workshop on preventing sexual abuse by teachers. It was his first introduction to the topic, one he had never given much attention to.

Sure, he remembered a male teacher he had in high school who had been fired for having a relationship with a senior girl. It was a big story for a few days but eventually faded, with many community leaders saying that it was an aberration; things like that didn't happen in their community. And they were right. There were rumors sometimes about some teachers getting too involved with a student, mostly a male teacher with a female student, but occasionally a female teacher with a male student. There were even rumors about same-sex relationships. But they remained rumors.

As Randy immersed himself in his mentoring role, observing his teachers in both their classrooms and coaching roles, he began to become more aware of how his teachers handled close, personal relationships with their students. He also remembered some of the data and suggestions about teacher–student sexual relationships that he had learned in his workshops:

- There were 110 documented cases of sexual abuse between staff members and students in New York City schools between 1991 and 1995. Most of the cases concerned some kind of willing involvement by smitten students.
- In a 1991 survey of former students at a North Carolina high school, 13 percent of the graduates reported they had engaged in sex with a teacher during their high school years.
- Many teachers lack training and supervision in how to carry on close and intimate relationships with students. If their own personal needs for love and affirmation become thwarted, they may unwittingly seek to meet these needs through a close involvement with a needy student, a student looking for a caring, loving adult, a confidante, whom he or she sees on a regular basis.
- Inexperienced teachers are often more at risk for teacher–student sexual abuse because they don't understand how to create clear boundaries with needy students. Initially flattered by a student's interest and response to their caring, novice teachers may not see the hazards and risks ahead.
- School administrators and colleagues need to recognize the danger signals when they observe them in other teachers' interactions with students, and they need to know how to intervene.
- Teacher–student sexual abuse knows no geographical boundaries; it can happen in any school. It is not just an urban phenomenon.
- Teacher–student sexual abuse is not unlike sexual abuse in other professions. Intimate helping relationships can go awry if the professional involved lets his or her own personal needs take over. Every professional involved in an intimate relationship needs ongoing supervision and mentoring.
- Professional training programs and having a professional degree are sometimes insufficient preparation for real-world helping issues.[1]

In mentoring teachers, it is important to observe how they interact with their students on a personal level. Yes, schools want teachers to be involved in helping students who are at risk and lack a significant adult in their lives.

Schools need teachers who are responsive and caring and who are positive role models for needy students. But mentors need to be alert when they observe teachers becoming too involved. There are hazards and risks and when mentors observe such behaviors, they need to act.

Sometimes their intervention is rebuffed, but it is still best to take the risk. Turning our backs on problem-creating situations or saying that it's not our job can leave protégés at risk. Like teachers with their students, mentors need to be able to address the nonacademic aspects of their protégés' professional lives and not focus only on the classroom issues. That is an important part of a mentor's work, but not all.

Randy has wrestled with how he is going to address a sensitive issue with Shawn. Shawn is his first hire and in a few short months he has turned into a dynamo, teaching two ninth-grade health classes, two physical education classes, and team teaching a class on tobacco addiction. He has made a quick, positive impact. The students, staff, and parents give him high marks.

He is also coaching the girls' volleyball and soccer teams. He seems to be everywhere—eating lunch with students, walking the hallways, greeting kids (he seems to know everyone), arriving early to supervise the weight training room. He's young and seems to have boundless energy, the kind of teacher every school needs to provide a shot of adrenaline. He's a prize that needs to be cherished, but he also should be taught a lesson about the complex life of school.

As Randy understands, Shawn is inexperienced and vulnerable. In spite of his boundless energy and enthusiasm, he makes mistakes, maybe more than other, more cautious first-year teachers because he is willing to take on many projects.

The sensitive issue Randy is struggling with is Shawn's seeming over-involvement with a ninth-grade student, Aileen Lopez. He has noticed that Shawn has been having lunch with Aileen in the school cafeteria on a regular basis. He has also observed Shawn giving Aileen a ride to school on some mornings. Aileen is also on Shawn's soccer team and he seems particularly supportive of her efforts.

On one level Randy is hesitant to say anything. Maybe all Shawn is doing is trying to help a student who is having troubles. Aileen is new to the district, having moved from an urban school in Philadelphia. Evidently her parents are divorced and she is living with a grandmother. Her younger siblings are living with other relatives in various parts of the country. She is in a new school with little family support. But she seems bright, eager to learn, and is a good athlete.

But the other students haven't welcomed her. She's very attractive and adult-like. It's as if the other students don't know how to react to her. She seems much older than her age of fourteen, as if she belongs in high school or college. Maybe Shawn is just trying to provide a safe place for her until she learns how to fit in.

On another level Randy has some concerns. Shawn is young, only twenty-four. And the female students think he is, as they say, a hunk. He gets a lot of eyeballing and contact from them. You know teachers like Shawn in your schools, more student than professional teacher, still wet behind the ears. While he may be trying to help and support Aileen, he is drawing attention to himself by eating lunch with her on a regular basis and driving her to school.

It may be perfectly innocent behavior, but some of the staff are beginning to talk. A few have come to Randy and voiced concern, not so much that something is going on between Shawn and Aileen but that it doesn't look good. It will hurt his chances of getting tenure. Should Randy let things be, hoping Shawn will resolve things himself, or should he speak to the issue and maybe sound a warning and show Shawn how to set some boundaries?

Randy: Hey, Shawn. Good to see you. Coffee? Oh sorry, forgot, you're a no-caffeine guy. Got some juice, though. Donut? Oh, wrong again. No sugar, right? Hey, here's a health bar. I keep them for you health nuts. Seriously, how are the classes and the coaching going? From what I observe, you're really moving and grooving. Kids, staff, and parents all seem to think you're doing a great job. And I do too. I haven't heard one criticism. It's very unusual for a young teacher to have such an impact. I guess I know how to hire the right people.

Shawn: Thanks, Mr. Edwards. I mean Randy. I keep thinking I should call you "sir" or "mister." Yeah, it's been great. The kids and the staff have been great, and so have you. I didn't know what to expect, really. I've been fortunately successful all my life but I wasn't sure how this experience was going to be. My student teaching was in a very conservative school and my mentor there was really out of touch. All he really did was turn the classes over to me and go out for a smoke.

But it helped make me independent and rely on myself. I couldn't do some of the things I do here, like Project Adventure, but I survived. The kids there didn't have any of the programs you developed. Looking back I feel like they were being robbed of things that could really help them, like the tobacco workshop. The students here are lucky and I'm just glad to be here. I'm up every morning and ready to go and the day goes by so fast. I can't believe it's February already!

Randy: That's great, Shawn. Your happiness and enthusiasm show. You've brought a great gift, yourself, to us—to me, the staff, the kids, and the parents. It's much appreciated. I want to do what I can to cherish and support you and your gifts. You have all the makings of a master teacher.

But there is one area I think we need to talk about. It has nothing to do with your teaching performance. You're aces there. And maybe it's not really a problem at all. I just feel we need to get each other's input on the situation and figure out how we should proceed. As your department chair and mentor, I am, after all, somewhat responsible for your well-being, learning, and career advancement. I need to address any issues that may get in the way of this process. Does that make sense to you?

Shawn: Sure. I know you're in my corner. I never imagined that you'd be in my classes and at my games so often. I appreciate your interest in me so much. I know you're not out to hurt me. What's going on?

Randy: Again, this may not be a problem, but I've noticed you spending a lot of time with Aileen Lopez. I know she is new and has some personal issues to resolve, and I know she doesn't easily fit in with the other students. Ivy Harrison, the school counselor, shared some of that with me. She's counseling Aileen on a regular basis. What concerns me is this. You may be creating the wrong impression by eating lunch with Aileen on a regular basis and giving her rides to school. And, my take, you seem to be giving her more attention than needed in soccer.

Now, this may not be true, but the wrong impression I'm talking about goes like this. Schools are political places. You're new and you may not grasp that yet. You have no ulterior motives but some staff members do, and they may draw attention, negative attention, to your seeming over-involvement with Aileen. Rumors can start and rumors can be vicious. Things can be said that may threaten your career, your tenure, even though you're the best new teacher we've had in years.

You have to be sensitive to the picture you're giving other people. Sure, help Aileen, but don't give the impression that somehow there is a friendship, or worse, a romantic relationship, developing between you. That's not fair to you and not fair to her.

Secondly, we are all human. Teachers, in trying to help students, become emotionally involved with them. It's part of the deal. We get to know them, their lives, their struggles. We feel their pain. Sometimes we want to do more, become their savior, confidante, even take them home so they can have a good meal or a decent night's sleep. It's part of being a concerned and caring teacher.

Sometimes our personal desire to help can go too far. I am not saying that this is happening with you and Aileen. But sometimes teachers can become too intimate— become friends, or even lovers—with students. It happens. And it can happen to any teacher in this building. That's why some teachers avoid becoming involved in personal relationships with students. They are academic teachers only—they teach their subject and go home.

You know why? Because deep inside they're unsure of themselves in intimate relationships with students. It's safer for them to keep their distance. Their stance is, "Don't tell me about yourself. I don't have to care about you if I don't know your story."

But if you are a caring and concerned teacher, which you are, you have to learn how to set limits and boundaries. We can't be the student's parent or make all the wrongs right. We can care, listen, give advice, be there when we can, but we have to draw a line. That's something you're learning, and in a way this situation is a gift because it provides a wake-up call about school life and creating boundaries.

Let me be specific here. I want to hear your response to my query. But here are some specific suggestions regarding Aileen. Stop having lunch with her on a regular basis. Some staff, students, and inevitably parents will pick up on this. Some may start unkind rumors. Don't expose yourself or Aileen to this threat. Stop driving her to school. Again, some people will misread your good intentions and assign less than admirable intentions to you.

Put a stop to the rumors before they start. Support her in soccer but be aware that you may be giving her too much attention. The other kids and parents aren't dumb; they see it. Don't let it become an issue in your coaching and teaching.

I am not saying end your involvement with Aileen. She clearly wants your support. Withdrawing that isn't useful for her. What I am saying is make the support and the lines clear. Be involved with her in class and in soccer. Be there for her. She will seek you out when she understands that's where the focus of your relationship is. But no phone calls, no rides home. Bluntly, don't be naive about school life. It can be cruel and hurtful, not just for kids but for teachers as well.

For some teachers, schools are dull places with little novelty and excitement. They live their professional lives on rumors and finger-pointing. Learn that lesson. You can be the greatest teacher in the world every day but if you're drunk at faculty parties or womanizing with colleagues, that's the image that gets talked about. Don't make yourself at risk and vulnerable.

Let me handle the politics. Learn from me how to do it. I'll try to silence any negative references to this situation that may be raised by staff. I don't believe in letting rumors go unanswered. I've learned from experience.

My record as first-year football coach was two and seven and we barely won those two games. I came on board after a championship season replacing Earl Allen as coach. Allen was a legend here. A lot of rumors started after that season. Getting rid of me seemed a given but I went to the athletic director and superintendent and made my case. They gave me cover, three years to turn things around.

I'll give you all the cover you need. I'm a local boy and I know how things work. You're in good hands.

Finally, don't worry. This will pass. In fact, as I said, this is a valuable experience for both of us. It's a lesson for you that there's more to learn about school life than teaching. It's good that we're going through this together. I am learning, too!

What do you think about my observations and suggestions? I've hit you fairly hard, maybe unfairly. But I need to say these things if I'm going to be true to my mentoring role and our relationship.

Shawn: Wow. You caught me by surprise with this one. You're right about Aileen. She lives around the corner from my place. Plus she's in my health and P.E. classes and on the soccer team. I met her at the deli one Saturday morning and we began to talk. She's pretty much alone here. Her grandmother is eighty-five and quite ill. She has a lot of worries about her family. Her dad went back to Mexico and her mother is living with some guy in Philadelphia who has a drug problem. I guess her mother does, too. And her two younger brothers are living in L.A. with an aunt and her sister is up in Boston with another relative.

She's literally on her own. I guess some of the other students haven't been too kind to her, using racial slurs. It's been tough for her but she's eager to do well and make a place here. So I've tried to spend a lot of my time listening to and guiding her.

No, there's no sexual stuff. Maybe friendship. But I never thought of that until now. It seemed normal, like I was trying to help a kid in trouble. I didn't realize that the spotlight would be on me as a beginning teacher but I guess it is. Jesus, what do people think? You're right about other things. I find myself spending more time than needed with her at soccer, even giving her a ride home. Whew! Never thought about this stuff. As for your suggestions, I think I'd better listen to them. I mean, I wasn't doing anything wrong, but as you say, the picture isn't good. Thanks for noticing.

Perfect ending? Who knows? But both Randy and Shawn learned a valuable lesson. Randy gets to affirm his mentoring skills and judgment. He acts, as Shawn suggests, as a guardian angel, warning and protecting his novice from two kinds of threats: threats from the institution that may derail his career, and threats that lie within himself that may propel him unwittingly into a more intimate relationship with a needy student.

This kind of relationship can happen in any secondary school to caring but unwitting teachers like Shawn. Intimate one-on-one relationships between caring teachers and needy students can lead to a surrogate parenthood or romantic relationship without intervention from wise, experienced mentors like Randy.

THE ASSISTANT PRINCIPAL AS MENTOR

One of the major themes in this book is the acknowledgement that bad times, failure, and burnout can happen to every teacher, even the most successful ones. It may be more difficult for star teachers to be aware that they are losing positive contact with their students and colleagues. It's not supposed to happen to them. These are the teachers who have won the teacher of the year awards and held elected office in local, state, and national professional associations, such as the National Middle School Association, the Association for Supervision and Development, and Phi Delta Kappa.

These teachers regularly make keynote speeches at conferences, lead staff development workshops, and serve on select state and national government committees on issues such as education reform. They are known throughout their school, district, state, and even nation as prime examples of professionalism and creative teaching. They are always in demand from an education, parent, or citizen group, receiving a steady stream of phone calls asking them to be the keynote speaker at a conference. They are the go-to experts that the media zeroes in on when an issue arises, such as student violence at Columbine High School. They are interviewed by the press and on television and radio.

In a sense, these teachers create another "expert" persona in addition to their teaching persona. In a real sense they have created another role that may increasingly take them away from their primary role, that of classroom teacher. On the fast track to stardom, their primary focus moves from the classroom to the speaking circuit. In the process, their teaching world, and the teaching world of their students, begins to change. The boundaries get rearranged.

At first, this new star role is met with support and enthusiasm by district superintendents, principals, school board members, and community leaders. The newly acclaimed teacher begins to draw rave reviews. It helps put the district and school leaders on the map. They have to be doing something right if they are cultivating such fine teachers. It helps pass budgets, raise morale, and move the educational climate away from a focus on problems to one of success. It's a win-win situation, or so it seems, for everyone.

Things often change, however, as the star teacher begins to miss more and more class time. A vacuum sets in and a sense of loss develops. The boundaries are different for students, parents, and colleagues. Students, faced with a succession of subs, grow disgruntled. Kids develop a close relationship with an effective and caring teacher. When that is taken away from them, they notice. Like children in a family affected by divorce, they develop a sense of loss or even betrayal.

Parents, too, sense a loss and betrayal. Although initially proud of the star teacher's success, they grow weary of the parade of subs and lack of continuity. They vow that next year's teacher will be classroom-based with a main focus on working with the class.

Fellow teachers also begin to react to a star teacher, as well. Statements are heard in the faculty room: "Is she ever here? I bet she's angling for a state education department or college professor job. Even when she's here she's always running out of her classroom to take a phone call. The secretary is sick of running up and covering her class. I wouldn't do it. I hear she's getting paid $500 a shot for her presentations and still collects her paycheck here. What gall. I hope the administration sets her straight soon."

This movement into a star role isn't viewed by the teacher as a bad experience, a failure, or a situation capable of burning them out. It feels good. It's exciting, novel, and a source of new energy.

But it is also a treacherous, seductive role, one that lures teachers away from their teaching role by offering the possibility of life in the spotlight. It can result in teachers giving less and less attention to their teaching role and eventually bring about failure as a classroom teacher. Some teachers naively, even foolishly, assume things will stay the same in their classrooms, that they can return at any time and things will be as they were—the students, the parents, their colleagues.

But they have changed and so has their classroom. The speaking circuit becomes a fool's-gold situation for them, giving teachers novelty, change, and a sense that they have become a "somebody." Numbers of teachers attend their presentations and cling to their words. They feel a rush they never felt as a classroom teacher. Is it unrealistic to think that they can be successful in this dual role they have created? Can teachers be both star presenters and effective classroom teachers?

When a star teacher returns to her regular teaching duties, she begins to sense that she has drifted away from her school, students, and colleagues. She essentially becomes a visitor, and the old parameters no longer exist. She pulls into the same parking space, but that's all the permanence that remains. When she walks into the building, she senses being viewed as "someone who used to work here."

Relationships have changed and she suddenly finds that while she may be succeeding as a presenter, she is failing as a classroom teacher. She finds she cannot successfully manage both roles, and one has to go. Do star teachers stay or move on? Do they try to recapture their lives as successful teachers or move on to being consultants or presenters? If they decide to stay, are they willing to give up being "somebody" and accept being "just a teacher"?

This vignette focuses on how mentoring can help a star teacher resolve the question of whether to stay or move on, how to reestablish boundaries or form new ones. As Dr. Seuss suggests, this teacher has come to a place "where the streets are not marked." She must make a decision but the way is not clear. The emphasis here will be on the mentoring characteristics identified in Chapter 3, characteristics that can help awareness and clarity:

• Mentors understand that bad times, failures, and burnout can happen to every teacher, even the most successful ones.
• Mentors understand that resistance to mentoring will take place.
• Mentors know how to help their protégés find and define their best teaching selves.
• Mentors know how to help their protégés clarify the many complex roles they play in the classroom.
• Mentors understand that their lack of in-depth knowledge of every subject and grade level does not reduce their efficacy in mentoring teachers.

This is the situation that assistant principal Linda Alvarez and teacher Myra Fryman find themselves in. Linda has been assistant principal of the school for three years. Prior to that, she taught eighth-grade Spanish and started the English as a Second Language program. She is very involved with the growing number of Latino and other immigrant students and is chair of the school's diversity committee. She has championed a district-wide effort to provide staff development workshops for teachers in the area of diversity and inclusion.

Her parents were immigrants from Cuba to America. Schooled in Catholic schools in Miami and at the University of Miami, she is a strong believer in discipline. She expects students and teachers to take care of business. Her philosophy of education, and life, is written on a poster behind her desk: "Be a responsible and responsive member of this school community. Don't make a mess that others have to clean up." She was a natural choice for the mentoring program because of her energy, clear focus, expertise in diversity and inclusion issues, and no-nonsense approach to leadership.

As prepared as Linda Alvarez is, she isn't ready for some aspects of the mentoring program. Her experience with Myra Fryman proves to be a novel learning experience.

Myra Fryman is one of the best, if not the best, teachers in the school. Her science students routinely finish in the top five in science contests. She is sought out by prominent parents who want their students to be in her classes. Her room is called "Fryman's University" by the students because of its many resources—computers, lab equipment, and research tools—acquired by Myra with grants from universities, government agencies, foundations, and other sources. Her school has more resources than any other school in the state and even some local colleges. She is a go-getter and an excellent grant writer and salesperson. She knows where the money is and she goes after it.

With grants, her budget is over $100,000 for the past five years, exclusive of district funding. It is her money to manage; she has an oversight board but she steers the money to create new programs of her choosing, such as a summer science camp and a mentoring program with Harvard University.

She has created an empire for herself in the district. The superintendent and school board regularly bring visitors to the school to show off Myra's lab. She is famous within the district and state and even on the national level, where she serves as a consultant and head of the Teacher Education Committee for the National Center for Disease Control and Prevention.

She is also on the governing board of the National Science Teachers Association and chairs the science section for the new national testing standards. A picture of her receiving the national Teacher of the Year award from President Clinton in 1995 hangs over her desk. Her achievements have created a situation where she is literally her own boss. Some colleagues say she is beyond supervision, and certainly no one controls her. She seems to come and go as she pleases, in a world of her own. The often-heard comment in the faculty room is, "Whatever Myra wants, Myra gets."

Things began to change for Myra when Brad Foley became principal and brought Linda Alvarez on board as assistant principal. It wasn't a dramatic change, but something was in the air.

In the previous administration, Myra came and went as she pleased. She regularly took part in presenting at local, state, and national conferences, and she was often away training other science teachers. She really had several different jobs—science teacher, grant writer, teacher trainer, and conference presenter.

The previous administration was eager to support Myra's multi-role situation. They basked in her national success when visiting educators from throughout the country made visits to their school, and a new secretary had to be hired to help Myra manage her grant process and greet the growing number of visitors. "Fryman's University" was an organization of its own and unconnected to the school except for the classroom component.

At first, both Brad Foley and Linda Alvarez were surprised by how often Myra was out of the building. Her requests for subs seemed out of bounds. In the first year of Brad and Linda's tenure, Myra missed thirty days of school, fulfilling commitments she had made with the approval of the previous administration. When Brad promoted the mentoring program, he asked Linda to serve as a mentor for Myra and in that role to look for an opportunity to address Myra's growing absence and the impact it was having on her students.

Although many parents want their children in Myra's classes, there is growing discontent that she isn't present to provide necessary continuity. For the first time, some students have asked to transfer to other classes. Even Myra is shaken. Cracks are beginning to appear in her star-teacher armor.

Early on, Linda recognized that these issues would be a major focus in her mentoring role with Myra, but Linda isn't naive. Myra is tough and she has political backing. She isn't about to allow herself to be mentored. Linda feels that to leave Myra on her own, increasingly removed from her students and the school community, is not fair to Myra or her students. Things have to be brought under control, and Myra needs some boundaries, like all other teachers.

Myra was surprised when Linda began to observe her classes and invite her in for follow-up mentoring sessions. She knew that Brad had started the program and was requiring every teacher to participate, but she thought that with her busy schedule, Brad would let her pass.

Brad indicates that this is not the case. Every teacher has to participate, including Myra. How would it look to the other teachers if Myra were not included? No, Linda would be her mentor, do class observations, and meet with Myra for follow-up conferencing. Several issues emerge from these sessions.

Myra: You know, Linda, I really don't have time for this today. I'm waiting on a call from a professor at the University of Michigan who wants to bring a team of educators here in January. I also have the summer science camp curriculum to review and two ninth-grade research classes this afternoon. Can't we say we met and skip this one? Besides, you know I'm a good teacher. You see the rapport I have with my kids.

I don't mean this as a criticism but you're not a science person. What do you really know about my subject? How can you mentor me? Wouldn't your time be better spent with a new teacher or one of those burned-out teachers? You know who I mean. Really, this is a farce.

Linda: Thanks, Myra, for coming in today. I know you are busy and yes, I can see where you might question how much I can be of help. But I want you to know that I want to be a resource for you and I do have some issues we need to discuss.

It's not about your teaching, per se. When you're in front of your class you are, as you say, a great teacher, one of the best I've seen. I feel it's a privilege to be working alongside of such a gifted person. You blow my mind with some of the ways you involve your kids. The issues I am referring to go beyond the classroom.

Myra: Linda, I really don't like being part of this mentoring program. You know I am an effective teacher, and you know I'm very busy promoting our science program and projects. Do I really have to be involved in mentoring? Can't you talk to Brad and arrange some sort of gracious way out for me? You know the science fair is coming up in two months. Plus my top science kids are involved in the Westinghouse Scholarship program. They are going to need a lot of help from me.

Linda: I know you're busy and very involved in many projects. Brad and I appreciate all you do to promote our science program. But every teacher is required to take part in the mentoring program. There can't be any exceptions. If we give you a pass there will be a group of teachers knocking on our door for the same exemption. I know I am asking you to be involved in a process that takes some time and getting used to. I know it's not easy for you.

My sense is it's hard for you to sit and talk. You're always moving and doing something, but I am asking you to slow down a bit and listen to what I have to say. How you use it is up to you. It's what I call necessary feedback. It can, I believe, help you to redefine your best teaching self.

Myra: Look, it has been a long time since I've been in any supervision or mentoring situation. I've operated on my own for twenty years. John Owens, the principal prior to Brad, never came into my room. Every year he wrote the same glowing evaluation report for me. We had a deal. He let me promote the science program and left me alone. You have to understand this is a big change for me and I sense this project could lead to changes in the way I do my job.

Linda: Whatever the case, Myra, I am concerned that you are missing a great deal of class time. You were out of the building more than thirty days last year. That's a lot of missed time for your kids. And it's not time out for illness; it's being involved in all of your presentations and speeches.

Your kids, it seems, are missing you because of all of this involvement outside of school. The reason they wanted to be in your classes was the expectation that you would be there for them, maybe not every single day but most of the time. Parents expect that as well. It's only fair. It must be hard on you trying to juggle all of the extra roles—grant writing, teacher training, presenting at conferences.

How can you manage to be successful in all those roles? Something has to give and from what I am seeing the kids are on the losing end. A lot of your energy is being spent on activities and projects that are unrelated to them. You're expending a lot of energy welcoming visitors from all over the country and the world. I'm not saying this is bad, but it takes away from your interaction with your students. You become a host, not a teacher. It seems like all of this should be difficult for you because teaching has been such a passion for you and you get such joy and satisfaction from it.

Here is the main question I have, a fastball right at you. Why are you giving up teaching, something you love so much and derive so much pleasure from, and focusing on the other projects that, while they build self-esteem, don't seem to be as fulfilling? You talk about being a leader on the national scene but what about your classroom? Are your continued absences fair to you and your students?

Myra: Look, what I am doing is not just for me. It's for you, the administration, my colleagues, for the district, for the community. I'm putting myself and this school on the map. We are known and recognized throughout the country because of my work. It's not something to sneeze at. I've worked my tail off.

You think being a presenter at conferences is a picnic? I come home drained. Sure, it feels good while I'm part of it but when these things end, I'm beat. Hotels, airports, restaurant food—I get sick of it after a while. At first it's a high—my picture in the paper, being on TV, getting the teacher of the year award, and having lunch with Bill Clinton. But it wears on me after a while—too many handshakes, Chardonnays, too much politicking.

In some ways I am sick of it and the question you're asking me is right on target, I hate to admit. Sometimes I think I'm running on empty. One more meeting, one more visiting team from God knows where, one more flight to Washington, one more delay because of bad weather. I come home dirty, sweating, tired, like I've been through the mill.

And you're right, I'd rather challenge you, set you back on your heels, than sit and listen and talk. It scares me. If I stop running, I think I might collapse. With the kids I feel guilty; I know that when I'm not here it's not the same. They miss me and what I can give them. When I'm in and out it upsets all the continuity, for them and for me. It's no good, a lose-lose situation.

I know some of the students and their parents are upset with me for being out so much. This is the first time I've had kids ask for a transfer. It's insulting, even hurtful. But I guess I can't blame them. Sometimes I think about throwing in the towel and getting a job at a university. But that's not for me. I honestly don't know where to begin to make things right. Got some ideas?

Linda: I am so glad you were able to talk about things and I appreciate your listening to my observations. These are things we can work on. I think that first you have to decide what you want. You can't do everything or be everything to everybody. You need to do what works best for you, what makes you happy. Clearly going on this way isn't going to work. It's too draining.

Maybe in a sense you've achieved your goal already. You've put the school, and yourself, on the national map. You are somebody and you've helped the school to be somebody too. But maybe enough is enough. Not to be funny, but being in the spotlight too long can burn you.

The conferences and presentations, hotels, airports, and travel—those are not the real world, are they? Sometimes they're places people go to run away, steal some time away from the daily struggles. Usually you're speaking to the converted anyway. Maybe you've done all that. Maybe returning to work only with the kids will get you off the star track and back to being a great teacher.

You seem to find great joy in that. Why take away something you love and replace it with something that drains you? Other people can take over the grants and projects, or they can just be put on hold. Think about what we've talked about and let's meet next week. I'll be anxious to hear what you have to say.

Myra: Look, you've given me a lot to think about. It has been a long time since anyone gave me such a direct reaction and honest feedback. Usually people in the school keep their distance and treat me with kid gloves. I'm going home to think this over.

Like Ellen, Myra needs to be asked direct questions by her mentor, questions that allow and encourage her to reflect on the negative aspects of her situation. We all have a better opportunity to communicate our hidden feelings when the questions are open-ended but hit on the issues we are struggling with. We may wish to evade these questions, but because they ask for the truth, we want to answer. Our defenses are down.

A nascent trust can create a window of opportunity. Sometimes our initial stance, like Myra's, is to want to fight and challenge our would-be helper. But if the questioning has sincerity and clarity, we are disarmed. Linda, with her skillful questions, becomes a friend, not the enemy. Myra is suddenly free from her defensiveness and open to reality.

Reality for Myra becomes a little clearer in this mentoring episode. The bottom line for her to grapple with is that presenting at conferences and being a star performer has its price. It can be costly. Spending time on the road can be draining and depleting. Speaking to some educators at a conference who have spent the previous night carousing is not fun.

As Myra describes, the entire scene has begun to wear on her. Teachers in her position slowly begin to lose their classroom-teacher persona and begin to focus on marketing and self-promotion. They enter a new reality.

Linda's wake-up call to Myra reminds us all of the price we may be paying and what we may be losing in seeking professional and personal growth. It reminds us that knocking on the wrong doors can lead to mischief and unmarked roads. There are risks involved in stretching ourselves too far and drawing our boundaries too wide. Linda wisely helps Myra decide for herself if she wishes to continue on the road she has chosen.

Maybe that is the greatest gift of mentoring, to be able to ask the right questions, to get protégés to reflect on their situation, to guide them to either accept where they are and accept the consequences, or to begin a process of change that will, as Myra suggests, unburden and free them. Perhaps it will allow Myra to be a great teacher of kids again, not a star teacher looking for affirmation in places that are temporary and ill suited to long-term professional and personal growth.

THE COUNSELOR AS MENTOR

This final vignette focuses on the pain of dislocation, of losing familiar boundaries—one's students, colleagues, seat in the faculty room, and daily coffee break with pals. That is what happened to fifteen-year veteran physics teacher Jim McDonald. In June, after the rush of final exams and good-byes to favorite students, Jim is told by his department chair that he is being reassigned to the junior high.

The reason? Some of the veteran teachers who were expected to retire have chosen not to. The department now has a surplus of teachers. In order for Jim to keep his job he would have to go along with the change. It's a simple matter of arithmetic, but not simple at all for Jim.

At first Jim was OK with the move. He took things in his stride and was not a person who made waves. He would go along with the reassignment. At least he had a job and maybe he could get back to the high school once his more senior colleagues retired. The real impact of the change did not immediately hit him. Cleaning out his room and saying his good-byes went on with little emotion, certainly no anger or resentment. He was told of the change after the year-end faculty party.

For him, it was unlike a retirement—he never got to hear the speeches about how much he influenced his students, helped them enjoy physics, and excelled as a tennis coach, faculty advisor for the National Honor Society, and intramural sports coordinator. He was exiting alone, out the door with no fanfare or thanks. This kind of exiting happens to thousands of teachers each year.

Reassigned: a non-emotional word, isn't it? It doesn't describe the emotional pain, the anxiety, the sense that everything the teacher worked for so hard has suddenly vanished. As suggested in Chapter 3, renewing yourself is often not easy, even under the best of conditions.

How do you renew yourself in foreign territory? You leave an assignment where you know the boundaries. Then suddenly you arrive in a new school where you don't know the staff, don't have experience teaching at that level, don't know the students, and don't have a routine. Will your teaching skills work here? Will you be given time to adjust and get settled in?

At first, Jim did not anticipate these fears and concerns, but by August the real impact of the move set in. He received his teaching schedule in the mail, along with the curriculum outline and textbook list. He was assigned to three seventh-grade earth science classes and two eighth-grade biology classes, both subjects he had never taught before.

He had less than four weeks to prepare. There would be a one-day orientation workshop designed to help him adjust to his new school. There was also a personal letter from counselor Ivy Harrison; she indicated that she would be Jim's mentor for the school year. In this capacity she would observe Jim's classes and hold follow-up conferences.

The basic thrust of the program was to help Jim adjust to his new environment and find his best teaching self. Ivy would seek Jim out at the new teacher orientation so they could get to know each other. Although the letter was very thoughtful, the mentoring program sounded like just one more thing Jim had to do. It was a new program and for now was offered only in the junior high.

If he had remained in the high school he wouldn't have to be dealing with any of this—new curriculum, new kids, new staff, and now mentoring. His resentment and anger began to grow. He feared this change was not going to be easy.

And it wasn't. In spite of getting some helpful hints at the orientation meeting run by principal Brad Foley and meeting Ivy Harrison (who seemed like a very helpful person who was serious about her mentoring role), things got off to a bad start.

Jim quickly learned that his students were different. They were like little kids, talking, jabbering, acting out. They weren't like his high school students, who were for the most part serious, high-achieving students. His high school classes had been almost like college classes, with quiet discussion and reflection. There were no behavioral problems. The students were intent on getting into good colleges and were not about to risk their chances for good grades and letters of recommendation. It was a quiet, highly professional routine; Jim was in charge and he had few distractions.

Junior high students, being early adolescents, don't focus on being quiet or reflecting. They make mischief, bully each other, and make the teacher pay for wavering or hesitating. If they sense fear or uncertainty, they pounce. There were certainly some talented students in Jim's new classes, kids who were studious and knew how to behave. But for the main part of his first month, Jim was constantly thrown into a disciplinarian mode.

Much of his teaching persona centers on control. In a few short months he had gone from having a professor-like teaching persona that focused on real learning to being a disciplinarian with a few precious moments left over for real teaching.

It has begun to wear on Jim. Each day seems endless, with the same issues of control disrupting the day. He has to continually stress to the students that he was in charge, not them. He is further handicapped by not knowing the students. What kinds of students are they? What interests do they have? What are their home lives like? It is such a slow process and there is no safe harbor for him.

In the faculty room, teachers cluster in groups. During his visits few teachers notice or acknowledge him except for some other new teachers. He had gone to a local bar where the junior high teachers hung out on Friday nights, but he felt like an outsider.

Everything seems so wrong after seeming so right in the high school. He has even thought about going back to his old haunts on Friday to have a drink with the high school staff, but he doesn't belong there either. He knows he should take it one day at a time, and maybe he will get the hang of the place. But what if he doesn't? This is not where he wants to spend the rest of his career. Who wants to control little kids all day?

Ivy has been a member of the school counseling staff for five years. While not a veteran, she is tough and clear on her role. She represents a new wave of school counselors, not like the ones from the 1960s and 1970s who thought of themselves as primarily there to assign students to classes and solve academic problems.

Ivy is different. She believes in a proactive counseling role, in helping students solve their nonacademic and personal problems as well as their academic issues. She also believes in educating and supporting parents so they can be more effective in the child-rearing process. And she believes in helping teachers become more effective by improving their skills and their ability to work with all their students. As an African American, she knows about isolation and labeling. She is committed to promoting programs that improve diversity and inclusion. She is an educational leader who has a number of skills and resources. She has highly developed one-on-one counseling, group facilitation, and program development skills.

Each week she sees over 100 students in one-on-one conferences and problem-solving groups and co-leads a ninth-grade tobacco prevention group with P.E. teacher Shawn Mallory. She also leads a parents' support group on Wednesday evenings and a "How to be an Effective Teacher-Advisor" staff development workshop on Tuesday afternoons. The main focus of the teacher-advisor workshop is to help teachers become more effective listeners and helpers.

Given these resources and skills, she was a natural selection for the mentoring team. She has demonstrated that she is able to listen to the concerns of teachers and help them solve classroom problems and often personal problems that impacted negatively on their work.

Principal Brad Foley was able to free up Ivy's schedule by working out an arrangement with a nearby university's counselor-education program. They assigned a master's degree candidate with individual and group counseling skills to the school on a half-day basis as a permanent sub who takes over Ivy's seventh-grade counseling duties. Ivy still leads the eighth- and ninth-grade programs and is available to support the new counselor. In turn, Ivy joined the adjunct counselor-education teaching staff, serving as a visiting fellow in a summer counseling institute.

At least on paper, Ivy seems a good match for Jim. Yes, they are different. Ivy is African American, twenty-nine years old, trained in communications, and a rising star in her field and the school. Jim has an Irish-American background, is entering middle age, and is trained in science; he has found himself, one might say, to be a falling star. Both enjoy students, aspire to be master teachers and educators, and have good track records. They have successes under their belts.

Their first interaction takes place in October, one month into Jim's junior high career. Their mentoring relationship focuses on several mentoring characteristics described in Chapter 3:

- Mentors understand that bad times can happen to every teacher. These bad times can be sudden, tumultuous, and even career threatening.
- Mentors understand that renewing themselves is not always easy.
- Mentors have a sense of history, of the good work that has gone on in the past by caring teachers, the creative responses to changing needs and times, and the good work that goes on in their school each day.

After Ivy has a chance to observe Jim's classes, they meet for a conference.

Ivy: Hi, Jim. Glad we could meet. You've got a hectic schedule and so do I, but this is great. We have some quiet time to talk. I enjoyed observing your classes.

It must be such a change for you from teaching juniors and seniors, mature young men and women, at least most of them. It's different here, isn't it? You have these preteens—their sexual awareness is developing as they go through all of their physical and emotional changes. They're little kids one day and they mature, they think, the next, with no real life experiences to guide them. Kids at this level make mistakes, some of them big ones. Their newly found freedom can lead them down many wrong roads—drinking, drugs, smoking, early sex. It's an emotional cauldron here.

Teachers have to work extremely hard to keep their kids focused on the subject matter. It seems a constant effort to keep the kids' boundaries defined and knowable. I notice how hard you are working at that process. I sense it must be different in the high school, although I'm no expert.

Most high school kids, I believe—you'll have to set me straight if I'm wrong—know how to control themselves and set boundaries for their school behavior by the time they reach eleventh and twelfth grade. As teacher, you don't have to spend half of your class time maintaining control and discipline.

It's different here. I think you're finding that. I admire that you haven't backed off the challenges the students are throwing at you. It takes three or four months just to get them in line. You're a respected, veteran teacher, and I see you have great skills, but this is a new set-up. It will take some time for you to adjust to the kids, and them to you, but I think you're doing just fine.

Do you remember what happened to Ed Frankl? He retired last year, but you and he share a similar experience. He came to the junior high four years ago. "Reluctantly" would be the kind word to use. He, like you, had been an outstanding high school teacher, winner of the social studies teacher of the year award in 2006. His first months were a nightmare, worse than yours. But he hung in there and by the end of the year he was in the groove. He got to know the faculty and found friendship and support.

I remember him telling me that the last years of his career were the most enjoyable. He didn't have to deal with all the pressure of state exams and grade-hungry college-bound seniors and their parents. Life, he said, was simpler and more enjoyable at the junior high level. What seemed like a career disaster turned out to be an opportunity for renewal. The same thing could happen to you. Hang in there. Keep your expectations low for now. Take it day by day.

Jim: Well, let me tell you I appreciate your every word. It's nice to hear some good stuff. It has been a major change for me. Every day is a new challenge and I'm learning as I go along. It just seems to move so fast here. It's all go-go-go and there's no quiet time for learning like I had at the high school.

And there are no real conversations and questioning. My kids in physics class were like adults. They asked great questions. In retrospect it was a piece of cake. Here, if I do succeed in creating some kind of order—and in some classes that's questionable—the kids just sit there. I have to ask all the questions. Sometimes I think to myself, "Hello? Doesn't anyone have a brain here except for a couple of the nerdy kids?"

I try to keep myself in check and not get angry with the kids or myself. My wife says things will get better eventually and she says, and I have my doubts about this, that I'll be a better teacher for this experience. I wouldn't take any bets on that one.

Ivy: Hey, maybe she's right. It's good that you have her support. I know enough about change to know that you're probably missing your colleagues at the high school as well as the kids. You've been asked to make a major career change, to give up a teaching life you've worked hard at for fifteen years. You're being asked not only to teach a different grade level but also to form a whole new set of relationships, all in a matter of a few short months and with no real training. Everything has changed for you.

I'm not saying you are, but I sense that you might be feeling some resentment at this reassignment. And I sense you might be feeling some loneliness as well. I see you struggling to make some connections in the faculty room and at our Friday afternoon get-togethers. It's not easy. Most of us have been here a while and, in spite of our best judgment, we tend to hang out with certain groups. We're like the kids, really, forming little groups—the jocks, the nerds, the party people, the young marrieds, the divorcees.

You're not a new teacher but still it will take a while for you to find your spot. It's great that your wife is supportive but sometimes that's not enough. I like to think that we can develop a friendship and a good mentoring relationship. You're beginning anew here, but your high school career needs to be honored and remembered.

From what I hear about the way your reassignment was handled, it didn't allow time for some much-needed affirmation and good-byes. That must have been tough. Saying good-bye to what once was, particularly if it was successful, is always hard. It takes time for the shadows to clear. But the bottom line is that you and I know you had a great high school career and you were a model teacher and student advisor. No one can take that away from you. OK, you didn't get the gold watch and accolades when you left. But you know, and your colleagues know, that you made a huge difference. Hang on to the good you did. You earned it.

But now that part of your life is over. Sure, maybe you were dealt a bad hand, but that's the way it is. It's time to move on and focus, as you are, on today. Luckily, from what I can see, you're not a whiner or an angry guy. You're not burdened with the kinds of negative stuff that would make you a candidate for burnout. You're trying to learn this new job and get to know the kids. You may think you are adjusting too slowly but I think you're right on schedule. I wouldn't change one thing you are doing, at least not right now.

Let's continue our meetings. I think things will continue to improve. All I ask is that you try to think of yourself more as a beginner. Put aside, if you can, what you were like in the high school, what the kids were like, and what your colleagues were like. Bury those memories in some safe place for a while. Feel good that you are more than surviving here. Many teachers don't.

Jim: I think you're right on target on a lot of things. I do feel many of the things you're suggesting. And I have been looking back a lot. I guess I can't help that; it's not easy to put those feelings and memories aside. But I agree with you that no one here, teachers or kids, is going to read my resume and press releases. No one cares that I had almost 100 percent of my students pass the state physics exams each year. No one cares that my students regularly won the county science contest in physics. To them I'm just the new guy on the block. I have to show them that I have the right stuff to make it here. The burden of proof, as always, is on the newcomer.

And you're right; that's who I am. That's my new identity. No one cares if I am the former great high school physics teacher. Yesterday's news doesn't count. That clears up some of the mist for me. It's hard to think of myself as a beginner again, but it is so. Thanks, I'll sleep a little better tonight.

Beginning again is never easy. Ivy focuses Jim on the reality of his situation. He is in a new and difficult role and yes, the way he arrived there was less than ideal. He could rightfully be angry and resentful. He could even use his resentment to fuel a career-long vengeance that could consume him and make him bitter with himself, his students, and maybe with his family.

But Ivy wisely suggests that he is made of better material than that. He has already chosen not to go down this road. Having harnessed his would-be demons, his job now is twofold. He must put his dreams of returning to the high school on hold for a while, and he must continue the course of learning new skills, the requirements of his new job, and more about this new breed of students. And Ivy is right. Jim is doing OK.

Both Ivy and Jim get the feedback they need. Jim is made aware that he is a newcomer again. Ivy learns that she is in step with Jim's feelings and suggests a necessary course of action that holds the possibility of bringing about new opportunities for success.

Effective one-on-one mentoring can help create a school climate that encourages lifelong learning for teachers. It is the first step in building an ongoing renewal process. Other steps are needed as well:

- The themes communicated by protégés in the mentoring process need to be identified; they provide useful data in planning ongoing workshops and staff development efforts in the school.
- Mentored teachers need to be encouraged to lead workshops designed to train colleagues in the best professional practices, workshops that highlight the personal hobbies and successes of teachers, and workshops that can add a little novelty and joy to the teachers' daily routine.
- Mentored teachers need to be encouraged to serve as mentors themselves. Mentored teachers are a valuable resource, not only as trainers for colleagues but also as one-on-one mentors. It's called putting our best practices and resources to work.
- Mentored teachers also can be the primary resource in creating a schoolwide mentoring network. That means passing on mentoring skills to other members of the school community such as support staff and students. Both of these groups are ideally positioned to help struggling students. All too often they lack the training or are advised that this is not their role. Simple training led by skilled mentor-teachers can ready them to pass on simple, useful advice.

A skilled mentoring team can use these themes to identify topics and build them into their ongoing renewal program They provide an accurate compass of the direction the team needs to follow to keep the learning pot boiling. In a sense, these themes help identify the curriculum for workshops to provide additional learning and support beyond the mentoring process, workshops presented by team members, mentored teachers, and community and university resources.

Teachers need learning hubs that are attractive, easily accessible, and focused on pertinent topics. The mentors in the vignettes presented in this chapter generated ongoing workshop topics in mentoring conversations with protégés Tom, Ellen, Shawn, Myra, and Jim. These workshop topics can be separated into two categories: classroom issues and professional/personal issues:

Classroom issues include the following:

- Identifying teachers' talents and areas of strength in the classroom
- Identifying areas in which teachers are experiencing difficulty
- Pinpointing the skills teachers need to improve
- Understanding adolescent development
- Developing effective discipline skills
- Developing effective listening skills
- Identifying how teachers hold effective classroom discussions
- Noting how teachers work effectively with students in groups
- Identifying how teachers hold successful one-on-one conferences with students and parents
- Pinpointing how teachers handle crisis situations
- Noting how teachers identify and solve classroom problems
- Identifying how teachers get helpful feedback from colleagues
- Assessing which students teachers tend to avoid and making a plan to include them
- Assessing which students teachers tend to spend too much time with and making a plan to reduce the level of interaction with them
- Designing an attractive classroom setting
- Understanding how to be an effective advisor to students and help them to solve personal problems
- Identifying and referring troubled students and parents to reliable sources of support

Professional and personal issues include:

- Saying "no" to too many outside-the-classroom responsibilities
- Staying well, physically and emotionally
- Identifying ongoing career renewal activities to avoid burnout
- Understanding the aging process
- Intervening and giving useful feedback to colleagues who are struggling
- Identifying possible mentoring skills: can you visualize yourself as a mentor?

Ongoing renewal opportunities should be attractive, easily accessible, and focused on topics that are real and needed by teachers. In addition, they should be enjoyable experiences that are held in a comfortable professional setting with the necessary props of coffee and snacks. These workshops can be built on some of the classroom and professional or personal themes identified above, or they can be built on the spontaneous ideas and needs of creative staff; for example, one teacher sharing her Ph.D. research or another talking about the article on discipline she coauthored.

The themes and topics don't have to be classroom related. Teachers need a little novelty, a little joy, and a little relaxation during their day. Non-

–school related topics shared by teachers add spice to the daily routine and are a wonderful morale-boosting exercise—a way for colleagues to know the personal side of each other's lives.

These forums don't have to follow the often stale after-school training model so often employed in a school's staff development efforts. Workshops can be held on a voluntary basis before school, during free periods, at lunch, or after school. The famous line in the film *Field of Dreams* applies here: "If you build it they will come."

Creative administrators like Brad Foley and Linda Alvarez can seek out funding resources to allow substitution services for teachers who are willing to put themselves on the line and lead workshops. This process encourages the notion of a teacher as a trainer of colleagues, a career alternative that's not costly but is highly effective.

Getting teachers to take on such a leadership role is not easy. At first it may seem to them to be an unnatural and self-serving role. Teachers don't talk a lot about their professional and personal successes. Putting their skills and resources on public display and promoting themselves as skilled professionals who know much about their craft does not come easily. Stepping out of the group to model effective teaching techniques requires risk and courage.

Administrators like Brad Foley and Linda Alvarez can encourage and support this kind of risk-taking behavior. They understand that it is a necessary extension of the one-on-one mentoring program. Well-trained teachers are a valuable resource, a necessary resource to provide ongoing training for colleagues.

Administrators like Brad and Linda serve as antennas to identify outstanding teachers who can be brought on board as teachers of teachers. This process provides an ongoing way to expand the learning community within the school, acquiring new talent that can help prevent stagnation, reach resisting groups, and expand the constituency of teacher learners. It is an ongoing process of forging new alliances and networks.

Every day schools across America are losing the valuable training resources of successful teachers. Many teachers have outstanding helping and training skills that can be used to help struggling colleagues. Many have participated in recent skill-building programs such as mentoring, conferences, and workshops. They come back to their schools eager to share what they know, but often no one asks what they've learned. Once excited to share, they slowly lose interest and retreat to the boundaries of their classrooms. No one harnesses or uses their new learning and energy. There is no vehicle in place for them to share with and teach colleagues who need stimulation.

Both the newly skilled teachers and their colleagues lose out on the opportunity for growth. This is not cost effective; the monies and time spent on training are limited to a single individual. The new learning never gets any exposure. Millions of dollars are spent each year on programs, conferences, and workshops to help improve teacher effectiveness, but too often these newly trained teachers are not asked, encouraged, or required to share their new learning. Money and resources are lost.

The same process can occur with newly mentored protégés unless they are encouraged to become mentors themselves. Again, many teachers do not see themselves as leaders or as having the skills to help colleagues. It's part of the group norm that teachers follow in most schools. The boundaries are fixed and based in the classroom. But moving outside of the classroom and becoming a mentor alters these boundaries and in a sense sets the mentored protégés free. They are free to be a resource for colleagues, to be of service, to see that others have an opportunity for renewal, as well.

To help expand the pool of mentors and avoid the stagnation that often comes when a new program settles in, the mentoring team need antennas to identify newly mentored teachers who seem to have the right skills to join the program. Mentoring, when done right, is a taxing process. In addition to skill, it requires energy and the will to win, to jump from the ledge into new, uncharted territory. It can be draining.

Because of this, being a mentor should not be a lifetime job. Team members leave for many reasons and new talent needs to be identified and brought on board. It's an ongoing process of beginning and ending, with newly mentored protégés taking over the reins again and again.

You now have some understanding of what kinds of themes and issues take place in one-on-one mentoring conversations and of how mentoring teams can use this data to build ongoing learning hubs such as teacher-led workshops. You also have an understanding that mentoring teams need to tap into the skills of newly mentored protégés and encourage them to come on board as mentors themselves. To do otherwise is irresponsible.

Teams need every resource within the school community to establish a climate that offers ongoing renewal. Teachers and mentors can't depend on outside resources alone. Too often outsiders don't understand the unique issues in individual schools. The reality a mentoring team embraces is that educational issues need to be addressed primarily by members of their own school community.

A mentoring team can easily transfer the mentoring skills identified here to other members of the school community, such as support staff and students. How can mentors transfer these skills, making mentoring a whole-school process? After all, support staff and students are themselves valuable resources who can, with minimal training, intervene to help troubled students and serve as additional antennas for a school committed to caring, inclusion, and community building.

A mentoring team can harness the skills and energy of recently mentored teachers to offer short-term training to support staff, often labeled the non-professional staff: cafeteria workers, hall monitors, secretaries, security personnel, teacher aides, and so on. They can all play a critical role in creating positive interaction with students. They are on the front lines of the school and are often the first people to spot trouble—students smoking in the bathroom, cutting classes, or drinking at a school dance or sports event.

Many school support staff have spent years in close contact with adolescents and they get to know students in a very intimate, unthreatening way. Students often confide in them and seek advice and information on personal issues.

While many support staff may lack degrees, certificates, and formal training, many have learned through experience how to be helpful. In their roles they have one clear advantage—they are not perceived by students as professional staff or as a threat. Rather, they are friends, neighbors, and confidants who will not reveal a secret.

Because they are easily accessible and usually trusted by students, they can serve as positive role models and trusted adults. They can serve, in a true sense, as a vital antenna to identify and guide teens to reliable sources of help within the school and community.

Formal training that helps ground them in practices and skills that work can enhance the resource of support staff. Many of the mentoring skills described in Chapter 3 can be transformed into a formal, short-term training workshop led by teachers committed to sharing and passing on their newly learned skills. A simple curriculum for such training could include a number of elements:

- Identifying areas of strength in helping and guiding students: what do you do well?
- Identifying areas that are not effective in helping and guiding students: what skills need improvement?
- Adolescent development
- Particular concerns and issues of adolescence
- How to build trusting relationships
- How to hold effective one-on-one discussions
- How to hold group discussions
- How to be an effective listener
- How to give nonjudgmental but accurate feedback
- How to address and sometimes confront risky student behaviors (alcohol, tobacco, drugs, eating disorders, family problems, and so on)
  - How to assess student problems that present a critical health or safety issue and thus require immediate intervention by school staff

- How to refer students to reliable sources of help in the school and community
- How to create ongoing opportunities for professional growth

The notion of everyone in the school as learners and of ongoing activities made available to ensure lifelong learning is a critical part of this book's message. To limit learning and professional growth only to teachers, administrators, and counselors leaves out important members of the school community—the support staff—and places them in a subservient role, suggesting that what they do requires minimal or no formal training.

That perception changes when we begin to offer them the opportunity for ongoing training and professional growth. In acknowledging their skill and value to the school community, we bring them on board as allies and partners and in the process expand their boundaries. Professional opportunities should not be limited to or the sole domain of the professionals in our schools. Effective training for every staff member should be the goal.

To make mentoring a whole-school process, the mentoring team can also transfer skills to students. Kids are smart. They observe the adults in their school—the teachers, counselors, and administrators—and they see how they treat one another. They see how students are treated as well. If some teachers and students are looked down on, they know it. They understand that the in-groups of teachers and kids get the praise and the out-groups get the ridicule and put-downs. The put-downs are not always purposeful or meant to hurt someone. It's just that someone has to be the target, the enemy, the scapegoat. That's school for many kids.

Jim Moriarty, whom we met in an earlier vignette, knows that he is one of those kids on the outside. He is a relative newcomer with few friends, is failing in school, has parents who are divorced, isn't into sports or clubs, is a smoker and a truant, and is known to the staff as a troubled kid. He is not on the top-ten list of troubled kids in school; he can still be reached, but the odds against that are increasing each day. He knows he is different from the jocks and the preps. He is on the outside looking in.

But all that separation, the building of barriers and boundaries, the isolation of some school community members, can change when a mentoring program begins and takes hold. Kids are apt to observe something much different—a building of a strong sense of school community, a school that counts every teacher and student and considers them useful community members with special gifts. Many teachers and students have gifts that are hidden because no one ever asked them to be shared.

As teachers begin to be listened to, helped with their problem solving and skill development, and encouraged to serve as mentors for colleagues, they begin to use these newly acquired skills with students. Students are no longer seen as belonging to separate groups but as individuals with hopes, dreams, and possibilities. And teachers, now that mentoring supports them and makes them aware of their classroom dynamics, can observe and see, often for the first time, the walls that have been built up among kids as well as between kids and teachers.

Caring schools in which students care for, support, and respect each other do not develop overnight and without hard work by many members of the school community. These schools evolve because the adults in the school model these behaviors. Kids are quick learners and they too—with a little information, training, and expectation—can become mentors as well.

Let's return to the story of Jim Moriarty and teacher Tom Murray. Since the incident with Jim's father, good things have happened. Tom Murray took Brad Foley's advice and moved Jim's desk to the front of the room. He also began having lunch with Jim once a week. Using the same listening skills that Brad modeled in their mentoring sessions, Tom learned a great deal about Jim's life. It's been a tough road for Jim. He has been in five schools and lived in three states. His father has been in and out of drug and alcohol rehab many times and has never seemed to settle down. There are always fights and violence between his mother and father but his mother refused to leave despite Jim's pleading and fear that something bad was going to happen one day. Jim's older brothers all dropped out of school and moved out as soon as they were old enough.

School had always been a problem for Jim. He was unable to learn the basic skills because he moved around so much. With moving so much, he could never fit in at the new schools and was always on the outside with both his schoolwork and relationships. One day, he just gave up. He was failing and had only a few friends in the band. It was easier to pretend he was sick and stay home than deal with class. His mother gave up on getting him to school. He went just often enough that child protective services didn't get involved and bug his mother.

Once Tom began to take an interest in Jim, things changed dramatically. Jim started coming to school on a regular basis, doing his work, and keeping his counseling appointments. Tom got him into the social studies club and encouraged him to try out for the basketball team.

One day in their session, Jim surprised Tom by saying, "I wish I could help other kids like you do. I know they have some programs in schools where kids get to help other kids. Do you think you and I could do something like that?" Tom was taken aback. Sure, he wanted to help Jim, but starting a mentoring program was out of his league. Tom promised Jim that he would think about it. At his next mentoring session with Brad Foley, Tom brought up Jim's idea. Brad, always looking for ways to promote a mentoring philosophy in the school, grabbed the idea: "Look, Tom, this is another opportunity to help Jim and other kids. Jim is ready to help others as he has been helped by you and Greg. Sure, you're uneasy about starting a big program. Why not start with a small group of seventh graders, maybe about fifteen? You and Jim can plan out a training program for kids to be mentors using the same skills you've used with Jim. Make it a six- to eight-week program with meetings once a week. We'll rotate the meetings so they don't miss too much time in any one class. I'd be glad to help.

"When you're ready, we'll announce it to the staff, kids, and parents. As far as expectations, once kids get through the training, let's keep it simple. We can give them certificates for completing the mentoring training. Then let's turn them loose and ask only that they try to be helpful and useful to other kids.

"You and Jim can meet with them as a group once a week, hear their stories, support their efforts, and continue to teach them mentoring skills as the need arises. You know they'll be able to help some kids but others will reject their efforts. Failure, as you know, is part of the mentoring program.

"It's early December now. Let's plan to start a small program after February break. By May, after a six- to eight-week training period and then practice time as mentors, we should have a better handle on how to train kids as mentors and where we can go with the program. For me, this completes the circle. I've got my administrative staff focusing on mentoring teachers, teachers mentoring each other and kids, and now kids helping each other.

"I've seen some real changes on the part of teachers who have been hard on kids. Maybe by mentoring, the kids will lessen the tension between the groups in the school. That's a good goal. I say go for it. Get back to Jim and work out topics for a training program. And keep a diary on the program as you go along. Who knows, maybe you could write a book about this and be a big-time conference speaker.

"This is good stuff that other teachers need to know about. The University School of Education is starting a Ph.D. program in leadership next fall. I'm teaching some of the introductory courses. Give some thought to applying. I'll get you the information. This mentoring program could be an excellent dissertation topic. I'll make sure you get some consultant money for planning the program. If you get it going, I'll also give you some release time to manage the project."

Tom and Jim went to work and came up with an eight-session training program. At Jim's suggestion they also asked Janine to be involved. Jim felt she would attract some kids who might otherwise avoid the project. They agreed on a list of topics to be addressed during the eight training sessions:

- Why do I want to kelp other kids?
- What are my strengths as a helper?
- What are my weaknesses as a helper?
- What kids do I want to help?
- What problems areas do I want to help kids with?

- What kids do I have trouble helping?
- What problems do I avoid dealing with?
- Where do I begin making plans to help?

Training students to mentor and help each other is a natural consequence of a teacher mentoring program. It gives everyone in the school a chance to get on board and be a useful citizen of the school community. It helps send the message that everyone in the school counts and that we make every effort not to turn our backs on each other. Remember, our working definition of mentor is "a wise, loyal friend, teacher, and coach." That's a role that can be played by students in advising peers who lack effective academic and personal problem-solving skills.

These vignettes, constructed from my own real-life experiences in schools, help expose the angst that teachers and mentors experience in their everyday roles. After all, the words *renewal, professional development, lifelong learning,* and *intervention to help students at risk* are neutral, unemotional words that do not describe what goes on in the process of mentoring and helping colleagues. They lack the image of the heat of the battle and the sweat and turmoil that novice and veteran teachers can experience in their classrooms, and mentors can experience in trying to help and guide their protégés.

These words, without the images of the real lives of teachers Tom Murray, Ellen Turner, Shawn Mallory, Myra Fryman, and Jim McDonald, do us a disservice. The words alone could make the mentors of these vignettes—principal Brad Foley, teacher Frank Bronkowski, department chair Randy Edwards, assistant principal Linda Alvarez, and counselor Ivy Harrison—unprepared for the tough issues that mentoring presents.

Schools cannot ignore the fact that a teacher's search for renewal and growth is a difficult journey. These vignettes help elucidate the perils involved in pragmatic, everyday mentoring. They also make clear the possibilities and positive alternatives that mentoring can yield. Effective mentoring can help create an environment in which teachers have a chance to turn their professional lives around.

This chapter is not Mentoring 101 with a simple list of the things mentors should accomplish. Rather, it is stories of teachers trying to right their careers with the help of mentors who are skilled and unafraid of going beyond mere suggestion into territory that leaves the teachers vulnerable to the involvement of their mentor. The strength of effective mentoring builds on the notion that the responsibility for teachers changing their negative behaviors rests with the teachers themselves.

The role of mentors is to help teachers become aware of their ill-conceived practices and identify approaches that are effective. Mentors give their protégés data on which they can base new, self-affirming decisions about their classroom management, their students, and their own careers. This data and feedback provide sources of new direction that can, as these vignettes demonstrate, alter the wrong directions of gifted teachers.

NOTES

1. Cary Goldberg, "Betraying a Trust: Teacher-Student Sex is Not Unusual, Experts Say," *New York Times*, 21 May 1995, L37.

Chapter Seven

Utilizing Mentoring to Jump Start the "No Teacher Left Behind" Era

This second edition begins with the observation that we are entering the early stages of the "no teacher left behind" era. While education leaders have created programs such as "No Child Left Behind" and designed intervention programs to prevent any child's being at risk, we have for too long failed to design similar programs for teachers, particularly novice teachers who, without the benefit of the support offered by mentoring, are at risk to failure and poor classroom performance.

Ironically, novice teachers are very much like some of their students, who are also at risk of failure, poor performance, and heading toward the margins of school life. They share a common bond, and the bond is possible failure, not an acceptable alternative. As a result many novice teachers who survive their first few years often lack the necessary skills to become competent teachers, a condition that can follow them throughout their entire careers, with these teachers never seeming to get things right in the classroom.

The failures of teachers and students are intertwined and can no longer be tolerated. Failure of any member of the school is costly because it asks the questions, "Did we do enough to help this teacher or student?" "Are we somehow responsible for this failure?" or more poignantly, "Who will come to my aid if my problems get out of control?" Our system has promoted a philosophy of zero tolerance for the failure of students but in the same breath has failed to develop similar interventions for teachers, meeting only half of its responsibility to the school population and failing to involve support staff in the equation.

The good news is that since 2002, when this book was first published, the mentoring of teachers, particularly novice teachers, has taken center stage in education reform efforts. However, Ellen Moir adds a cautionary note by suggesting that over the next decade, more than two million new teachers will find themselves facing a full classroom on their first day, charged with the mission of transforming it into a learning community. She adds that it is easy to forget what it was like to be a beginning teacher, having to acquire curriculum and classroom strategies while at the same time balancing practical concerns with lofty ideas.

Moir suggests that veteran teachers may well ask themselves, "If I were starting my career today, what would help me to develop into an outstanding, caring and accomplished teacher?" According to Moir one answer stands out among the rest: "I can only imagine how much better a teacher I would have been that first year if I had a mentor."[1]

Moir's comments state the obvious truth. Novice teachers without real school experience and veteran teachers who have to learn how to cope and survive without mentoring are both at risk of failure and poor classroom performance. One group, the novice teachers, are beginners trying to find their way; the other group, the vets, are still trying to get it right in the classroom and make up for the mentoring they never had. Both groups are in need of intervention that is tailored to meet their needs.

The majority of novice teachers, even with their youthful enthusiasm, idealism, and years of training, are at risk of failure or not becoming the competent teachers they might be unless they are involved in mentoring to help pave their way in the early, often problematic years of their careers. This scenario seems to be more prevalent in our large junior and senior high schools. These are often crowded schools, many with student populations of over 2,000—places where novice teachers, like at-risk students, can find themselves quickly involved in a school culture guided by a philosophy of sink or swim.

Sink or swim is a philosophy well known to many veteran teachers who had to learn on their own how to survive. There was often no mentoring or helping hand when they began as young novice teachers. For them, many of them in their early twenties at the time, it was a battle for survival. Some succeeded and some failed. It was a combat scene they were never taught in teacher education.

Many veteran teachers, while sympathetic to the plight of novice teachers, have no real role model to follow in coming to the aid of novice teachers or sharing their own hard-earned experience. As one veteran teacher told me,

It's a big boy's and big girl's world here. New teachers have to learn early on to be tough just as I did. They can't communicate weakness or in any way suggest they are not up to the job. If they do, the kids will eat them alive.

This may come as a surprise to you but most of the veteran teachers here do worry about these rookies. They remember what it was like to face a class of savvy students without a clue of what they were getting into. The word 'naive' doesn't do justice to the danger they find themselves in. They understand that these new recruits are just kids out of college and thrown into this crazy place, a high school with over 2,500 students.

But there's no role or support for us in giving the newcomers any help. We're not needed even though we are the teachers who have the most experience. But there is another reason for our lack of involvement, a reason that's rarely talked about. In the tough world we occupy, it's frowned upon, not cool, to go around coddling these rookies and trying to act like a big brother or camp counselor. There is peer pressure from the older teachers here not to be a savior for either the new teachers or the kids. It's simply not the way the culture works here.

Our job is to teach. We are not trained or paid to be counselor types. Advising and helping new teachers and kids is the job of the administration and the guidance office. Right now there is nothing in it for veteran teachers to go out on a limb and help a colleague no matter how much it hurts to see a teacher being literally run over by the kids. Believe me, when one of the veteran teachers tries to become a savior and be a counselor type, he or she is in big trouble, taken to the woodshed and told to knock it off.

Peer pressure isn't only a kid's thing here. There is plenty of peer pressure going on among teachers that forces them to behave in certain ways. In fact, that's the way it's been ever since I started teaching here twenty-five years ago as a rookie. Nothing much has changed.

There is also the issue of aging. Many of us veteran teachers started teaching here twenty-five or thirty years ago. We are getting older and beginning to confront health, motivation, and retirement issues. We'll all be gone from the school in the next ten or fifteen years. The major theme in the faculty room is trying to navigate through our final years here, knowing somehow when to stay and when to leave.

Personal issues and concerns dominate our conversation. I know they do for me. This school has been my second home for twenty-five years and you know what? This final stage of my life here is the most worrisome. I wonder if anyone will remember me and the good things I did to help kids and parents.

Both novice teachers and veterans need each other, with each group involved in mentoring that is designed to meet their needs. This chapter is about how to change a school culture in which teachers are left on their own to survive or fail. We need a new model, a new culture, that provides many open doors for help, such as mentoring—easily accessible doors through which novice teachers can walk and get the help, training, and support they often desperately need. We need to provide intervention for teachers in the same way we do students, not letting one teacher fall through the cracks.

The question is, where do we begin to make the "'no teacher left behind" era a reality? Our first step begins with examining two critical issues that have emerged in the mentoring process since the early 2000s, when mentoring came upon the national scene to help bring about needed school reform. These issues need attention if mentoring is to be truly inclusive and offer an open door for training every teacher, bringing about the "no teacher left behind" era.

First, school leaders need to move beyond offering mentoring primarily for novice teachers. The process of mentoring novice teachers is now in place and needs to be extended to veteran teachers. Second, mentoring for veteran teachers needs to be very different from mentoring for novice teachers.

The needs of novice teachers are not complex. They need to learn the ropes of what is required to be successful and gain tenure, such as classroom skills, the politics of the school, what behaviors are OK and what can bring trouble, and sources of help and support. As novice teachers they are an easy sell for the administration. They understand that they have to go along to get along—no resistance from this group! They have no power. Their goal is crystal clear: get tenure and hold onto their jobs in these tough times.

Mentoring for veteran teachers is more complex. These are teachers who have tenure, fifteen to twenty years or more in the classroom, in the middle adult years of their lives, usually ages forty to sixty-five, and on a path to retirement. Many veteran teachers have had their fill of failed education reform efforts. They are, and rightfully so, a tough sell for any new school change efforts. As *New York Times* columnist Maureen Dowd suggests, "It's nice to talk about change, but you can't wipe away yesterday."[2]

The "yesterdays" for many veteran teachers often include being involved in a series of failed education reforms to which they devoted great time and energy, only to be left with the same conditions as the visiting reformers abandoned their efforts and left town. These memories can't be wiped away unless veteran teachers actually see that a new change, such as mentoring, has something in it for them. They need to be sold on the value of becoming a mentee and perhaps moving on to becoming a mentor for novice teachers and veteran colleagues alike.

However, many school leaders are leery about making mentoring for veteran teachers a priority and developing a sales campaign to get them on board—one that addresses their needs. One of the primary reasons for leaving many veteran teachers out of the mentoring mix is that they can offer great resistance, use their positions of power in the school to block a mentoring program, and, if disgruntled, be a negative model for idealistic yet naive and sometimes gullible novice teachers.

For many school leaders getting veteran teachers on board any new change effort appears to be just too much of a challenge. Many feel a better strategy is to focus the mentoring process on novice teachers, a strategy they feel can have a big payoff not only in novice teachers being trained but also in offering good community public relations. The process often involves utilizing a small cadre of outstanding veteran teachers as mentors. These are often star teachers who have gained local, state, and sometimes national recognition and have the favor and ear of the administration.

Who can find fault with mentoring novice teachers and using home-grown star teachers as mentors? It's a win-win, feel-good story for school districts that are under attack from many quarters. Many school leaders rightfully ask why they should use their energy, resources, and capital to involve veteran teachers in mentoring when the chances for success are questionable at best. It's a sort of field-trip scenario—the well-behaved kids get to go on the trip while the kids who are at risk and potential troublemakers are left behind because they might act out.

It's time to frame our view of veteran teachers in a new, more positive way and develop a new narrative on how we speak to them, involve them, and acknowledge their contributions to the school community. Clearly we have our work cut out to reach this goal, an important goal in making the "no teacher left behind" era a reality. This chapter gives recommendations on how we can proceed.

RAISING THE AWARENESS OF SCHOOL ADMINISTRATORS ABOUT THE NEED TO INVOLVE VETERAN TEACHERS AS MENTEES AND AS POTENTIAL MENTORS FOR NOVICE TEACHERS

Our first step is to help convince school leaders that indeed there is an urgent, doable need to involve veteran teachers in mentoring. That means encouraging them to revisit the landscape of veteran teachers and become aware that many veteran teachers have pressing personal issues that often overshadow the need to improve their classroom skills—issues that impact on their professional lives, such as aging, retirement, health and wellness, family problems, addictions, and attempts to combat the stagnation, burnout, and malaise that often visit veteran teachers.

School leaders need to raise their understanding about the personal sides of the veteran teachers' lives. This information is often deemed private, unspoken, and better kept under wraps, but it is a key factor involved in these teachers' success or lack of success in the classroom.

In conversations with veteran teachers, many report that their resistance to any new change program such as mentoring isn't just aimed at school leaders. Rather, the real reason for their resistance is that, in their present form, new programs such as mentoring, with a singular focus of improving classroom skills, do not address the needs that have emerged as these teachers have aged and entered middle adulthood. As one teacher union leader reported,

> Most of the staff development programs the district offers are about improving the teacher's classroom performance and test scores. But there are no workshops, men-

toring, or counseling to help my veteran union guys and gals deal with the professional and personal issues involved in getting older.

And believe me, the aging issues are what they're concerned about. They are simply not interested in attending workshops on themes such as classroom management, especially with novice teachers. Their heads and needs are somewhere else. I've been working on my school administrator to push for more programs such as mentoring to help our aging teachers but he's having a tough time figuring out how to sell the program to the district administration.

But I swear to God my veteran teachers would be a lot more committed to teaching if they could develop better personal skills and information to deal with aging. And my guess is that they'd be a lot more positive in dealing with kids, parents, colleagues and the administration.

Clearly this union leader's thought that suggest developing a mentoring program to help veteran teachers improve both their professional and personal lives offers an exciting new approach, but it presents a difficult selling role for school administrators.

As Maureen Dowd said, "It's nice to talk about change, but you can't wipe away yesterday." It does take rethinking and reassessment—thinking outside the box—which can create a learning model based on meeting the real learning need of teachers in the trenches, not what those far removed think they need and should learn. It requires packaging this new model in ways that involve engaging veteran teachers while also helping to sell the need for such a new approach to district administrators who hold the purse strings.

Mentoring novice teachers in improving classroom skills is an easy sell, but mentoring that offers veteran teachers ways to improve their personal as well as professional needs is a big change in the direction of training veteran teachers and the way we do business. It's a process that adds a new dimension to staff development interventions, and it offers a new kind of training that can appeal to the vets. It can be a win-win addition that can "wipe away yesterday" and offer veteran teachers a place at the table with a menu tailored to their needs.

Clearly it's not an easy sell, but it is doable because it offers school administrators an intervention model to at last engage veteran teachers and get them back on board as contributing members of the school community. Given our aging school population, one can make a strong argument for a three-step mentoring process that can offer veteran teachers the opportunity to:

- Address their personal issues and concerns
- Move on to improving their classroom skills as they begin to develop a sense of self and professional renewal

- Become mentors for both novice and veteran teachers, for those interested and skilled

Research by Tom Ganser can help school leaders raise their awareness about the need to involve veteran teachers as mentees and mentors and develop a strong selling case for such an effort.[3] Ganser suggests that mentoring is an idea that has gained considerable momentum in recent years. He cites the results of a survey of 5,253 teachers in fifty states and the District of Columbia by the National Center for Educational Statistics (2001) which revealed that 26 percent of the respondents have been mentored by another teacher. Ganser points out that most states now recommend or require induction programs such as mentoring for beginning teachers.

He also points out that a recent report of the National Commission on Teaching and America's Future (2003) indicates that the number of state induction programs has increased from seven states in 1996–1997 to thirty-three states in 2002. Ganser also reports that more and more school leaders readily support mentoring programs.

However, Ganser raises an important note of caution to the rapidly growing mentoring effort. Ganser suggests that because of the retirement wave of teachers hired in the 1960s and 1970s, there are fewer veteran teachers to serve as mentors. As a result many mentors have fewer years of teaching experience.

Ganser also points out the irony in this situation. He suggests that it is ironic that just as expectations for mentoring links are rising, the number of desirable mentors who can both articulate how they conduct their work and guide beginning teachers in mastering rigorous teaching standards and qualifying for more strenuous licensing requirements is getting smaller.

Clearly the battle to institute mentoring in the public schools is being won. The success of mentoring novice teachers has now provided an open door to involving veteran teachers as mentees and encouraging some to become mentors. However, the rules of how we engage veteran teachers as mentees and mentors need to be changed..

For example, we have limited our invitation for veteran teachers to become mentors to only star teachers with track records of leading workshops and similar accomplishments, but have not tapped into the expertise of the vast number of veteran teachers who have been left on the sidelines. Maybe they are teachers in the trenches who haven't led workshops or presented at conferences, but they do know a lot about their craft. No, they are often not self-promoters like the star teachers, and if asked about their successes they can become speechless—speechless because no one has ever asked them that question or seemed interested in what they have accomplished, teaching thousands of kids over a twenty- or thirty-year span, and maybe in the process directing kids to a better life or even saving the lives of kids who were suicidal, addicted, homeless, or on their own.

They are teachers who wake up each day, grab their coffee and a bagel, and walk into their classrooms at 7:30 in the morning, some ready and prepared, some not. But they understand, sadly, that being ready or not doesn't matter because all too often it appears that no one cares what they do as long as they don't create problems with kids, parents, and the school administration. When it comes to being affirmed, recognized as a vital part of the school community, given positive feedback, or offered support and encouragement to improve their craft, there is often only silence. They are like at-risk kids who are reminded that being quiet, not acting out, and flying under the radar is what the school culture wants from them—don't be noticed, don't draw attention, and you'll make it out of here.

If mentoring is to become available to more teachers, the question we need to begin asking is how to connect with every member of the veteran teachers' community, one at a time, and get them on board as mentees and mentors. We need to find a better way to let them fly above the radar screen, in full view, and be noticed—to see that their experience is needed, and to be given the attention their experience warrants. They are, after all, the only group available to help further our mentoring efforts. Veteran teachers have the manpower needed and their hard-earned experience to share. We need them.

SELLING VETERAN TEACHERS ON GETTING ON BOARD AS MENTEES AND MENTORS

Though it may make great sense to school reformers, the road to involving veteran teachers in their own professional and personal renewal will not be easy. We have a huge sales job on our hands. Veteran teachers are like school administrators in one respect. Both groups talk a lot about change, the good and bad of the process, often on and on until the word becomes overused, cliché, and repeated far too often in any memo or speech on school reform.

The only conversation that makes the word *change* come alive and enter the reality of school life comes about when teachers are asked to make a commitment. "Hello, we need you on board." "Where do you stand?" "What are you going to do?" Deciding to make a commitment to get on board is never easy. There are often too many reasons not to do it and too few reasons to overcome one's resistance and say, "Yes, count me in."

You have probably heard many of the reasons teachers offer when they say "no" to their involvement. Maybe they've even mouthed these reasons themselves. "We've tried that stuff here before and it was a disaster." "This is just one more thing you want me to do. I'm up to my ears in work already. No more." "Why can't you guys just leave us alone to do our job? Enough of this change talk."

Risks and new beginnings are rarely sought out or wanted by teachers or administrators who function in a school culture that favors the status quo and is highly resistant to the turmoil that can come about when the tide begins to flow in a new direction. Change comes only when one is convinced that help is needed now. It's a process similar to deciding to go into therapy in one's personal life. One develops a glimmer of a new and better life and begins looking for a path, and the skills, to reach this new place. One hears a new message, faintly at first, that makes one think, "There has to be more in this life for me."

The message we need to offer veteran teachers is similar: helping them to hear and believe that they are needed. We need to offer veteran teachers who are resisting and uninvolved a different, more personal message, a message that says, "We need you to be involved in the mentoring program as mentees and mentors; your skills, wisdom and experience are needed and we understand that the training we need to offer you is designed specifically for veteran teachers."

Many veteran teachers have been allowed to just settle in with little chance for change. This is particularly true in our large junior and senior high schools. Many veteran teachers in these schools report a sense of malaise and being dead-ended. They report, often with a combination of sadness and anger, that they are not going to become administrators, department chairs, or star teachers who always have their pictures in the district newsletter; write educational books and professional articles; present at conferences; become adjunct professors at school of education; or be the American Federation of Teachers (AFT) or National Education Association (NEA) teacher of the year.

They understand the truth—that they are not going anywhere except to the same classroom each day in which they have taught the same subject and grade for their entire career, a one classroom–one subject career, a prescription or sentence for boredom, negativity, and burn-out.

It is no wonder that many veteran teachers look upon the opportunity to learn new skills with disdain. Yesterday's memories of failed staff development efforts only remind them that this new effort at mentoring will probably be more of the same. And they fear that novice teachers will be the new victims of another school reform effort. Not surprisingly, some veteran teachers say they don't want to be coupled with beginning teachers. It can be degrading, even humiliating, to be coupled with novice teachers after many years in the classroom.

As a result, the only life-giving path open to many veteran teachers appears to be retirement. They have nowhere to go, no new ladder to climb, and the one sure way to avoid stagnation is to dream about the future and retirement.

Their early dreams, often beginning as novice teachers, to become star teachers have withered away, as have the challenges and excitement of the job. Many veteran teachers feel there are no more puzzles to solve, such as how to run their classroom, create exciting lesson plans, involve students and parents, and develop a legacy about their contributions. This is a scenario with the caption, "It is what it is." It's all about counting the years, months, and sometimes even the days until retirement, a period in their career when one foot is in the school and the other out the door.

The key to bringing about an era of "no teacher left behind" lies in involving veteran teachers, many of whom have literally dropped out and closed their doors to new learning. They are our target group, in need of intervention such as mentoring that can present them with clear alternatives for confronting the negative school culture they live in. It's a culture that suggests to veteran teachers that "the only path for you is out of here; play it safe, take no risks, count the days. They'll never miss you when you're gone. Another warm body is waiting to take your place."

However, many veteran teachers don't think they have a problem or, more important, that their skills are needed. Maybe their teaching life is not great, but they know the work, get paid well and get summers off. They have to be sold on the idea that things can be better and they need to be shown how. What is now required is a message so welcoming and attractive that it is embraced by veteran teachers even when their memories of the failure of earlier school change efforts cannot be wiped away.

It means giving veteran teachers mentoring that meets their present needs, not the same training offered to novice teachers or mentoring training based solely on retooling their classroom skills. We can offer them something that catches their desire for novelty, affirmation, personal and professional growth, and the opportunity to be a contender, or as one veteran teacher told me, to "not go out as a loser who everyone wants out the door." Veteran teachers must be viewed as valuable members of the school team who have made and will continue to make great contributions.

This dire situation of veteran teachers presents such an opportunity. Many veteran teachers are waiting to be asked to the dance. I argue it is the responsibility of the suitors, the school leaders, to offer them a proposal they can't resist.

This proposal has to be worded so that it offers the hope for veteran teachers to address the many subtle and often unspoken personal issues and concerns that affect their teaching performance, commitment, motivation, morale, attendance, energy, and level of participation. It must include issues and concerns about aging; health and wellness; changing family dynamics that come with the aging process; wellness issues such as addictions, health, obesity, and so on; and ways to improve their classroom skills in a safe, trusting, and affirming mentoring process.

This mentoring or intervention process for veteran teachers should couple ways to improve both their personal well-being and their classroom skills. Both components, career and personal development, are intertwined and need to be addressed simultaneously if we are going to restore the dignity of veterans in the face of a school culture that often labels veteran teachers, sometimes subtly and sometimes in a loud chorus, as *not up to the task, over the hill, out of date, dead wood*, and so forth.

Admittedly it takes a great deal of effort and will to win to overcome the resistance from veteran teachers to once again opt for renewal and to develop a trusting relationship with school leaders. Here are some aspects of such a sales campaign.

Understanding the School Culture that Gives Rise to Veteran Teachers Resisting Mentoring and Renewal

Facilitators for the program need to literally enter the bastions held by veteran teachers. I say *held* because there are territories in our large secondary schools that are the sole province of veteran teachers. For example, there are faculty rooms that are taken over by veteran teachers in which no novice teacher, department chair, or administrator is welcomed. The culture of these faculty rooms often features a drumbeat of negativity toward students, new teachers, administrators, parents, and others. These are settings that have not changed over time, with teachers often occupying the same chair until they retire.

An example of this extremely isolating scenario confronted me on a tour of a large high school in Hartford, Connecticut. My tour guide, an assistant principal, showed me a cluttered and dirty faculty room and pointed out, "That's Mrs. Fitzgerald's chair. No one dares sit there but her. And many of the other chairs are literally owned by teachers who've been here a long time. It's a rite of passage. Many of our teachers bring a chair from home or bought at yard sales. They even bring couches, fridges, and microwaves. It's like a home away from home for them. Not a place that offers much hope for renewal or to heal one's wounds. We are trying to offer veteran teachers an alternative to hanging out in this dump but it's a battle we are losing right now. We tried to have the room painted and new furniture put in but they threw the painter out before he could even get started."

And then there are isolating departmental wings in our large secondary schools, such as English, mathematics, social studies, science, language, health and physical education, guidance, music, athletics, art, and so on. These are departmental wings in which veteran teachers usually dominate the culture and set the unofficial rules of combat. I use the words *rules of combat* because competition among departments for funding, recognition and publicity is just that—combat. Each department is doing what it can to survive in hard times and trying to outsmart and outmaneuver each other. Departmental life, then, is highly political.

There is no role for novice teachers who, while struggling to gain competency in their classrooms, are also thrown into a political cauldron, a situation for which they have no preparation in undergrad or grad school. When veteran teachers say to novice teachers, "Welcome to the real world," many newcomers go home at night wondering what they have gotten into and where they have landed.

And let's not forget the faculty meetings. Faculty meetings often have sections set aside for different groups. No sign is posted that says *Reserved for Vets*, but it is their territory. Here again, veteran teachers often have their assigned chairs. In this forum they are in command, often seated in a rear area but close enough to observe *the show*, as some call it, and close enough to mount an attack if some issue arises that they find problematic.

Any school reformer can surely expect the wrath of the veterans if a proposal involves asking them to do more. It's combat at close quarters, where reformers can expect to be hit hard with every reason why a new project can and will fail and to hear cries of, "We tried this before and it didn't work. Can't we move on? We are already over time. If we keep running late the union is going to have to step in."

And finally there are the social functions of the school. The school cafeteria often has long-established tables designated for veteran teachers, again with no sign posted—but everyone knows the rules except newcomers, who are quickly sent packing to another table. In some schools veteran teachers have their own chairs in the cafeteria as well. Many vets eat together, go to meetings together, and hang out in the faculty room together. It's an extremely isolating experience for veteran teachers that translates into little or no positive contact with other members of the school community, such as novice teachers.

This isolation is not limited to the school setting. There are the traditional Friday after-school get-togethers at local bars, where veteran teachers gather to talk about the good old days and what it was like to be a rookie way back then. There are the war stories: "Hey, remember when that crazy kid, what was his name, Frankie Testa, came after Joe Sheridan, the gym teacher, with a knife? Sheridan hit him with a bat and gave the kid a concussion and thirty stitches. Believe me, if it happened today, Joe would be brought up on charges, maybe lose his job, for doing the same thing. Everything has turned upside down. The kids and the parents are winning."

They tell tales of combat between teacher and teacher, administrator and teacher, teacher and student, and parent and teacher—tales that send a subtle message to newcomers to follow the lead of veterans and adopt a "we are all in this together" persona, or else risk being isolated, not in the club or "one of the boys or girls." Novice teachers quietly drink their beer at the end of the bar and probably wonder once again where they have landed.

Novice teachers have no role in each of the areas I have described above. They are observers who, while receiving little advice concerning their classroom problems, have entered a world far removed from kids, curriculum, and parents. It is as if they have stumbled upon a secret door that, when opened, reveals a hidden part of school life, a life in which many veteran teachers have traded their focus on teaching for a role that is dominated by school politics, negativity, rumors, gossip, and plans for retirement.

It's as if there were two worlds in the school, one a positive one with a picture of the classroom with teachers, students, books, computers, and so on all involved in learning, and the other a negative one focused on the myriad of settings in which veteran teachers are involved in various forms of resistance and negativity, chained to their chairs until retirement sets them free.

I believe we have abandoned many veteran teachers in our large secondary schools to this negative role and left them trapped behind walls of indifference. Theirs is a world often unseen by students, parents, and community members, who think, naively, that school is all about kids and learning. Welcome to the real world of school.

Changing the Culture of the School to Open Up Renewal Opportunities such as Mentoring for Veteran Teachers

The closed-door world that exists for veteran teachers is the world that school reformers need to enter to make their case for mentoring for aging teachers. This is the only approach that can work to engage veteran teachers: meeting them on their own turf and showing them that mentoring is in their own best interest. One can send out e-mails, memos, and program descriptions, but that's a no-win strategy.

These overtures are usually quickly dumped into the school and e-mail wastebaskets. They are faceless invitations that can be easily discarded. The real opportunity to involve veteran teachers can come only with face-to-face conversations that sometimes take the form of combat. Venturing into these walled fortresses presents an opportunity to explain what's in it for veteran teachers, how they can be involved, why they are needed, and what suggestions they have to make the intervention attractive.

One must be tough, committed to the change process; persuasive; able to withstand criticism, name calling, and even personal attacks; and willing to take a big risk in order to sell, invite, and utilize the skills of vets.

Most reform efforts fail because there is no direct contact, live, with dissenting groups in the school. There is no sales pitch to get them involved, no effort to get them on board as both participants and leaders. In a real sense it's a political effort. One is changing the rules by entering the opposition's bailiwick and confronting resistance head on. There is much failure in the process, and one has to continuously engage resistance and play in all the areas veteran teachers dominate: faculty rooms, department areas, faculty meetings, faculty cafeterias, teacher bars, and so on. It is one way to get respect for the program one is offering.

Teacher groups who resist education reform are often impressed with reformers who have the courage and will to meet them head on in their own setting. School reformers need to be courageous fighters, good listeners, talented facilitators, able to be involved with different and divergent groups, and able to shine and share the light of success on those veteran teachers who have come on board and are making a positive difference in helping programs such as mentoring and "no teacher left behind" be successful.

This model of engaging veteran teachers in face-to-face contact is similar to the counter-insurgency model used by the military—an approach to win the hearts and minds of the resistance and, one by one, win them over and tip the scales from defeat to victory. It is a process aimed at not leaving resisters isolated and vulnerable to negative controls and outdated beliefs. The main weapon in this model is face-to-face communication with the message that teachers' professional and personal lives can be better.

If school reform facilitators stay committed to this aggressive process, they can change the way the business of reform is carried out in our secondary schools. Reformers need to keep in mind the reality that most resisting teachers are left alone, unchallenged. Yes, they get the memos and e-mails on change efforts, but no one comes knocking on their doors to offer and invitation and explanation. They seldom experience the feeling of being wanted and needed. Veteran teacher are often described as the problem that needs to be fixed but as simply not interested in changing—a faulty assumption.

A different strategy is needed. That strategy consists of going aggressively into the lion's den of uninvolved teachers and selling one's wares, that is, school reform such as mentoring. This is a seemingly simple process that targets resisting teachers by offering an olive branch that says, "Come on board, we have something for you." It's a simple process that suggests, "No, we are not going to leave you alone; we are coming after you with our tank full of opportunity and we will be back often to get you on our team. We are here to stay."

That process leads eventually to getting some dissenters on board, seeing that this could be a good deal. For school reformers, turning the reform process upside down by going directly to resisting veteran teachers can be fun and exciting.

The process raises one's anxiety and level of risk, and in its raw form is life-giving for both the reformer and resisting teachers. It's an act of courage they have never seen before. It's like a former husband showing up at his ex-wife's wedding and wanting to meet the groom. It's unexpected and out-of-the-ordinary behavior that catches everyone by surprise and off guard. It's an olive branch that can over time reduce the isolation between reformers and resisting groups, shifting the playing field from exchanging charges and offering resistance to establishing real conversations and respect.

Most successful school reform efforts have this stealth quality, which can paralyze the opposition, albeit temporarily, and allow one to make a safe landing on a beach usually covered with mines and strafed by artillery fire. Remember, school reform is like combat. Surprise is an important component in securing victory. You have to hit them where and when they least expect it.

The most vulnerable area for resisting teachers is their feeling secure that no one will dare to violate the seemingly safe cocoon they have established to fight off change. Change is often brought about with surprise and new tactics unseen or unexpected by the opposition. The opening can be as simple as, "Hi, I am Bill Fibkins. I'd like to talk to you about this new mentoring program I am helping to start. I know this is your free period and I promise I'll only take a few minutes of your valuable time."

Making Sure that the Mentoring Offered to Veteran Teachers Is Something to Improve Their Personal and Professional Lives

Involving veteran teachers is in many ways similar to the evolution of a romantic relationship between two people. In the beginning there is often a lack of trust. Both sides may wonder, "Is this the real thing for me? What if he or she turns out not to be what I expected? Maybe I should put off a decision for a while. Some of my friends tell me this could be trouble and not to get involved."

In a sense it's like a dance between two people not quite sold on what's in it for them. They wonder if this is a real romance between two equals. The beginning push and pull involved in a serious romantic relationship is like a dance in which two people, not partners yet, dance in two colliding worlds, sometimes dancing far apart, checking each other out, and at other times dancing closer together, thinking, "I've found something for me."

Committing oneself to a romantic partnership can be a big risk, and so it is with saying "yes" to mentoring relationships. While mentoring is not about romance per se, it has some common ingredients, such as a relationship built on trust, mutual respect, and openness, a relationship in which one can reveal to a partner or mentor one's fears, concerns, hopes, and dreams.

Therefore, in addition to carrying the sales message directly to those veteran teacher groups who have long been isolated and resistant to change, education reformers leading the effort need to take the next step of making sure that the mentoring process is actually doing what it is intended to do.

They must demonstrate to veteran teachers that there is something in it for them, something that can improve both their personal and professional lives.

Mentoring veteran teachers is different from mentoring novice teachers. Veterans need to be engaged on a personal level, their concerns heard and respected, and their value as both persons and as teachers affirmed before there is any talk of how to improve their classroom skills. A personal bond must be developed between mentor and mentee, a bond that involves having the mentee feel safe, have trust, be affirmed, and be convinced that the mentoring process does not involve any hidden agenda other than helping his or her renewal.

It is a process, then, that involves the opportunity for the mentee to reappraise and modify both her personal and professional life, a process that allows her to consider her past and future and what she needs to do to create something new and, perhaps, become aware that stagnation can be a part of the aging process and a destructive force, closing out hope for creating something new on all levels.

The early stages of the mentor–mentee conversations are, then, not about curriculum and teaching skills. They are about creating a welcoming setting and establishing a tone of acceptance and caring, a setting that can help veteran teachers develop new dreams, feel renewed, and begin to believe that they are on the right path and have something worthwhile to offer students, parents, colleagues, their families, and the world in both the present and future.

It's a process that can help them to be contenders again and rid themselves of a negative persona, a mask that communicates to everyone in school, "You can't count on me. I'm not really here. My body may be here in the classroom but my mind and spirit departed long ago."

Perhaps you know teachers like this. They get to school late, leave early, are absent a lot, complain endlessly, resist any new ideas, and talk, talk, talk Florida and retirement. In the end our effort to raise awareness about the current plight of many veteran teachers is really an effort to save their professional lives. It's a mentoring process based on uncovering the hopes and dreams of teachers, many of who have long ago lost their will to hope for real novelty and change, to help them to understand that being an aging teacher doesn't necessarily translate into stagnation and giving up. They can, with mentoring, become models of success for themselves, colleagues, students, parents, families, and community.

Part of our work as school reformers is to remind ourselves that veteran teachers are human, that is, vulnerable and not made of steel. They have lived a life and have scars to prove it. Many arrive at school each day carrying emotional and sometimes physical baggage. As the reader knows, good intentions in life don't always work out. Life intrudes and we go down wrong roads. No one is spared from troubles, not even professionals like veteran teachers who have many achievements. They've gone to graduate school, become certified teachers, earned tenure, and early on found their niches in the classroom.

But life intrudes. As they age many veteran teachers find their personal lives having a negative impact on their classroom performance. Some find themselves in failed marriages or love relationships, divorcing, or getting involved in addictive behaviors, risky relationships, conflicts with grown children, poor financial decisions, sickness and death of their parents, and facing their own health problems as they age. Loss and failed dreams are part of adult life, and veteran teachers are not spared.

It should come as no surprise that the classroom performance of some veteran teachers deteriorates over time. They are trying to navigate through a personal and professional world that is always changing. Many do not want to just exist and spend the last twenty years of their careers gathering in faculty rooms with talk about the good old days, complaining about the present situation, trapped in the past, present, and, without intervention, the future.

Understanding why It Is Imperative to Close the Deal to Get Veteran Teachers on Board as Possible Mentors for Novice Teachers

It is time to act. The research by Ganser tells us we need to increase the number of mentors to help novice teachers. The main source of mentors for novice teachers is the great number of veteran teachers who have until now been uninvolved, except for those star teachers. They need to be invited into the process and shown they are needed.

Deborah Wadsworth, president of Public Agenda, paints the need for such an invitation in dramatic terms in the Public Agenda report "A Sense of Calling."[4]

Her comments are a wake-up call to the need for school leaders to act now to involve veteran teachers as mentors. She suggests that what is clear from interviewing novice teachers is their fundamental belief that the heart of good teaching comes not from the pages of a book but from what happens daily in the classroom—how teachers engage children's interest, how they get kids to persevere, how they explain difficult material, how they communicate its importance, how they inspire effort, and how they manage a respectful and productive classroom. All these things, teachers tell us, are as important as "knowing your stuff."

What their preparation lacks most, they say, is not content but the training needed to manage a classroom, bring classes alive, and make their students actually learn. Most beginning teachers tell us that when they first entered a classroom, they were often at a loss when they tried to help struggling students, yet they had every desire to do so.

Wadsworth argues that we have all stumbled into situations where it's clear that experience is something you don't get until just after you need it. Our beginning teachers understand that all too well. They speak powerfully about the shock of going from the theory of teacher education into the reality of the classroom. Wadsworth states, "To leave them there, eager to help out but lacking the skills to intercede, seems almost cruel."

Wadsworth has it right, a vivid picture—leaving novice teachers with just hope and desire is cruel, sort of like putting a young, untrained boxer into the ring with an experienced champion. Some new teachers are like raw meat. They are going to be chewed up, cut into ribbons, by October. It's like a war scene in which we put soldiers into combat without the necessary training, equipment, and support. The human stories of the struggles of these new teachers are seldom reported. They arrive in September, and some are gone by mid-year or June, taking their stories of failure with them.

Other new teachers survive based on the luck of the draw, but not drawing negative attention that would lead to firing does not mean they are necessarily effective classroom teachers. It may mean they lucked out with an easy class, which allowed them to go unnoticed, to fly under the radar screen. They may be at risk in the future when difficult students come their way.

Meanwhile, as in war, as the body count mounts with the attrition of novice teachers, often the only solution is to send in more raw recruits. The data on the attrition of novice teachers, like the deaths of young recruits in battle, is cloaked in numbers. Numbers don't tell the real story of human loss, failed promise, what went wrong, and what might have been if things had gone well.

It doesn't have to be this way. Things can change. The opportunity is there. Wadsworth states,

> Understanding what matters to people, what motivates them and why, can be of inestimable value in crafting policies and reforms that might actually make a difference."
>
> The "Sense of Calling" report reveals a passionate group of young adults who believe teaching is a calling. The strength and vibrancy of their morale and motivation are striking. It seems almost criminal to ignore what they have to offer by turning a deaf ear to what they have to say. [5]

I believe the words *almost cruel* and *almost criminal* help frame the seriousness of both the need for mentoring for novice teachers and the utilization of veteran teachers as mentors. There is a lot at stake for both groups: survival, proficiency, and success for novices, and for veterans the opportunity to intervene to help novice teachers be successful and, in the process, improve their own classroom skills.

As Jean Casey and Ann Claunch suggest, Daniel Levinson has provided the most contemporary view of mentoring.[6] Levinson points out that the act of mentoring includes providing a model of adult conduct and involves the acts of giving and receiving. The activities of a mentor are varied, and Levinson asserts that true mentoring is not defined by formal roles but by the character of the relationship.

Casey and Claunch add that other researchers, particularly in business and industry, have characterized the mentoring relationship as having two distinct functions: career functions and psychological functions. The career functions of mentoring center on enhancing career development and professional opportunities for the novice. A mentor in this case acts as a sponsor, protector, promoter, and guide. The career mentor opens doors for the protégé, challenges, provides opportunities for wider exposure, and introduces the protégé to those with influence and power.

The psychological functions of mentoring are aimed at personal development. In this case the mentor acts as a role model, quasi-counselor, teacher, supporter, and close colleague or friend. The protégé receives reinforcement, affirmation, acceptance, and confirmation from the mentor. The mentor's role becomes one of offering opportunities for enhancing self-esteem at both the personal and professional levels.

Here again we return to the importance for both novice and veteran teachers to join together as partners in meeting each other's needs to be successful in the classroom. As Levinson suggests, there seems to be a natural inclination in youth to seek out mentors. Developmental tasks in early adulthood include the development of life and professional skills, and respected, mature, adult role models aid in that process.

As a degree of security, confidence, and competence is developed in young adulthood, the tasks shift from development of self to concern for the development of others. Middle adulthood often brings on the need to lead, teach, counsel, and coach young people. In this way the developmental tasks of each life cycle are complementary.[7]

Clearly, selling veteran teachers on the need for them to be involved as mentors and mentees and opening the door to this process becomes a critical component in ensuring that teachers at various stages of development can successfully navigate through their various life cycle changes. Novice and veteran teachers alike need each other to overcome failure, boredom, and lack of affirmation and recognition that often accompany teachers as they move along their career paths.

The connection between novice and veteran teachers enables them both to secure a role of importance in the school community and develop a legacy that can be respected and emulated. As Levinson suggests, in this process the mentor and protégé are both connected to achieving a common dream.[8]

I believe this common dream is what Wadsworth describes as the need to manage a classroom well, bring classes alive, make sure students actually learn, feel that they are truly making a difference in helping students, and believe that they indeed have a special calling to be teachers. I believe we have the know-how at hand to make this common dream a reality in our schools. We have the right idea, the dream idea. What we need is the will, skills, determination, and courage to overcome resistance and make our sales pitch so compelling that resistance erodes. The stakes are high.

Wadsworth's assessment leaves no room for equivocation, looking the other way, or looking to tomorrow to solve the problem. Action is needed now. The professional and, coincidentally, the personal lives of many young and aging teachers are at risk. Failing professional lives do have an impact on personal lives.

Therefore, to leave novice teachers floundering as they face the reality of the classroom, eager to help but lacking the skills to intercede, seems almost cruel. And it seems almost criminal to ignore what they have to offer by turning a deaf ear to what they have to say. We must be reminded that each member of the school community—students, teachers, counselors, administrators, department chairs, central office staff, school boards, and parents—is part of the problem and part of the solution.

Our intervention efforts to make "no teacher left behind" a reality must include clear-cut ways for the school community to respond to the cries for help by struggling teachers, whether they be novices or veterans. We need to show the school community members how to move away from a school culture that says it's OK to ignore the cries for help they hear and observe from novice and veteran teachers. We must show them how to intervene so they can truly make a difference in saving professional lives. That means creating and demanding a culture that puts a stop to staff looking the other way, saying "it's not my job," casting blame on others, and closing one's door to silence the cries for help.

If the school culture allows some teachers to flounder and fail without intervention such as mentoring, the same avoidance and looking-the-other-way behavior patterns are often carried over to troubled students who are crying out for help as well. An effective mentoring program helps to combat the notion that it is OK for some members of the school community to be allowed to fail when trouble surfaces in their lives.

Clearly, teachers and students headed towards the margins of school life and failure have much in common. Each group is struggling to survive and looking for an open door to find a respite from failure, a renewal of hope, and the skills to become a successful and contributing member of the school community.

The "No Child Left Behind" and "no teacher left behind" interventions are interconnected. Successful schools need both interventions, sending the message that any member of the school community can become at risk and there are many open doors for help, including mentoring. The interventions must be guided by the philosophy that states that no member of the school community is dispensable and each person matters.

Serving as a mentor can open many doors for both professional and personal growth for veteran teachers. As Levinson suggests, being a mentor with young adults is one of the most significant relationships available in middle adulthood. The distinctive satisfaction of the mentor lies in furthering the development of young men and women, facilitating their efforts to form and live out their dreams and to lead better lives according to their own values and abilities. But this is not simply a selfless act on the part of the mentor.

Levinson says the mentor is doing something for himself as well. He is making productive use of his own knowledge and skill in middle age. He is learning in ways not otherwise possible. He is maintaining his connection with the force of youthful energy in the world and in himself. He needs the recipient of mentoring as much as the recipient needs him.

Levinson suggests that nurturing the development of children and adolescents is a major, age-appropriate function in early adulthood. At the same time veteran teachers in middle adulthood are ideally positioned to nurture young adults such as novice teachers.[9]

A marriage between the younger and older adults in the school community, then, is a win-win for the students, parents, novice teachers, veteran teachers, administrators, and community. Here is why:

- It offers the opportunity to novice teachers to hold onto their dreams of becoming successful teachers and for veteran teachers to form either new dreams or return to the dreams they had as novice teachers but long ago gave up on achieving.
- It allows the elder partners to demonstrate their concern for the young adults who will one day take their place.
- It gives veteran teachers the opportunity to avoid the stagnation that often visits older teachers—a chance, a lifeline, to again feel useful and invested in the school and to overcome their feelings of boredom, of being stuck or out of date, or of being on their way out.
- It provides veteran teachers with the opportunity to create a legacy that highlights the contribution they have made as mentors, one that has helped both their novice mentees and their students lead more successful lives. Mentoring reminds veteran teachers of their worth.
- It can help veteran teachers to feel tested once again, as they were as novices, presented with an opportunity to alter a daily routine that may have remained stagnant for years.

Taking on a new role can be unsettling. There is no easy script to follow when it comes to taking on a mentoring role. It's not like lecturing students. It's learning to really listen, accept, confront, be open to sensitive issues, share a part of one's self, and suggest alternatives to problems that demand a solution. Being a mentor can make one feel uncomfortable, anxious, tested, even exhausted—the same feelings classroom teachers have until they opt out for settling and playing it safe.

What is needed—and mentoring is one small cure for malaise—is to help veteran teachers feel human again by jolting them out of their long-term sleepwalk and into becoming learners again, in the end helping them to be grateful that they can feel something deeply again. Anxiety is not a bad thing for veteran teachers mired in the same old stagnation.

Veteran teachers are akin to therapists who understand that they need regular feedback from other therapists on how they are proceeding. Mentors must raise their awareness concerning the kinds of teacher personalities they have trouble relating to in mentoring sessions. They must be aware of why they may be avoiding some kinds of problems that teachers bring to them.

These types of quasi-therapeutic conversations among mentors serve to help the mentors be motivated to learn new skills in order to embrace colleagues and problems that so far they have chosen to avoid, personalities and issues that have posed a threat to their safety level and that they have pushed away. As important are self-awareness conversations, which can be valuable to veteran teachers who have also kept certain students and problems at arm's length, avoiding their presence in the classroom and, as one teacher told me, "wishing they would disappear, be absent, drop out, be suspended, move."

HOW MENTORING CAN IMPROVE THE EFFECTIVENESS OF CLASSROOM INSTRUCTION FOR BOTH NOVICE AND VETERAN TEACHERS

An often unreported aspect of mentoring is that the process can help mentors become more aware of the dark side of their classroom behavior, offering a vivid picture for them of which students are "in" and which are "out ." For me the value of this process, the exchange of "how are things going?" conversations among mentors, is that mentors can begin to face up to their humanness, accepting what was but beginning to learn new skills to open up their classrooms to every student who walks through the doors regardless of color, ethnicity, intelligence, dress, behavior, health, or wellness. As Levinson suggests, mentoring has a psychological function, and clearly teaching students has one as well.

Being both a mentor and teacher at the same time can trigger some unexpected new learning that can prompt the need for new skills. However, the process can also be unsettling. Veteran teachers have often taught their classes in the same way for many years. They have brought the values they learned as children, teens, and young adults with them and have incorporated these values into their view of how students should act and how a classroom should operate. It is no wonder that, as human beings, they are attracted to certain student personalities and behaviors.

It is often easier for teachers to like students who are high achievers, motivated, and well-behaved, and who share the same values or even background of the teacher. As one teacher told me, "They're my kind of kids. Like me, they work hard, play by the rules, don't act out, and are responsible. I'll take a class of fifty of these kids if I could get rid of some of the dirtbags they send me."

And so it is that for many teachers who were raised as rule followers, having students in their classes who are anything but can be unnerving. As novice teachers they were no doubt aware of how threatened they felt by such students. They probably had no wise mentor to show them how to reach these students and in the process reduce their own fears of being threatened by their differentness.

The wise mentor knows he does no good and in fact is harmful if he coddles his mentee and pretends that the element of confrontation, the duel between teacher and student, will magically go away and all will be peaceful. Prayers and hopes for new beginnings are usually not enough to arm teachers for the daily battles they face.

Rather, mentors need to teach their mentees classroom skills and political survival skills, the importance of having the will to win, how and when to show a tough take-charge persona and how and when to be a caring facilitator, how to overcome resistance, and how to sustain these skills in order to do well. Overly nice guys and gals do not usually make it as teachers, particularly in large junior and senior high schools. In the classroom there are times to be soft and caring with students, but there are also times to be tough, to know how to confront, and to be in charge. We do our novice teachers no favors in suggesting otherwise and leaving them unprepared for the arena they are entering.

The mentor–mentee sessions offer prime time to teach mentees how to be in charge and to be assertive while at the same time choosing to be open and caring with students. Perhaps the most important lesson a mentor can impart to a mentee is the notion that the classroom is not always about cooperation and goodness. To think it is constitutes a willful flight from reality. Kids are kids and some don't always play by the rules, willingly go along with what the teacher says, or act eager to learn.

The streets are filled with fired ex-teachers who naively entered the profession hoping to encounter docile students, no bullies, peaceful classrooms without acting out or confrontational students, total acceptance and respect by students, and playgrounds absent fights and name calling. They were unprepared and paid the price. Hope simply is not enough to be a classroom teacher.

In the end survival comes before proficiency. In order for novice teachers to successfully navigate the path from survival to proficiency, they require the easily accessible, ongoing support of training offered by mentoring.

USING MENTORING TO CREATE NEW ROLES FOR VETERAN TEACHERS

Mentoring for veteran teachers can bring them full circle, back to a time when they, like the novice teachers they are trying to help, were intent on their own survival, cultivating only those students who didn't rock the boat, act out, or ruin their goal of tenure by challenging the teacher's authority and inviting the negative attention of the principal. In a sense their mentoring is quite a marvelous and exciting process, a gift really, for mentoring teachers.

The process can put them in touch with their own beginnings as novice teachers and help them realize that they don't have to play it safe any more. They have tenure and are now involved in teaching and training adults as well as students. This new and necessary beginning is often exciting, challenging, and anxiety-provoking.

However, the initial good feeling of achieving tenure and the security that comes with it is short-lived and often results in a growing sense of boredom. Security is not always a friend when it comes to being a continuous learner.

In one study, Seymour Sarason observed that without exception teachers with more than five years of experience had lost enthusiasm, excitement, and a sense of mission and challenge. Sarason suggests that in one way or another, these teachers indicated that they now rarely experienced a sense of personal and intellectual growth. The shape of the future was dismally clear, repeating a routine with which they were already too familiar.

Sarason also suggests that as teachers grow older, organizational isolation and boredom erode their sense of purpose on the job. Most people need a *belonging* sense of responsibility and purpose, feeling part of a group or community they can depend on and contribute to. Sarason concludes his remarks with the questions, "Can we teach our children to live in a community when we ourselves lack a sense of community in our work?"[10]

Sarason's comments help explode the myth that receiving tenure allows novice teachers to relax and feel they have at last entered the club, that they can breathe a sigh of relief, and that they've won the job and the pressure is off to keep learning. As Sarason points out, there is a dark side to the process. In receiving tenure there is no longer the risk of failure or the anxiety that is often present to a rookie, being onstage and trying hard not to get on the wrong side of the principal, department chair, colleagues, parents, and students. It's a little like being a coach of a football team that is ahead, choosing to run out the clock to preserve a victory. The focus is on protecting the ball and not trying anything fancy.

As a result there is no longer the element of risk. Without the risk and anxiety that come with change and novelty, teachers, as shown in Sarason's research, often lose their enthusiasm, their excitement, and their sense of mission and challenge. Mentoring can lift the veil of boredom by offering veteran teachers the life-giving chance to begin anew.

As Sarason argues, mentoring offers the veteran teachers a sense of belonging, responsibility, and purpose and the opportunity to see themselves as master teachers and doers in the present. Mentoring offers them an opportunity to keep both feet in the school and avoid using their energy to chase the god of retirement. Buoyed by the mentoring experience, they can continue to feel part of a school community they can contribute to and depend on.

Robert Bellah and his colleagues echo Sarason's call for the need to help teachers regain a feeling of belonging, responsibility, and purpose by suggesting we need to develop a sense of calling in our work settings, a calling that links a person to his or her fellow workers and to the larger community. What we *do* often translates into what we *are*.[11]

In terms of veteran teachers, a sense of calling implies that they are in the right place, they are contributors, and they have found their niche; they are not professionals trying to get out but are firm in their belief that what they do matters, that it offers something good to others and contributes to the common good.

But middle adulthood can be a risky stage for veteran teachers, a state in which they are faced with the dilemma of choosing either to renew their sense of calling and create new dreams for themselves or begin the process of slowly extracting themselves from their career identities as teachers.

Bellah and colleagues suggest that midlife often marks the end of a dream of progressing in a career. It's when the trajectory of a career flattens out and dreams tend to die as the excitement of the job diminishes. For many in middle age the world of work then dims. As a result I believe one's sense of calling evaporates unless an intervention such as mentoring is available to rekindle and expand one's dreams.

Mentoring can help veteran teachers to become professionally alive again, or for some, for the first time in their careers. Through mentoring, they are able once again to experience being a contributor and also receive much in return if they become involved in helping novice teachers find their way.

Sarason reminds us of the importance of such partnerships when he suggests that Freud and Dewey both stressed that it is nonsense to think and act as if helpers and helped, teacher and pupil, are different kinds of people or that one can change or help the other without experiencing change in himself.[12]

Let me conclude this chapter by summarizing these important points:

- The mentoring of novice teachers has increased dramatically since the first edition of this book came out in 2002.
- In the early stages of mentoring novices, star teachers—those with a track record as excellent teachers, workshop and conference presenters, authors of books and journal articles, and education consultants—were utilized as mentors.
- With the rise in mentoring, there now exists a deficit of mentors available to fill the need.
- Veteran teachers, those in the trenches who are not known as star teachers, are one group with experience who could serve as mentors.
- Many veteran teachers have been turned off by participating in school reform efforts that have failed. They have tended to isolate themselves rather than to pursue further training, and may end up focused solely on retirement.
- Veteran teachers must be engaged on their own turf and sold on their value as mentors, using their experience, wisdom, and guidance to ensure that no teacher is left behind.
- Once engaged and brought on board as mentees, those veteran teachers who display the skills needed to be mentors can be encouraged to serve in this new role.

In Chapter 8 the focus is on a case study involving my own experience to demonstrate how veteran teachers can be engaged one on one and brought on board a school reform project. The same model can be used to get veteran teachers on board the mentoring process.

NOTES

1. Ellen Moir, "Launching the New Generation of Teachers," in *Teacher Mentoring and Induction*, edited by Hal Porter (Thousand Oaks, CA: Corwin Press, 2005).

2. Maureen Dowd, "Port Mortuary's Pull," *New York Times*, 1 November 2009, 9 WK.

3. Tom Ganser, "Learning from the Past—Building for the Future," in *Teacher Mentoring and Induction*, edited by Hal Porter (Thousand Oaks, CA: Corwin Press, 2005).

4. Deborah Wadsworth, "A Sense of Calling," Public Agenda (2000).

5. Ibid.

6. Jean Casey and Ann Claunch, "The Stages of Mentor Development," *Teacher Mentoring and Induction*, edited by Hal Porter (Thousand Oaks, CA: Corwin Press, 2005).

7. Ibid.

8. Ibid.

9. Ibid.

10. Seymour Sarason, *Creation of Settings* (San Francisco: Jossey Bass, 1972).

11. Robert Bellah, Richard Madsen, William Sullivan, Ann Swidler and Steven Tipton, *Habits of the Heart* (New York: Harper and Row, 1985).

12. Sarason, op. cit

Chapter Eight

Utilizing Mentoring to Provide a Second Act for Veteran Teachers

Chapter 7 questioned the assumptions that are often heard in schools and communities about veteran teachers:

- They are not interested in improving their classroom skills.
- They are not concerned about the well-being of novice teachers.
- They are just biding their time until retirement.
- They don't want to be their brothers' keepers and help colleagues.

However, these faulty assumptions are not the fault of veteran teachers. Rather, the real reason is our problem—that of the leadership in the schools and of education reformers. We have misread the opportunity to engage veteran teachers in continuous learning activities that speak to their needs in the middle adult stage of their lives. We have tried to sell them on improving their classroom skills, without support to address the personal needs and issues that are so much a part of midlife.

We thought teacher training was simply about the classroom instead of the entire life spectrum of veteran teachers. This half-empty-glass approach has resulted in our literally turning them off from making a commitment to renew their classroom effectiveness. What is needed is a selling campaign and program that offer the opportunity for both professional and personal renewal, a program such as mentoring that speaks to teachers' needs in midlife, not a one-size-fits-all approach that is offered to every teacher from novice to aging veteran.

The needs of veteran teachers are unique to their development stage. Attention needs to be paid to our senior staff members if we are to engage them in forming new dreams, new roles, and new hopes. In midlife they are on a search for a "second act," and as school leaders and reformers we indeed have the responsibility to provide them with such an opportunity and not abandon them to living out their careers focused only on retirement.

We say our goal is to leave not one child behind, to not abandon children in need of hope and support in avoiding the margins of school life and becoming a dropout. How can we not offer our teachers the same message, a message that says we will leave not one teacher behind, not abandon teachers in need of help and support in avoiding the same fate?

It is a fact of school life that many members of the school community need a second act to successfully navigate through difficult developmental stages, whether they are students, teachers, administrators, support staff, or counselors. Here are the whys and hows of providing our veteran teachers with their second act and, in the process, helping novice teachers.

ENGAGING VETERAN TEACHERS ONE BY ONE TO CREATE CONDITIONS FOR RENEWAL AND A SECOND ACT

In Chapter 1 Michael A. Ballin, president of the Clark Foundation, advises school reformers that "addressing the system rather than the specific actions of individual teachers leads us to commit the cardinal sin of education . . . confusing treatment with cure. I have only one bit of advice to aid escape from the futilities of school reform. Stop trying to make schools great schools and take up the task of trying to make teachers great teachers. We engage in school reform teacher by teacher."[1]

Engaging teachers one by one on their own turf can play a major role in breaking down resistance and opening up new, exciting doors for teacher renewal such as mentoring. I learned this lesson the hard way when I helped found and became director of the Bay Shore Public Schools–Stony Brook University Teacher Center in Bay Shore, New York. Here is my story and the personal anecdotes that were so important to me in my personal and professional life. It was an experience that inspired me to study and explore a variety of helping interventions for teachers, such as mentoring.

The evolvement of the center and my interests in teacher development, how the aging process affects veteran teachers, and how to overcome teachers' resistance to change began with receiving my Ph.D. from Syracuse University. I was excited about returning to the junior high school from which I was on leave for two years.

My dream was to start a unique teacher training center. I envisioned a center that would offer workshops during the school day that teachers, support staff, and administrators could attend on their lunch breaks and during free periods. My vision was that the majority of the workshops would be led by the school staff, with outside resources such as faculty at Stony Brook University also on board as workshop presenters.

Teachers who volunteered to lead workshops would be released from their teaching duties for the day. A grant from the university would enable the school to hire substitute teachers as replacements. The plan was for teachers to offer their workshops at each of the three faculty lunch periods and be available during the other periods for informal conversations with interested faculty.

My initial goal was to encourage teachers to decide on what workshops would help them to be more effective in the classroom. It was a homegrown effort specifically designed to meet the needs of teachers at the junior high, a reversal of the usual staff development offerings, which usually involved in-service workshops focused on meeting the goals and mission of the entire school district.

This was an exciting idea that was given full support by my principal, George Forbes. He understood that the project could have a major impact on improving the morale and effectiveness of teachers. Teaching at the junior high was not easy. The community had more than its share of low-income and at-risk kids. Forbes, a former counselor and school psychologist, knew the staff needed an infusion of new ideas and training and that the center might be the vehicle for change. He understood that he couldn't take on such a project himself.

Forbes told me, "I am so busy with everyday crises I have no time for staff development. I am hoping your experience at Syracuse can help us out in the area of teacher renewal. And I like the idea that you have cultivated a relationship with Stony Brook University. That relationship gives us some credibility with the district office, the school board, and the teachers' union. Maybe we are in the beginning of offering courses here toward a master's degree and certification. Wouldn't that be great for our teachers? Save them from having to take courses at night at some faraway campus."

The foreword in this book is dedicated to Forbes. He could see opportunity for change and knew to get out of the way. Forbes reduced the demands of my student assistance counseling job, allowing me a half day to help set up the center.

I was also supported by the involvement of a cadre of teachers who were involved in an in-service course I was teaching at the school on teacher burnout and by the education department at nearby Stony Brook University. A graduate student at Stony Brook came on board to help facilitate our growing relationship with the university. Full steam ahead, I thought.

But as you know, good ideas are not always successful. The good feeling involved in implementing a grand design that everyone would love quickly turned sour. As I suggested earlier, one can send out memos, program descriptions, and clear goals and speak to the converted, but not everyone is going to buy into your plan.

And so it was when we opened the center in a room next to the faculty room, an attractive room with comfortable furnishings, coffee brewing throughout the day, and a beginning library of education books and journals. It was a professional, welcoming setting. Our initial program offering featured workshops led by supportive teachers and university faculty. We were ready and set, we thought.

Reality soon sank in. The only teachers who showed up for the workshops were members of the in-service course I was teaching. Even they were ambivalent because of pressure they were getting from veteran teachers who questioned the project. Ninety percent of the teaching staff chose to ignore our efforts, especially the veterans.

They made comment such as, "Hey Fibkins, oh, excuse me, Dr. Fibkins, are you using this job to get on the faculty at Stony Brook University?" I was labeled as a person interested only in promoting himself. Rumors abounded: "He's changed big time since he got his doctorate." "Who is he to think he can waltz in here after being gone so long and expect us to like his big ideas?" "He's not in the classroom so what does he know about us teachers on the front lines?"

Some veteran teachers were intent on driving me away and getting me off my game. At one faculty meeting, where I was making a presentation on the center, a group of vets got up and turned their chairs backwards to my talk. Welcome to the real world of school, Bill Fibkins. But I learned. And that learning was a gift.

Here are some of the lessons I learned that helped me to understand the world of veteran and novice teachers:

- "Outsiders," even ones who have roots in the school, are often not trusted or quickly accepted by the teaching staff. One is tested anew, sometimes very aggressively, by veteran teachers who are suspicious of educators who want to use their turf, even if it involves a former colleague. I returned to Bay Shore different in the eyes of many teachers. I had a Ph.D., had written professional articles, and spoken at district, state, and national conferences. I had become a star teacher, a somebody.

    Although I saw myself as humble, eager to help others shine their light, and definitely not self-promotional, in the eyes of many teachers, particularly the veterans, I was no longer in the club. I had moved on while they remained in the trenches, teaching the same subject in the same room for years with no hope for novelty or change. In their eyes I had escaped.

    The school grapevine was active with doubts: "Why should we get behind a program to support a star who is probably going to use this experience to move on to some big job at a university or at the department of education?"

- Because many teachers have little opportunity for positive affirmation, they are at risk for and vulnerable to anger and resistance to any colleague who appears to have, as one teacher described it, *made it out*. I learned first-hand that the anger and resistance to me and my idea for the center was not so much about me as a person and a professional, but were reserved for anyone who had gotten out of the sometimes stagnating daily grind of teaching.
- For many veteran teachers, even though they feel trapped and without novelty, the opportunity for change is also anxiety producing and risky. For example, offering teachers the opportunity to lead workshops for their peers and to be released from their classrooms for the day was frightening for many. Many felt uncomfortable teaching their peers. Some anticipated negative feedback and rejection. It is not easy moving from teaching kids to teaching adults who know how to tune you out. Adults can't be silenced by threats such as, "You're out of here. Go to the office."

Education reformers sometimes think they are helping veteran teachers by opening new doors to opportunities for renewal, but help is in the eye of the beholder. We need to understand that we are dealing with teachers who have never experienced a world outside their classrooms. While they may know their stuff, they don't see themselves as having something to offer their colleagues. They are not star teachers, experts, conference presenters, or authors. Their first inclination when asked to be a workshop leader is to run for cover or say, "Are you sure you have the right person? I'm just a classroom teacher."

This sense of risk also exists for novice teachers who, just out of undergraduate or graduate school, do come on board with knowledge about new practices. However, they don't see themselves as contributors and are hesitant to take on this additional role. As one novice teacher told me, "I can't take a chance on telling the older teachers what to do. I could risk not getting tenure if that group turns on me. Got to keep my mouth shut." Being a mentor, workshop leader, or, in my case, an education reformer can get you thrown out of the club, subject to name calling, and at risk of appearing to dare to think you know something more about the teaching process. Most teachers in the school culture march to the same drum and it's risky to step out in front of the parade. Support, and plenty of it, is necessary for us to extricate ourselves from the sameness and lack of challenge of our work. In that respect the teachers at Bay Shore Junior High, both novices and veterans, and I had much in common. We were all trying to escape the risks of stagnation and boredom, yet at the same time hesitant to open a new door and take our place in a new kind of club.

As dancer and choreographer Twyla Tharp, quoted in Chapter 2, stated, "Cynicism is very de-energizing. And dance needs energy to go on. You have to believe what you are doing is important. That what you have to offer has something good for them . . . so there is no point in being cynical if you want to dance. So get over it."[2]

In teaching, as in dance, getting over it isn't so easy. Cynicism can reign in places where teachers congregate and be an obstacle to believing what you do is important and what you have to offer has something good for the teachers. Teachers, like dancers, have to be told in person and often that what they do matters. They have to hear that message loud and clear in order to drown out the cynicism that clouds their daily lives. The creation of a teacher center was my way of helping to erase that cynicism and help teachers believe in themselves.

- I could play a teaching role by modeling helping behaviors for the school staff. For example, while many teachers reported being concerned about the well-being of a teacher having problems in the classroom or in his or her personal life, they didn't see it as their role to intervene to help that teacher. Some said it wasn't their job and they didn't get paid to be a counselor. However, their reluctance to become involved in helping a colleague going through tough times was more about not knowing how to offer support. They lacked the skills to intervene and help direct colleagues to sources of help in the school and community and to stay with them in their time of need, gaining the understanding that they too might need the same kind of support someday.

Over time I came to realize that in modeling these helping skills at the center and in other interactions with teachers, I could play a role in teaching helping skills and making these behaviors part of the school culture.

Simple helping queries can make teachers aware that they can be their brother's or sister's keeper. For example, say "I notice that Gerry has been out of school all week. Someone said she is going through a difficult divorce. Maybe we should call her and offer our support," or, "How is Harry doing? Every time I walk past his classroom it seems the kids are out of control. Has he talked to anyone about what's going on? Maybe one of us should get involved."

Teachers need to be called on to help and be taught simple skills in order to be successful in the helping process. *Called on* means encouraging teachers to take responsibility for the care of each other, not look the other way. This process at first seems alien to them and somehow far removed from what they conceptualize as their teaching role. They have to learn that not only is it OK to help, but it is a responsibility that comes with being a member of a caring community. Learning helping skills adds a new dimension to their work with both students and colleagues, not letting one member fall through the cracks.

• By meeting teachers face to face in their classrooms, things can change for the better. In these kinds of exchanges, Dr. William Fibkins, the new Ph.D., became Bill Fibkins, a colleague and sometimes mentor and friend. I became a colleague who was convinced, as Twyla Tharp says, that what I had to offer teachers was important and had something good for them. In visiting a teacher's classroom I could quickly assess if that teacher believed I had something to offer and where resistance or opportunity existed.

A five-minute conversation can tell you a lot. Does the teacher seem ready, involved, motivated, confident, and eager to teach students? Does she or he appear healthy, energetic, ready, and set to deal with the resistance some students are sure to offer? Or does he or she seem uninvolved, not confident, and unready for the challenges that await beginning with the first period? Is the classroom clean, organized, and welcoming, a place that kids want to come to—or is it shabby, worn, piled with books and papers that never seem to get put away, with pictures on the walls that haven't changed in years? If a former student came back to visit, would he or she find the classroom the same as it was when he or she was a student ten years ago?

Classroom visits can assess how a particular teacher feels about your project. In my case, inviting a teacher to the center, asking for ideas for workshops, and also floating the idea that maybe she or he might offer a workshop could help with the assessment. The teacher's verbal feedback and body language can tell you if he or she is with you, against you, or maybe a little bit of both. That data is critical in helping to develop a plan to get the teacher involved, most often involving a soft sell. Showing up in a classroom early in the morning before students arrived, I could share idle chatter—weather, sports, vacation plans, and so on—then gently share information about the day's workshop at the center and convey a message that I wanted the teacher involved.

This kind of interaction is not confrontational, but is carried out with the expectation that you can win this teacher over if you can begin to develop a personal relationship with him or her, with the understanding that it is OK for the teacher to reject you and your ideas, but also with the understanding that if you keep coming back and developing a relationship, good things can happen.

When we began the center, over 90 percent of the teachers, the majority being veterans, boycotted the program. When I left five years later, over 90 percent of the teachers were participating as workshop presenters and learners.

Patience, accepting others at they are, persistence, offering a soft sell, looking for openings to bring about involvement, and being able to take on harsh feedback about my personal and professional life brought about needed change. Change is all about numbers. By going teacher by teacher, striving to reach the tipping point where we had the majority of teachers involved, we shifted the balance in the direction of reform. Meeting teachers face to face, calling on them to act, and encouraging their support helps build a caring, involved community and reduce isolation.

- Leading a successful education reform effort, such as opening a teacher center or mentoring program, cannot be accomplished without having the time and support necessary to get the job done well. School administrators are so involved in a number of complex leadership issues that they simply don't have the time to lead and sell staff development programs.

Yes, they need to be involved on a number of levels, such as gaining funding, selling the program to district administration, developing support from key teacher and union leaders, and serving as a political cover for the program when it comes under attack. They know the political world they inhabit and understand how to leverage a good idea, but they don't have the time to put together all the nuts and bolts.

George Forbes understood his role and what he could and could not do, and was so secure in himself that he was able to delegate his staff development role to me. Why did it seem a no-brainer for him? We had established a level of trust between us. He knew I was interested in developing the center, not in becoming the next principal or building a resume so I could move on and become a teacher center guru.

We were both committed to the job at hand—improving the professional lives of teachers, improving the school climate for students and parents, and affirming members of the support staff whose helping roles were often taken for granted. Secretaries, custodians, cafeteria and hallway monitors, and teachers' aides are seldom given positive feedback for all the help they give to students.

George Forbes selflessly turned over part of his role to me and as my mentor freed me to do what I did best—listen, engage, involve, support, and help others. Like me Forbes enjoyed helping others to shine their light; he was a mentor in the truest sense of the word.

I learned these lessons by arriving early every morning and visiting each classroom in the school. I made my presence known. Many of these visits involved a simple conversation and invitation: "Good morning. How are things going? We are having a workshop today on discipline. Mike Wallace, the eighth grade social studies teacher, is leading it. Hope you can drop by. Got any ideas for workshops? I hear you are taking a course at Stony Brook on at-risk children. Maybe you could share your learning at the center. Give it some thought."

But sometimes my visits took on a more personal tone. Some teachers needed an ear, someone to talk to about problems with kids, parents, colleagues, or the administration. As my daily routine evolved and the level of trust rose, there emerged conversations about personal issues—aging parents, trouble in their own families such as divorce or conflict with children, health and wellness issues such as substance abuse or obesity, and among veteran teachers, fears and concerns about aging. I realized that in visiting the room of every teacher each morning, I was not only opening a door for each teacher to get involved in the center but also becoming a confidant on personal issues. I was a regular presence in their lives and a good listener, had training in counseling, and could be trusted to keep their stories private.

But while honoring their privacy, the themes in the personal issues they described were also themes that could be explored via the workshops we offered at the center. I was learning a simple truth: the concerns of teachers, more pronounced in the lives of veteran teachers, were often more important than academic issues.

Teachers at all levels of experience needed both an ear to talk to about their personal issues and a resource, such as the center's workshops, to gain more problem-solving information. To my surprise, concerns about aging and avoiding stagnation were at the top of the list for veteran teachers.

It was true that I had "gotten out" of the day-in-day-out routine of school life as we know it and found a new role for myself. And in the beginning many school staff rightfully asked, "What is this guy up to and what does he do? He's not a teacher, an administrator, or even a full-time counselor." My new role was a little mysterious because neither the teachers nor I had a grand design of where we were headed together. We were both taking a risk, buying into a new vision and trusting it would benefit the staff, students, and parents. It was not an easy role for me. Rather it was one filled with anxiety, self-doubt, rejection, and a few victories to make each day a challenge. I had no script to follow, just a hazy vision of creating a helping setting for teachers and reducing the anomie so prevalent and so destructive.

In my daily visits I was a living example for veteran teachers that things could change. I was not only expanding my mission and role in new ways but I was also providing a resource for teachers to help them to explore new dreams. In a sense it was missionary work, asking teachers to join with me. I needed them and believed they needed what I had to offer. The teachers and I had something to gain from each other.

However no matter how one tries to open up new doors there are some teachers who dig in their heels and won't buy the education reform you are selling. There are some veteran teachers who are polite and appear to listen, but who, as they say, want out of the school door as soon as retirement day comes. One keeps trying to involve them but at some point it is a standoff. One can't win everyone over in school reform efforts..

And there are veteran teachers who the staff want "out of here, now." They are described by colleagues as burnt out and as creating a bad name for the school. When it came to intervening to help these teachers I soon realized I had arrived at their door too late. They appeared depressed, tired, isolated, and not well emotionally or sometimes physically. They were like an alcoholic who stays in his or her room, with no one visiting, their family and friends no longer caring and perhaps secretly wishing that the alcoholic would go into rehab, simply disappear, or even die. Support has vanished and it's only a matter of time before the alcoholic does as well. Help is not on the way.

Such was the case with Harry Walker (a made-up name to conceal his identity). Harry wasn't an alcoholic. He was more like the teachers I have described as appearing worn out, passive, having low energy, and conveying a sense of not being ready for the day or the challenges to come. It was as if he had surrendered his teaching role and was waiting for someone, a savior, to come and lead him out of his misery, out of the school, and guide him home where he could rest and heal his wounds.

But that help never came. After teaching the same subject in the same room for thirty-eight years, he had arrived at a terrible place. He never left his room all day. He brought his lunch and ate alone. His students controlled the class while he sat at his desk, seemingly untouched by the chaos all around him.

As you know, students, even the most polite and kind, can act out when there is no discipline, focus, or attention being paid. Harry's behavior was the talk of the school. In the faculty room veteran teachers talked about wishing he would retire or simply not return one day. Many were angry with him and wanted him gone, out of sight.

One teacher said, "He gives all of us who work our butts off a bad name with parents and taxpayers." The more compassionate teachers voiced fears that they might become like Harry as they aged and would have to endure the same kind of name-calling from peers.

The novice teachers had a different reaction. They didn't fear becoming like Harry but expressed puzzlement at seeing him arrive each day, often unkempt, unshaven, and wearing clothes from another era. To them it was as if Harry were stuck in another time zone, the early 1950s, when he first began teaching. They too wanted Harry gone. There were a few novices who saw an advantage in Harry's plight. They wanted him gone because it could open up a vacancy for a tenured job for them.

The administration, while concerned about Harry, was ambivalent about how to intervene. Harry had tenure, never missed a day of school, had until the last few years enjoyed a successful career, and had the support of the teachers' union, who feared that if Harry were forced to retire the district would not replace his position in those tough budget times.

The union seemed to feel that a passive, even troubled, Harry was better than no Harry at all. In those bad economic times it was all about preserving jobs at any cost. The union leaders warned the administration that they would fight any attempt to force Harry out. The administration didn't need that kind of battle. The district was planning a buyout package for teachers over fifty-five. Maybe Harry would choose to leave quietly and go out with a nice package.

So, ironically, it came down to Harry and me. My daily visits offered, slowly at first, the chance for him to talk about how he felt as his career had fallen on tough times. On some days I never made it to visit other teachers; I stayed with Harry. He was like some of the at-risk kids I counseled in my other role as student assistance counselor, overcome by the deterioration in their lives, too many school failures, too many moves from town to town, too many new homes (if one can call some of the dumps they lived in a home), too much violence seen in their young lives, too much of everything, often leaving them with a shell-shocked, dazed look.

But there was no getting Harry to the teacher center or out of his room. He wanted the comfort of my presence and the chance to tell his story in private. I thought that if only I had been around earlier, maybe I could have helped him somehow to climb out of his stagnation and explore alternatives for survival and a way to be back in the game again. Harry took the only way out for him—he retired that year. He was a no-show at the district retirement party. The superintendent lauded his service while some teachers in the audience raised their glasses to toast his departure. Harry left quietly—just got in his car on the last day of school and drove away.

I wondered what he was feeling on that last day. Did anyone get a chance to say good-bye to him? Nobody knew he was retiring, but just hoped that he would. The administration was told of his decision a week later by the union rep. Rumor had it he moved to North Carolina. Many teachers reported that they felt a sense of relief with Harry gone. I remember one teacher telling me, "He was burnt, toast; at least we don't have to look at him suffering any more."

I realized that while it was too late for Harry, maybe the story he told me might help other teachers raise their awareness about the perils of aging as a teacher and motivate them to take an active role in staying well and useful.

To this end I wrote a play about Harry's plight, *Is There Anyone At All?* again keeping his identity private but including the themes that emerged in his story. The year after Harry retired a group of teachers and I put on the play at education conferences throughout the Northeast. The response of teachers, particularly veteran teachers, was overwhelmingly positive. We touched a nerve with Harry's story. To our surprise, the presentations were so well received that often we could not get off the stage because of the number of queries and comments.

The most interesting part for me was the revelation by many teachers that they had colleagues like Harry in their schools. Some also voiced the fear that they might become like Harry as they aged, feeling abandoned and left to silently slip away.

Here is Harry's story, which I adapted from the play for this book.

IS THERE ANYONE AT ALL?

This is a story about a teacher, an older man, in his early sixties, a solitary man somehow out of touch with his colleagues because his pain is so vivid, so real. His daily struggle with his students and his home life can no longer be hidden. He cries out and asks for help even when he knows he should be quiet. He knows people are looking at him as if he were some kind of freak. He knows they see him as unsure of himself, stumbling.

What he does not know is that they see themselves in him. Will they become like him at sixty-three? Is it somehow the destiny of all teachers to stumble, become less sure? Seeing him every day only increases the fear of his colleagues for themselves. If only he weren't here. If only we didn't have to see his pained face every day. If only we could rid ourselves of the struggle within us to both reach out to him and at the same time, to run away, not wanting to struggle with him and ourselves over the meaning of such words as *caring*, *powerlessness*, and *dying*.

The scene is a classroom in a large junior high school, thirty-two seats in six rows. It is two o'clock in the afternoon. The students are coming in slowly for their seventh-period class. The room is hot and smells of sneakers, sweat, perfume, hairspray, and deodorant, all mixing to give off an aroma of decay. Into the room comes a group of boys about fourteen years of age, pushing each other, shoving the desks around. "Faggot." "Your mother."

In the middle rows four very obese girls appear to be helping each other with the homework; they appear frightened by the noise and commotion. Outside the door students continue moving toward the room. Somehow the scene looks like a dance, moving toward the room and away again. "You got snagged." "I'm not going to detention, man." Are the voices for practice, for show, to be heard by others? Or is the message for real?

A girl comes into the room and suddenly everyone is quiet. She is strikingly beautiful. The obese girls look up and quickly away, somehow not wanting to see this lovely girl. Another boy comes in, slamming the door behind him. He throws his books down on the desk. "I'm bored. And this room stinks. Hey, you stink. Did you fart?"

The windows are dirty. The pictures on the walls are of former presidents; they have a yellowish, diseased look. The American flag hangs limply in one corner, no wind, no vibrancy. Like the room, it is just there. The teacher's desk is in the front center of the room. Books are lined up along the edge.

The desk is filled with booklets, papers, plan book, late slips, report cards. It is a small desk that seems to sag with all the paper.

Sitting at the desk is the teacher, about sixty-three years old. He sits, feet outstretched, meter stick in his right hand. His eyes seem tired; his body, with slumping shoulders and paunchy stomach, has the appearance of a ticket taker at the merry-go-round ride on a rainy afternoon, a "no business today" sign across him. He appears sad, exhausted, not up to the moment.

In the scene being played he is like the merry-go-round operator, about to start yet knowing that the story to be played out will be a repeat of the class before and the day before and the year before. The faces change but the movement and the music stay the same. And he is part of the scene that remains unchanged. He's part of the furniture, not part of the play.

The bell rings as the teacher being to speak to himself, oblivious to the students in the room. The shapes of the students blur, fade, as he speaks to himself in his fantasy.

"I'm tired. How long has it been? Plattsburgh, B.S., 1955; NYU Masters, 1957; three in-service courses, four professional certificates, five summer workshops, and six more damned meetings than I can remember. I've lost track. Thirty-eight years of doing this. The mornings don't seem so bad but the afternoons become more and more unbearable. The heat from that damned radiator is driving me crazy! I've complained about these rotten radiators for years and nothing is ever done. The heat along with the smell of these kids makes me want to run out and vomit. They don't want to be here; they want to go to McDonald's.

"And I don't want to be here. How can I compete with McDonald's? I find myself disliking so many of them; it scares me to see me as I am. Ten years ago I would never have thought twice about the heat, or even dared let myself dislike one of these kids. But now the feelings and the words come easy. I hate the way I am."

Now, looking up from his desk, out toward the students who seem to be swirling around in space on a merry-go-round, he yells, "Johnson, one more time and you're in for it. I told you to sit down and be quiet. How come you're finished already? No one else is done yet."

He looks for a long time at the students, then lowers his head again and begins to talk, alone in the room. "Christ, I'm not doing the job. The kids know it, the parents know it. They want the administration to get rid of me."

The other teachers say, "We know what you're going through. What can we do?"

"I'm still living on what I was. Almost every day I see kids I used to coach. They're grown up and have families now. They talk to me as if I were still 'coach,' the super jock of this town. I bet they'd be surprised if they knew I don't even follow basketball and baseball any more. I haven't been to one school game this year. What a phony! I'm still living in the past, pretend-ing. All I do is sit in front of the TV with a beer can in my hand.

"And it's strange, strange—nobody knows it and yet everybody knows it. I thought I'd be happier. No traveling with the team two or three nights a week, no more getting home at one or two in the morning after boozing it up with the boys. No more graduate classes—all those goddamn hours. What do I have, M.A. plus sixty? Shit, I should have gotten a doctorate and been an administrator. At least I would have something to show for all these years. Now I'm home every night. What the hell, is this all there is to life?

"I don't feel anything any more. I wish someone would jab me with a pin, somehow be able to touch me. I don't remember when I last felt excited about my job. My work used to be my entire life—coaching, teaching. God, I felt up all the time, trying to be the best, doing everything I could to help kids get scholarships, putting up kids who were running away, coaching the church team on weekends. I was going day and night. I had so much energy. And now. . . ."

Looking up, he speaks softly, as if to no one, "OK, the assignment for tomorrow is to read pages 79 to 83 and do all the questions on page 83. Yes, you will need your books for tomorrow. If you've lost your book, you'll have to go. . . ."

And to himself, "Look at this room. It's a shithouse—paper on the floor, writing on the desks. God, twenty years ago no kid would have dared write on *my* desks. Now I don't give a shit. Christ, listen to my language even. Ten years ago I was somebody, knew all the teachers, and they respected me. Now I'm old. I don't know the young teachers at all.

"When they built that new superhighway through town, it seemed to cut off the junior high from the rest of the schools. We used to have big faculty parties with all the teachers in the district. I was the bartender. Everybody knew everybody else; there was none of this union and management bullshit.

"We were like a big family. When a teacher or a member of his family died, we went to the funeral. We did something if someone got sick. We cared about each other. But now nobody gives a shit. Nobody cares about school spirit. We don't have time for that any more.

"Everybody tells the kids they can do whatever they want. You know, 'experience.' No wonder the SAT scores are off. The kids don't read any more. The teachers are out of the parking lot before the school buses leave. Nobody else gives a shit so why should I? When there was talk of a strike here, the union wouldn't let any of the teachers work overtime to help the kids. I can't understand that.

"Things are so different. I'm all for security and protection but now all you hear is that the administration is out to get us. The administration doesn't seem to understand how tough things are in this school. They're over there in some nice clean air-conditioned building making out their reports and listening to their soft music. Christ, those guys wouldn't last an hour with these kids I've got.

"And then they talk about curriculum objectives. Curriculum, my ass! I'm just interested in getting through the day. And I've got three more years of this before I can retire. These are supposed to be my golden years, you know—fade out in a burst of sunlight. Christ, the way I'm going, they'll have to carry me out.

"Why don't I try something else and get out of here? Screw it, what would I do? Where else would I make what I'm making here? I'm too fucking old! I'm only sixty-three. What the hell is wrong with me to let this place beat me down like this? Sometimes I think I'm really going crazy, like really going nuts. Some days I'm so anxious that I sweat all over before each class begins. My knees get so weak that I have to hang onto the desk to keep from falling down.

"That's why I sit a lot, so I won't fall down. I'm falling, falling, and I don't know if I can hang on. Twenty years ago I never sat at my desk. I was always up, moving around. Where did my strength go? When did the slowing down, the drifting feeling start? If I only knew, maybe I could do something different. Maybe I could take a sabbatical and try to figure this out.

"But with the way the economy is going, maybe something would happen to my job. Besides, how could I get to go on a sabbatical? What can a guy of my age learn? And who would want to hear about my experiences? I'd be out of place anywhere, an old fool, wandering around trying to find himself."

This story raises awareness that aging teachers do sometimes need to be rescued from the fate that befell Harry. They need and deserve a lifeline. Mentoring the Harrys of this world might avoid the sad ending of a once-successful and highly regarded teacher.

It is important to keep this portrait of Harry in mind as we explore the use of mentoring to ensure no teacher is left behind. We are encouraged to intervene and offer at-risk students our assistance, but somehow fail to see our role in helping at-risk teachers as well.

The philosophy of a supportive school culture should be that we can all go down wrong roads and get hit by life; there is no group in the school that is trouble free. As we know with kids, being noticed and affirmed counts for a lot. Teachers can stop the slide of their colleagues by taking the time to listen and reach out. Mentoring is one way.

Harry's story is probably not representative of the majority of aging teachers. But it demonstrates in stark terms what can happen if intervention such as mentoring is not offered when veteran teachers are observed heading toward the margins of school life, a journey that they themselves are perhaps not aware of. In our large secondary schools it is usually fellow teachers who first notice a colleague who is becoming at risk.

Teachers on the front lines work in close contact with at-risk teachers and can sense that things are not as they should be. These teachers are ideally positioned to serve as first responders and offer help. However, sometimes the rapid deterioration of a veteran teacher frightens colleagues. They are often unprepared for what to do, how to intervene, and what their role is in an evolving crisis. They are on their own, asking, "What is my responsibility?"

Those charged with a helping role in the school, such as guidance counselors and school psychologists, usually define their roles as primarily helping and advising students and parents. Their role in outreach to teachers is ill defined and murky. No one says to do it and no one says not to do it. In our large schools these specialists work in offices often far removed from the classrooms. They don't observe or hear the cries for help from teachers like Harry. Then there is the third option for help, the school administration. They are the ones charged with the role of supervising teachers.

However, school administrators like George Forbes are often so overwhelmed with dealing with the daily crises that arise in large secondary schools that they rarely have time to supervise teachers in any great detail. This is a major downside of the job, as many administrators were very gifted teachers before giving up that role. In fact, they were hired as administrators because they had excellent classroom skills and experience and were respected by their colleagues, students, parents, and community members.

But once on the job their role changed to resolving problems with students, parents, and staff before they got out of control. They are left with little time to supervise teachers and act as a source of support for them. For many there is little time to consider a second act or reflect on finding a new career dream. Some die, as the saying goes, in the saddle.

Such was the case with George Forbes. He had the responsibility of supervising over 150 teachers and fifty support staff. He often shared with me his desire to spend quality mentoring time with his teachers, but the reality of life in a large junior high school dictated the opposite.

Indeed, he struggled over how to help Harry Walker as he increasingly received reports of his deterioration. He and Harry had begun teaching in the junior high at about the same time and had been buddies as well as colleagues for over thirty years. They shared family gatherings, vacations, coaching responsibilities, and leadership in the unionization of the district teachers.

But George found himself unable to fix what was wrong with Harry and was hoping he would just leave quietly. He knew Harry was troubled and didn't want to expose him to a battle between the union and the district. As he told me, "That's the least I can do for him." As a former school psychologist he knew Harry's mental condition was not good and he feared Harry would lose what control he had if he were to be forced out of his job.

Many administrators care deeply for their teachers but are left with very little time to really supervise them, especially the veteran teachers. To commit to more intense supervision requires a major, often personal, commitment that most administrators can't sustain. There must be some element of identifying with the failing teacher that makes them put aside pressing issues and act to intervene to help a teacher failing and being left behind.

George Forbes understood that reality and acted unselfishly to utilize my experience and skills to help teachers. It's not easy for an administrator to have such an ego. It's a job in which one is usually on the defensive.

Giving up a part of one's role and duties doesn't come easily. As a result, what we have in most schools is an organization that is not ready and set to respond to teachers heading toward the margins, whether they be veterans or novices.

The three major sources of intervention—colleagues, guidance counselors or psychologists, and administrators—all have other roles. Colleagues are not trained to help; guidance counselors and psychologists have no defined role; administrators are too overwhelmed. In our current school organization, their roles have been reduced to those of observers. They are not responsible for the problem or to be blamed for it.

What is clear is the urgent need to develop new mechanisms in the school organization—such as mentoring—that can provide the kind of support highly functioning teachers need to continue on a successful path. There is no mystery here in terms of what is needed. Many of our schools are stuck in a no-win situation, always playing a game of catch-up when it comes to giving novice and veteran teachers what they need to be more effective. Let us not be fooled by the illusion that this is an easy path. But it is a path of necessity. Here are some details of the path I recommend.

WHAT DOES THE NEED FOR A SECOND ACT FOR VETERAN TEACHERS IMPLY?

The phrase "second act" often refers to well-known politicians, sports stars, professional or college coaches, actors, musicians, authors, and so on. But it can refer to veteran teachers as well, people who early on in their careers became successful but ran into periods in which they seemed to lose their gift and skill to compete. The original dream that sparked their ascent changed, and they entered a period where they floundered, searching to create a new dream for their career.

For some the search for a new dream paid off. They found the path, a second act, to reinvent themselves and once again become contributors. Not everyone gets the opportunity to have a second act. Sometimes we remain stuck in self-defeating behaviors, with skills that are no longer relevant, and lack the necessary support and a vehicle to bounce back and be in the game again. We keep waiting for the lifeline to arrive but, as in Harry's case, it either never arrives or if it arrives we can't quite hold onto it. It slips away.

Some are lucky; they learn from the past. As one football coach told me, "They fired me when the losses began to mount. There was a long period when I couldn't even get an interview for a coaching job. But thanks to the support of my wife, friends, and former players, I persisted and finally found my niche coaching at a good program. Thank God I got a second chance. Being fired helped me to take a good look at myself, my skills, and my attitude. I think I was too cocky and arrogant at my old job, clearly not skilled in how to engage and get the best out of my players and assistant coaches. The journey to this new job was difficult, but I am glad now that I went through it. I am a better person and coach now because of it."

As I know from my own personal experience (as documented in Chapter 4 in my book *Students in Trouble: Schools Can Help Before Failure*[3]), retraining, mentoring, and counseling veteran teachers and creating a second act is no easy task. The hard reality is that there are often days, years, even decades when one is not able to move on from a stalled career. Even though colleagues may not notice our plight at first, we know things have changed and the change is often not for the good.

Second acts are about a search for new behaviors, skills, and opportunities for continuous growth, both professional and personal. It's a process that, when successful, involves coming to believe that we have found a new calling that represents who we are, that the new career offers a clear opportunity to make a positive difference in the lives of others, that we have become a role model for others who will learn from our work and contributions, that we will be missed when it comes time to leave this work setting, that the legacy we leave behind suggests that we leave it a better place than when we first entered it.

As we walk out the door and drive away to maybe a third act, a new journey, we will feel fulfilled, along with our colleagues, and proud of our career and craft, even with the mistakes and missteps along the way. It's a very different exit from that of the Harrys of the world, who drive away alone and questioning, as in my play: "Who would want to hear about my experiences? I'd be out of place anywhere. An old fool wandering around trying to find himself."

Some experts on the midlife and aging process also use the phrase "second journey" to describe this experience. For example, Margaret Newhouse suggests that a second journey is an opportunity to give birth to an ethic of service and mentoring in midlife. She reports that among the things that make the second journey something to anticipate rather than dread are the developmental "tasks" or "urges" that we now understand come with the territory. Most salient among these catalysts to continued growth are finding purpose and leaving a legacy. Newhouse argues that our most authentic and powerful legacies come from living "on purpose," that is, giving our unique gifts, guided by our core essence. These gifts of ourselves, both tangible and intangible, the imprint of our lives that reflect our purpose, are necessarily legacies of the heart.[2]

Newhouse offers some clear markers in our efforts to offer veteran teachers a second act, such as the need for mentoring, continuous growth, finding and living on purpose, leaving a legacy, and being guided by our core essence—a core essence that I define as searching and finding the teaching self we are proud of, at peace with, and able to share with others.

A MENTORING PROGRAM PROVIDES VETERAN TEACHERS WITH THE OPPORTUNITY FOR A SECOND ACT AND THE POSSIBILITY OF MENTORING NOVICE TEACHERS

I believe mentoring is an effective way to illuminate the path to a second act for veteran teachers. The following is an example of the kinds of components that I recommend to be part of mentor–mentee conversations, reflections, and journal writing, a process that can include both individual and group mentor-–mentee sessions.

Sometimes utilizing a group process can offer mentees support from colleagues and remind them they are members of a caring community, that they have a role in not letting one teacher fall through the cracks. These components are divided into two categories: career and personal.

- Career development components

  - Reflecting on past, current, and future dreams and hopes
  - Identifying career and personal goals for the next year, five years, ten years, and twenty years
  - Developing a legacy based on contributions to students, parents, colleagues, supervisors, and the community
  - Addressing relationships with students and parents
  - Addressing relationships with colleagues and supervisors
  - Identifying successful classroom skills and those skills that need improvement
  - Developing a plan for professional renewal and concrete efforts to stay current and retain a commitment to teaching well

- Personal development components

- Developing skills to affirm oneself and be affirmed by others
- Addressing health, wellness, aging, and family issues
- Developing a plan for personal renewal
- Assessing the pros and cons of retirement—when to stay and when to go

These components can serve as a basis for creating a veteran teacher mentoring inventory, which can be utilized as an icebreaker in individual and group conversation. It's a tool that can help veteran teaches gather data and awareness about their personal and professional lives, data that can help them create new dreams, goals, and career alternatives, such as mentoring a novice.

Here is a sample list of questions for a veteran teacher mentoring inventory that veteran teachers can respond to in writing and in conversations with a mentor:

- When did you first become aware of your interest in teaching?
- Please describe your dream of what it would be like to become a teacher.
- What was your experience as a novice teacher like?
- In becoming a veteran teacher, how has your original dream of becoming a teacher changed for the better or the worse?
- Please describe the positive parts of your current teaching life and the skills that seem to work well for you.
- What is your plan to maintain these skills at a high level?
- Please describe the negative parts and the skills you would need to acquire to turn these negatives into positives.
- What resources in the school can you turn to for help in acquiring these new skills and that offer support for renewal?
- How would you describe your relationship with students? With parents? With colleagues? With the administration?
- Have you found your niche as a teacher or do you long for something different?
- In looking at the future, do you find yourself trying to form a new dream for your career, a dream that would present you with new alternatives to your present teaching career, such as becoming a mentor for novice teachers?
- What are your career goals for the next five years?
- What are your career goals for the next ten years?
- What are your career goals for the next fifteen years?
- How do you see your career unfolding over the next fifteen to twenty years?

- Please identify those colleagues and members of the school community who are available to offer you support, affirmation, and help in solving problems that may arise.
- As a veteran teacher do you find yourself more and more focused on aging, health and wellness, and personal issues such as family life?
- Do you find yourself thinking more and more about retirement issues, such as when to leave?
- Whom can you turn to in the school, community, and family life to help you with this important decision?
- Which aspects of your current teaching role do you find discouraging and to be factors in considering retirement, even early retirement?
- How would you describe your legacy as a teacher? For example, what have been your contributions to students, parents, colleagues, and the community?

These open-ended, inviting questions can serve to help veteran teachers to become aware of the professional and personal issues affecting their careers. Some of the issues may be positive and deserve embracing, while others are problematical and act as barriers to success. These kinds of intimate inquiries also help mentors and mentees form a trusting bond by encouraging the mentee to respond honestly and the mentor to also share his or her own professional and personal experiences.

As Sarason suggests in Chapter 7, it is nonsense to think and act as if helpers and those they help, teachers and pupils, are different kinds of people or that one can change or help the other without experiencing change in him or herself. These kinds of queries also move the focus from being solely on classroom skills, which are included, to other pressing issues of veteran teachers, such as the need for novelty and change in their careers; health, wellness, and personal problems that may be having a negative impact on their teaching role; and retirement.

The veteran teacher mentoring inventory also offers a new narrative for the way in which we describe veteran teachers. The personal stories that emerge from intimate conversations with aging mentees can offer an open window to their lives and help us to better understand the world they inhabit. That knowledge can help school leaders and reformers to resist designing one-size-fits-all staff development programs.

We need a process such as the veteran teacher mentoring inventory to help vets reconnect to the excitement of their early careers, to remember when they were most alive and engaged as teachers, and to reflect on what is needed—what they need to do—to rekindle that excitement in their present and future teaching life. Mentoring offers veteran teachers a lifeline that says, "We are in this together."

In closing this chapter let me suggest that the statement "We are in this together" also implies that veteran teachers have a responsibility to come to the aid of novice teachers. They are the only ones who can share with novice teachers what it is like to labor in the tranches and who can teach them about the unglamorous and dark side of teaching that can leave even the most committed teachers spent at the end of the day, wanting to call in sick the next day but somehow dragging themselves out of bed and back to it.

Veteran teachers can also help their novice colleagues understand the very hard choices that teachers face at each developmental stage and career level to either continue the hard work required to be a successful teacher or choose to settle and rely on worn and out-of-date skills.

In a sense, both the younger novice teachers and the elder veteran teachers need each other to be successful. The younger teachers need the guidance, wisdom, and open window into school life provided by the elders, as mature adult role models. And the elders needs the enthusiasm, hope, and freshness of the younger teachers, an experience no retirement can offer.

It's a simple equation, really. Veteran teachers need mentors who can understand, accept and be available to them to help them change their world. Novice teachers need veterans to teach them about the world they have entered and help them navigate through the choppy waters they are bound to face.

NOTES

1. Peter Temes, "The End of School Reform," *Education Week,* www.edweek.org/ew/ewstory.cfm?Slug=29temes.h20 (4 April 2001).

2. Jennifer Dunning, "Twyla Tharp Finds Virtue as a Cause for Dancing," *New York Times*, 12 January 1995, C1, C13.

3. William Fibkins, *Students in Trouble: Schools Can Help Before Failure*, Lanhan, MD: Scarecrow Education, 2005.

Chapter Nine

Serving as a Mentor without a Formal Mentoring Program

While school leaders and education reformers can strongly advocate for a formal mentoring program, we must also face the reality that some school districts lack the funds, leadership, and political will to implement such a program.

However, that doesn't mean efforts to mentor novice and veteran teachers should not be encouraged. There are teacher leaders and administrators in our schools who can quietly offer teachers headed toward the margins words of encouragement, support, and advice and share the wisdom gained from their experience. They can be a source of support in a school climate that may seem unwelcoming and uncaring, especially for novice teachers, a beacon of hope they can turn to to receive the guidance that will help them make a positive difference in their classrooms. These teachers and administrators can identify themselves as someone who is available to offer support, creating a second act in the process.

This kind of second act emerges from the decision by some teachers and administrators that, in spite of the burdens they may face in their daily work, they will not look the other way when they see a teacher in trouble. They can choose to act rather than hide. They can carve out a few moments from a busy schedule to engage a troubled teacher on a personal level and offer a lifeline.

Yes, maybe they are reluctant to take on this role alone, not sure of the words to use in trying to help and fearful of the rejection that may come their way. Offers of help are not always well received. They need both a strong will to help and the belief that what they have to offer is worthwhile. Persistence can pay off in the mentoring and helping process. Teachers and administrators using mentoring to save one teacher at a time is doable and can provide positive alternatives from the negative aspects of the job. It's a second act focused on doing a good deed.

This chapter presents a vignette about how a mentoring relationship developed between a principal and a novice teacher in a large secondary school in an impoverished urban community. This vignette represents a composite of observations of novice teachers filled with dreams of helping children, and caring administrators who make the choice to involve them in a mentoring relationship to help ward off the troubles and pitfalls they face with students, parents, colleagues, and their own rapidly shrinking self esteem.

This vignette brings the process of informal, one-on-one mentoring to life and suggests one administrator's caring can make a great difference and save a professional career.

School principal Dr. Ralph De Feo and novice special education teacher Gary Smith had both dreamed of becoming educators in an urban secondary school, and both had a calling for their work. De Feo was a highly regarded junior high principal who had been an excellent classroom teacher. Smith was a highly motivated but inexperienced teacher. Smith needed De Feo's advice and guidance to survive. De Feo needed the kind of informal mentoring engagement that Smith required in order to "get out of the office and do what I am supposed to be doing—helping teachers." They needed each other.

Working in a large urban junior high school can be traumatic for a beginning teacher as well as wearing for a principal. Much of their work involves relationships with students whose families are impoverished, out of work, with problems that have been a part of the family landscape for years. These students don't recall having carefree days or expectations that things will improve. Their parents are not the kind who show up at parent–teacher nights or parenting workshops. They, like their children, live at the margins of school and community life, knowing they don't fit in and never will.

These students and their families are used to the bottom falling out and things going wrong. Violence is no stranger in their lives. Many of these children come to school each day to find safety, relief from their dreary world, a little fun, and just maybe a mentor who can help them find a way out.

In De Feo's school there were also children who came from middle-class families, many being affected by a failing economy, with parents suddenly finding themselves out of work or forced to take a lower-paying job, behind in their mortgage payments, and fearful about their future. The children also came to school burdened by the uncertainty in their lives. Like their peers who lived in poverty, their school represented the one place where things had some degree of order, routine, predictability, and hope.

Maybe there were problems in the school with troubled kids and some teachers who didn't seem to care, but De Feo worked hard to make sure that no child fell or was left behind. As he told his staff at faculty meetings, "Attention must be paid to every child, not just the high achievers."

Gary Smith had a dream and a calling to be a mentor for these students. He had experienced many of the troubles facing his students and understood the risky territory of a fragmented family life—what it was like to be a frightened child—the lack of safety in the home, the abuse of a parent, no answer to one's cries for help.

But Smith also understood the need to fight back against abusers and develop a determination and the mental set to survive, to save oneself, and to be hopeful that things could change. He was successful in finding a way out of his own troubled home thanks to educators who helped guide him and his own desire to become a teacher, to do for other children what his teachers had done for him.

However, being young and perhaps a little naive about the school world he was entering, Smith thought he could succeed as a teacher on his own merits. After all, he was tough, a survivor, and had the will to win. But one can go only so far having a dream and being a hard worker. He didn't understand the danger he was in and how easy it was for a novice teacher to lose his way, quickly. He needed a Ralph De Feo more than he realized.

Mr. Smith was by all accounts the most popular special education teacher at O'Neil Junior High School in Deep River, Massachusetts. Many of the special needs students and their parents at O'Neil wanted Mr. Smith for a teacher. Smith taught a seventh grade self-contained class, which meant he taught every subject area except gym to twelve to fifteen students who had been identified as having learning, emotional, and sometimes physical problems that affected their ability to learn. Smith was with his students all day except for gym and made himself available after school for support.

Smith had special gifts as a teacher of the learning disabled. He had a reputation for helping students with a history of academic and social failures turn the corner and become successful achievers, with many going on to college. He had a 99 percent yearly passing average in getting his students to pass the Massachusetts Comprehensive Assessment Test (MCAT), one of the highest among special education teachers in Massachusetts.

Many students entered his class in September hampered by a variety of learning disabilities that served as barriers to learning and left in June filled with hope and a new confidence that they could succeed. But there was no mystery to Smith's success.

First of all, he worked very hard. He usually arrived at school by 6:00 a.m. with his bagel, coffee, and bag lunch. And he was often the last teacher to leave the building, long after the extracurricular activities and events had ended. Smith was no eight-to-three, out-the-door-as-soon-as-the-last-bus-leaves kind of teacher. He made himself available after school to offer tutoring and support to his class and also served as a mentor to students in the regular academic program who were having academic or personal problems. Students and parents knew that he was available and his door wass always open.

Walking the halls of O'Neil, one could hear students giving advice to their peers: "You should go see Mr. Smith. He'll listen and give you good advice on what to do." No, he was not a professionally trained or certified counselor, but he had a knack for helping kids who were heading toward the margins of school life. Yet he seemed very humble, "comfortable in his own skin," as the saying goes.

He was not looking to be a star teacher like some of his colleagues, who were into promoting themselves by lecturing at conferences and extolling how wonderful they were as teachers. Smith appeared not to need applause. His needs appeared to be simple: to demonstrate in every possible way that his students could count on him to help them navigate through their academic and personal problems, and to listen to their hopes and concerns and use the information they shared to better understand his students and the family dynamics going on outside the school setting.

Smith had an extraordinary ability to store data about his students, data that he readily used to create a more personal relationship with his students and their parents. Smith was also available as a source of support for other teachers who were having teaching-related and sometimes personal problems. His door was always open and his colleagues, like his students, knew they could trust him with their struggles and get the help they needed to turn things around.

Needless to say, he knew every student in his class, and his knowing process was detailed and ongoing. I am not simply talking about remembering data like first names and IQ scores. Mr. Smith, as many of his fellow teachers say, *really knew* his students. He worked hard to get to know every aspect of their lives: home life, parents, siblings, home problems such as divorce and abuse if they existed, abilities and strengths, hopes, dreams, fears, past failures, relationships with peers and teachers, health issues that could be getting in the way of school success, what made them laugh and light up or what prevented them from laughing. He seemed color blind, lacking in prejudices, and evenhanded in respecting and valuing each student. He didn't cultivate favorites or need to be worshipped by students and parents seeking his favor.

This is no easy task for a teacher, even one as gifted as Mr. Smith. And he did his work without too much probing and without being too intimate. His listening, observation, and caring skills did the job. He noticed when students came to class with a bruise, a look of worry, or appearing anxious or out of sorts. He used simple words to help them talk and tell their stories: "How are you today? You've been absent for three days. That bruise on your face looks serious. Let's meet at lunch and talk about what's going on." He used simple words and questions that teenagers understand and can feel safe in answering. In Mr. Smith they had someone to whom they could tell their personal stories and really be heard.

Yet Mr. Smith understood he was not his students' parent or friend. He was their teacher. His job was to ready his charges for the academic demands and tests they were facing until graduation, making sure they had the skills to navigate through this increasingly pressurized school world and pass the MCAT. But he also realized he could use his teaching skills to help his students with their personal problems so they could become successful achievers.

He understood that his teaching role needed to include being an advocate and source of hope when dark times visited his students. Smith knew that every one of his students had experienced or would experience bad times. He was committed to being there for them but also realized that he couldn't make everything right or eliminate the emotional pains that come with life's problems.

He walked a fine line, caring for his students but at the same time understanding that they had families, sometimes imperfect and troubled ones, to go home to after school. He understood that he could not take on the role of a surrogate parent. He did what he could, and he did a lot. His goals were to have his students leave class each afternoon better prepared to handle the academic and personal problems they faced.

In a real sense Mr. Smith was different from many other teachers at O'Neil. This is not a put-down of other excellent teachers, but rather a realization that Smith seemed to have a special gift for keeping his students out of harm's way. His extraordinary ability to listen, tease out what was bothering his students, and help them resolve problems seemed unique and special. Early on in his career he appeared to possess an unusual gift for helping kids. It's as if he had years of training as both a master teacher and psychologist.

While there was something unique and special about Mr. Smith, his mission and desire to help each of his students didn't just happen. You see, Mr. Gary Smith—or Smitty as he was called growing up in Pittsfield, a small city in western Massachusetts—had a tough, abusive life as a child. His father, George, a logger for a local lumber company, came home drunk almost every night and took his alcohol-inflamed anger out on his wife Mary and on Smitty and his younger brothers, Mark and Jim. George created chaos and confusion almost every night, yelling about dinner not being ready, criticizing Mary's cooking, complaining about money and unpaid bills, and constantly bullying his three sons, telling them what losers they were. Smitty and his family never heard a word of love, praise, respect, or caring from George.

In spite of the daily terror, Mary was so intimidated by George that she could not allow herself to think about taking her boys and leaving. In her mind divorce was not an option. A deeply religious person, she attended church every day to ask God's help in saving her children and finding a way out of their misery.

But her main reason for not leaving was her fear that George might kill or harm her and the kids, a threat he made often enough to paralyze Mary with dread. Taking the children and leaving could push George over the edge. So Mary, Smitty, Mark, and Jim tried to survive and hold on to the fleeting hope that maybe one day things would change. They kept looking for a crack in the door that would set them free from their lives of terror.

It was during these rough times that Smitty made up his mind to not allow this kind of abusive behavior to happen to other kids. He would study hard, play football, basketball, and baseball, win a scholarship to college, and become a special education teacher. This was a career in which he would be able to help kids with disabilities that needed fixing.

In his junior and senior years he served as a mentor for peers in the special education program at school and was told by the teachers that he had a gift for helping kids with special needs. He vowed he would also help his mother and brother get free. He knew his father was headed for trouble with his increased drinking and poor health. Nothing could stop his self-destruction.

Smitty was determined not to allow his dreams be destroyed by George. If he became a teacher he could help other kids who might be going through the same turmoil he was experiencing. He understood that there were many kids with abusive parents like George. He focused his mind and his will on a way out of his awful life and on his determination to resist George's baiting. George's ongoing put-downs of him for his good grades, "sissy" friends and "pansy" decision to go into teaching—"a field for women"—were relentless. George knew no limits in verbally assaulting Smitty, even suggesting that his decision to become a teacher was because he was gay.

Gary fantasized about striking back, beating his father with his fists while he lay in a drunken stupor, or even worse, plunging a knife into George's heart. It's easy to become violent and abusive yourself when you're constantly under attack. But he didn't. He studied hard, played sports, and got a part time job in the evening mentoring kids at the local afterschool program. That kept him busy and out of the house, and he waited patiently for his time to come.

His determination paid off. He graduated third in his class and was accepted on full scholarship to the University of Massachusetts at Amherst. There he soon found great joy in learning to become a middle school special education teacher. He was, as one professor said, a natural.

As he neared graduation Smitty felt a renewed confidence. He was free at last from his abusive home and on the road to becoming a teacher and helping kids to survive their own hard times. He hoped that his mom and two brothers would see that they too could find new lives and leave George to his own demons.

His confidence in his teaching ability was about to be tested, however, when he began teaching in a real school setting. It was an experience that nearly forced him to abandon his career and feel that maybe he was not up to the demands of the job. Mr. Smith was scheduled to graduate early in January 2009, and his final requirement was to spend his last semester as a student teacher.

He was assigned to teach a self-contained seventh-grade special education class at O'Neil Middle School in Deep River beginning in September 2008. Deep River was a decaying factory city in Massachusetts with a high unemployment rate. Many of the students at O'Neil were poor and in need of counseling and health services that had been eliminated in school budget cutbacks. Yet it was a place where Smitty, now Mr. Smith, felt he could put his helping skills to good use.

More importantly, and as yet unknown to Mr. Smith as he started this first stage of his teaching career, his experience at O'Neill would help him to become aware that he possessed a natural gift to relieve the pain and suffering of his students, a gift to champion students who were at the margins of school life and in danger of failure and falling prey to personal problems not of their doing.

Mr. Smith was to discover at O'Neil that he could count on his special gift as needed and it would not fail him. At O'Neil he would develop into a master teacher, like a natural athlete who needed no coaching to be a star player, a natural who seemed to stand out among his colleagues, even the veterans with many years of experience.

At O'Neil he learned many subtle and valuable lessons about the teaching process, lessons that one doesn't learn in college but only, as the saying goes, in the line of fire in a real classroom where there is no protection from the fury of acting-out adolescents.

A professor at the university had warned him that veteran teachers don't like newcomers who tend to want to help their students. She said, "Many veteran teachers like student teachers who talk and act tough, newcomers who, like themselves, are not afraid to dole out harsh discipline. They don't want student teachers coming in who are quasi-psychologists who coddle kids and try to change the school. Be careful not to appear too close to and supportive of your students, as these veteran teachers have the power to ruin your student teaching experience."

Smith was no fool. He had had enough bad experience observing tough-talking people like his father, George, who live a life of threatening others. He understood he had to lie low and not become a target of the veteran teachers' hostility. That meant avoiding the faculty room and the Friday afternoon staff cocktail party. His goal was to keep his distance and avoid the limelight, the same behaviors he had used to distance himself from George. He would use his gift quietly but he would not back down when it came to helping kids. He knew early on that was the primary reason he was a teacher. He had a job to do at O'Neil and he would do it well.

Mr. Smith's first few weeks at O'Neil were very difficult. He soon learned how naive and inexperienced he was. He quickly learned that simply wanting to make contact with students and have them trust you didn't work. As a new teacher, he had to win them over.

However, his class was not into being won over easily. Frank Murray, the classroom teacher who was supposedly there to supervise his student teaching experience, warned him the first day that the class was a bad mix, with one group who were troublemakers and another group who had major personal problems and withdrew from any social contact with each other. Murray said there were a few good kids but not enough to change the negative dynamic of the class. Murray said he was a former teacher in the school and was only substituting for a teacher who had quit over the summer. He was leaving in January and heading to Florida.

Smith's first two weeks with his new class were a nightmare. Some of the students shouted out, had no respect for each other, and left their seats without permission. His only break was when the class went to gym.

Meanwhile, Murray seemed indifferent and unwilling to help him. All Murray did was sit at his desk and issue hollow warnings abut keeping the students after school, which he never followed up on. He left the teaching role to Smith and took long breaks, saying, "I'll be right back," and then disappearing for hours. Murray had replaced a Mrs. Fogarty, who had taken over in April for another teacher who quit.

Smith was beginning to see why these teachers had quit and was concerned and beginning to panic. He worried that he too could end up being replaced and ruining his career before it even started.

Smith spent each night tossing and turning in bed, wondering if he had made a poor career choice. Thinking about becoming a teacher and helping kids was proving to be a lot easier than actually being in a classroom. All his efforts to create some quiet and cohesiveness in the classroom seemed to fail.

To make matters worse, teachers in classes next to his room kept interrupting with "please keep the noise down and get your kids under control." The student teaching supervisor from the university, Dr. Moreno, wasn't much help either. He often canceled or showed up late for classroom observations.

Finally, in desperation, Smith made an appointment with the school principal, Dr. De Feo. De Feo suggested that they meet on Saturday morning so he would have time to listen to Smith's concerns. However, as they began their meeting, De Feo was clear that he couldn't be of much help to Smith.

"I am afraid I won't be able to be much of a mentor to you. Our budget was voted down last May and the budget cuts have been devastating for the school. The board cut my assistant principal and two counselor and psychologist positions so I am overwhelmed, to say the least. All I can offer you is this advice. You inherited a tough group. They are kids with special needs and have many failures in school. They got rid of Fogarty and her predecessor. They both tried to be nice and supportive but they didn't have the right stuff to make it in this school. You're lucky in the sense that three of the biggest troublemakers have dropped out. Most of the kids who are left can be won over.

"As for Frank Murray, he is there because we need a warm body in the classroom. He is a retired O'Neil teacher who is relocating to Florida in January and has no prior experience teaching special ed kids. Keep in mind that he is also a close friend of the school board president. He does as little as possible and knows I can't do anything about his lack of effort. You are on your own so don't look for any help from Murray or the other teachers.

"This is going to be a real test for you but hang in there. It's going to be a rough ride. You can call on me if you need to, but the kids have to see you as the man in charge. If I come in and discipline them, it won't work in the long run. They'll just start all over again as soon as I leave. That's how it works in junior high, especially with this group.

"Also, keep in mind that these are not wealthy kids from the plush suburbs like Newton or Wellesley. Many of their parents lack high school education and are working in poorly paying jobs or are unemployed. Needless to say, the majority of our kids have no health insurance. To make matters worse, many live in run-down neighborhoods with high crime rates and are at risk of abuse and bodily harm on a daily basis. Last year three kids were murdered and ex-convicts out on parole raped two of our seventh-grade girls.

"We've had a terrible record for special education kids passing the test, mainly because of the constant turnover of staff who move on to higher-paying or less problematic school districts once they get experience here. Over 90 percent of the special education kids never make it to high school.

"O'Neil, as you will find out, is considered the bottom of the barrel by other school districts and the state teacher education programs. I am trying to change that perception and need all the help I can get.

"The Deep River city motto is, 'We'll Try.' That's fine, but I want more for our school than simply trying. The image I'm trying to create here is that we can succeed as a school community—students, parents, and staff. The past is done. The opportunity for change is now, not tomorrow, not next year. That's what President Obama said in the election campaign, so I think we are in good company.

"You probably wonder if there is any good news. Yes, there is. The good news is that O'Neil and the education we provide represents the only chance for these kids to find a way out of their desperate lives. Our teachers are probably the only positive role models in their lives. I am telling you all this because in order to survive, and to do well here, your first priority is to establish control over the class and win their trust. I can't do that for you. You have to find a way to create those conditions yourself.

"One way to get your students to listen to you is to talk sports with them. I am not sure you know that Deep River has a large Portuguese population and there is great interest in soccer here, as well as Red Sox baseball, Celtics basketball (the NBA champions last year), Bruins hockey, and the New England Patriots football team—a Super Bowl winner. The kids love Tom Brady, the Patriots' quarterback, who is unfortunately hurt this season, and the Red Sox' David Ortiz and Manny Ramirez. Manny has been traded to the Dodgers and the kids are still upset about that.

"So use their interest in sports to your advantage. And stop wasting your time looking to Murray, Moreno, or the other teachers to help. It's sink or swim here, and sad to say, no one is going to throw you a life preserver, not even me. I'm up to my ears in problems and I don't have the time to be your mentor or babysitter.

"I know this is a tall order for a young guy straight out of the university. You seem like a likeable guy who is easy to relate to. Those are great qualities but not enough to cut it here. You also have to develop a *get tough* face and demeanor and do it fast. I am betting on you.

"My guess is that you'll learn. If you keep these kids in line, I'll write a glowing recommendation for you. Also, I see from your university record that you're graduating in January. That's when Murray plans to leave for Florida. Maybe if things work out we could hire you as the full-time teacher for the class. Then we would be rid of Murray and at least have someone in the class who cares about the kids. We'll talk more about this after we see how you do.

"However, there is one thing I can do for you right now. Let's walk down to Ed Daley's office and I'll go over the records of the thirteen kids you have in class. I probably should have done this earlier but it's been crazy here the first few weeks with school opening. Ed is the school psychologist and an ace at what he does. He has all the students' Individual Education Programs— that's the IEPs—on file.

"Ed's not in today but I am sure he will follow up with you. Don't hesitate to call on him. But the reality here is that Ed, like me, is over-whelmed with demands from students, parents, and staff since we had to let the other psychologist go because of budget cuts. Hopefully our discussion will help give you a leg up on what to expect concerning your student's backgrounds and problems and lends some reality about what you're up against.

"Let's start with Reggie Miller. Reggie, as you can see, has some serious speech problems as well as emotional disabilities. His family, what there is of it, moved here from Springfield a few years back, and he's struggled ever since he arrived. Part of his problem is that his father committed suicide last year and his mom has never recovered. Reggie has three younger sisters in elementary school and they, like him, have serious learning and emotional problems. The family is on public assistance and he gets free lunch at school, but my sense is that there is little to eat at home.

"The social worker assigned to his case told me his mom has developed a serious alcohol problem and Reggie is left to take care of his sisters, make dinner, do laundry, and take over as a parent. The kid's a good kid but he is, as you can see, very overweight, tired and worn out, I guess, from all his parenting chores and worrying about what might come next.

"The one good thing is that he is interested in sports, particularly the Red Sox and baseball, but has never been to a game. Nor does he have cable TV, so he never gets the chance to see a game unless he goes to the neighborhood rec center. He talks about going out for the baseball team at Durfee but it seems more a dream than a reality. He's way out of shape, probably weighs 250, no doubt due to his diet.

"I talked to Nancy Duran, the school nurse, and Rod Jackson, the physical education teacher, to try to give Reggie some help but they say he never showed up for their meetings. Maybe you can find a way to get him motivated to seek help. He's a good kid lost in a nightmare world and, like many of our students, needing a parent but having to be a parent himself.

"One final note on Reggie: he is African American, and although we have had a steady increase in black students they are still very much a minority here. So breaking into the peer culture of the Portuguese and white students isn't easy. It's not necessarily a racial thing but the reality is that most of the students are white and many have been together since elementary school. Their circles of friends have been formed. It's just another barrier that Reggie and many of your special needs students have to overcome together since many are minority students.

"And there is the new girl, Caitlin Dwyer. Caitlin at first seemed an odd fit for our school population. According to Ed Daley, Caitlin and her family moved here this past summer from Newton, which as you know is an upscale suburb of Boston. Her father is starting up a computer company that is promoting services to the military.

"According to Ed, Caitlin was involved in a terrible car accident with her mother last year, an accident that left her with brain trauma resulting in visual and hearing impairment. You'll notice she sometimes appears as if she is not focused and is in another world. She is still undergoing tests and Ed is monitoring her condition very closely. She is well-dressed and well-mannered so she stands out among your other students.

"You are probably wondering why she is here in a school of many troubled kids and not in a private school, which her father could afford. Her father told Ed that he wants her in a school where she can get the best special education services and that is one thing we do very well at O'Neil, even with our budget and staff being stretched to the breaking point.

"But there is also a personal dynamic going on. Her father has a live-in companion who has two younger kids in the elementary school. According to Ed, Caitlin is still in mourning for her mom and flatly refuses to talk with her dad's companion, Ella. So this is a kid who is going through all kinds of hell—losing her mother, moving to a new community that is very different, dealing with her dad's girlfriend and her kids, and then being thrown into a class of troubled kids. She probably comes to school each day scared to death. It says here her dad is trying to take the pressure off her by enrolling her in the local YMCA swimming classes. I guess she is a pretty good swimmer.

"So you've got your work cut out with her as well. I think you're beginning to get a sense of the challenge you are going to face.

"Ed Daley contributes a lot by providing counseling for each of your students on an individual basis once a week plus involving them in a group counseling session. He also, as I said, prepares their individual education programs and meets with their parents on a regular basis. But Ed, as he admits, is only skimming the surface. The dire picture is that we have one psychologist for over 1,800 students, of which over 200 are classified as special education students. And that number is growing.

"So, buddy boy, you're being asked not simply to teach but also to be their counselor, parent figure, and model. I am sure you had no idea what would be asked of you when you got the O'Neil placement. But here we are. It will definitely be a learning experience!

"Let's move on. Vicki Salazar is also one of your students. Vicki is something else. She is thirteen years old but acts as if she is twenty. She hangs with an older crowd of high school students, mainly guys. She dresses in a very provocative way and when she walks into a room the guys go wild and the female students get angry. Vicki was crowned queen of the Portuguese festival in July so she has become a major somebody in the school and community.

"But that's not the whole story. She has severe learning problems, and in spite of her physical attractiveness she has a very low self-concept. She tries to get attention with her good looks and cover up the reality that reading, math, you name it, are very difficult for her. She probably has one of the lowest IQs in the class.

"The good part of her story is that her home life appears to be much better than many of your other kids. She is the youngest of seven children, the baby of the family. Her parents are both caring and hard working. They own Café

Marigal, one of the best Portuguese restaurants in Deep River. They always show up at conferences and IEP meetings and do everything they can to help Vicki. But she is very stubborn and, as her father says, boy crazy.

"So do everything you can to help her but be sensitive to the issue that you're in your early twenties and she is a needy teenager. Keep your distance. Working with Vicki can be a valuable learning experience in the sense you'll have to learn how to be helpful but at the same time maintain the teacher–student relationship with a very attractive and needy young girl who is trying to find her place by wooing males.

"One other piece of information in her IEP might help you. The report says she is a very good soccer player and has played in the Portuguese Soccer League, even made the twelve-year-old all-star team last year. Maybe you could get her to go out for the school team.

"Let me see if I know any of the other kids. Oh yes, I see you have Than Kwy, known as Tommy. Tommy's family are immigrants from Viet Nam and own a laundry and a deli that caters to the Asian community. We don't have a large Asian community but it is growing rapidly. Most of the Asian students are in competitive academic programs and are encouraged by their parents to be high achievers in order to get into name colleges like Harvard, Massachusetts Institute of Technology, Radcliffe, and so on.

"But there are Asian kids like Tommy who want out of school and going to college is not in their plans. Tommy is a troublemaker with a capital T. He is a member of a gang and has been in and out of juvenile court. This past summer he and some members of his gang were arrested for firing paint balls into a crowd at the Portuguese festival. Kind of sad because he is very bright but refuses to play the game here at O'Neil. He is classified as having emotional disabilities and we are pretty much reaching the end of the line with him.

"The good news is, he has some good relationships with some of the coaches, such as Randy Sullivan, the basketball coach, and Lou Testa, the athletic department trainer and weight room manager. Tommy played on the seventh-grade basketball team as a sixth grader last year before he was suspended for punching out an opposing player in the school parking lot after a game. He's hot-tempered and ready to fight.

"But Coach Sullivan still keeps in contact with him and hopes he will try out for the team again this year. Lou Testa has him working out in the weight room. Tommy has a nice three-point shot and is a demon on defense, and the basketball coach at Durfee High, Jerry Maloney, has him on his radar screen as a potential playing guard. Durfee, by the way, is a perennial basketball favorite and has been for years.

"On the home front, Tommy's parents have had it with him and don't know where to turn. They are hard-working people and can't fathom Tommy's acting-out behavior. They are considering having him move in with an older brother who lives in Boston. He's a tough kid who might be salvaged by playing sports but again, I believe his days here are numbered.

"Who's next on the list? Sonia Krynski—now here's an interesting kid, and she has a story. First you should know she's adopted—adopted by two nurses who work at Charlton Memorial Hospital here in Deep River. She came to this country when she was three. She started having school problems in fourth grade when the Krynskis divorced. Sonia's mother received custody after a very hostile divorce. Last year the mother and a coworker, a woman, were married in the first civil ceremony in the Deep River area as a result of same-sex marriages being approved in Massachusetts. So the kid has had a hectic life so far, coming from Russia, doing poorly in school, the divorce, and now her mom's new relationship.

"Her IEP lists multiple learning problems and there is a suggestion that perhaps she was sexually abused as a young child in Russia. She is very quiet, timid, and tends to stay removed from her classmates and not socialize or interact.

"The one thing she has going for her, according to her mother, is that she is an excellent swimmer and swims for the local YMCA team. But she keeps that to herself. According to her IEP your intervention priority is to somehow increase the level of her socialization with her peers and try to get her involved in school activities. Maybe the new girl, Caitlin Dwyer, might turn out to be a newfound friend for her. Ed told me she swims at the Y and knows Sonia. Clearly, Vicki and some of the other girls dislike Sonia and Caitlin and make no effort to include them. You have quite a group, Mr. Smith, don't you?

"Hey, here's a kid you'll love. Tony Broccola. He is a real nice kid and often goes out of his way to help other kids who are being bullied—a real peacemaker. But he is also tough, a body builder and a starting tackle on our school team as a seventh grader, very unusual and probably the only seventh grader in the starting line-up. Tony is one of our best leaders in the peer counseling programs and is not afraid to speak his mind. Granted, he has big learning problems but he never lets up.

"He's one of the few students you have who will, I bet, not only make it to Durfee but will also go on to college and play sports. There's a college for him somewhere.

"How did he get to be such a great kid? It's truly a hard-luck story but somehow the family hangs in there. His family is on public assistance and has had their share of problems. His father worked as a fisherman and got injured while fishing off Newfoundland. He got himself tangled in a fishing net and almost lost both hands and leg. He's had over fifty surgeries. The owners of the fishing boat had no insurance so he is dependent on social security disability. He is always going to be very handicapped, wheelchair bound, and living on social security and public assistance.

"His wife Maria is a saint and has done her best to raise three boys. Tony is the last. The older boys, Don and Bobby, played football in high school and are now on the team at the University of Massachusetts at Amherst, where they are on scholarship. So, Smith, Tony is going to be a big asset. He is warm, positive, and courageous. Take him into your confidence and depend on his. He is mature beyond his age and he can be a good leader if you let him run with the ball.

"I don't know much about the next kid on your roster, Gene Wright. He's new to the school, a foster child who is living with the Claires. Mr. and Mrs. Claire have had many foster kids go through O'Neil. They are great people, kind, supportive, and tough when they need to be. I think they have three foster kids now. Two, John Sibona and Ron Luiz, are at Durfee and are good students.

"It says here in the IEP that Gene's father is in prison at Walpole State Penitentiary for armed robbery. It's his third time in the pen and he's there for thirty years. The kid doesn't want to see him. The mother abandoned Gene and his two younger brothers last summer when they were living in Watertown. Seems she just took off one morning and never came back. A neighbor finally called the state department of social services and the kids were placed into different homes here in Deep River.

"Gene is with the Claires while his brothers are with the Reynolds family in the same neighborhood. The brothers are in grades three and four at Fallon Elementary, so they see each other on a weekly schedule, which is a good thing. During the summer Ed Daley, who felt Gene had emotional problems, feelings of loss and abandonment, and very poor reading and math skills, tested him. According to Ed's records, Gene was on the track team at Lewis Middle School in Watertown.

"But again, I don't really know this kid. We'll have to monitor him closely. The good news is that the Claires will be a big help to you and will no doubt be scheduling a meeting with you soon to introduce themselves. Again, they are super responsible and take no crap from the foster kids. They know more about how to deal with problem kids than most of our teachers. Don't tell anyone I said that!

"Let's take a break and get some coffee at the cafeteria. They keep a pot on for me. I'll tell you a little about the next kid, Kashine Movray.

"The kids call him Mr. K. Very popular kid, outgoing, and probably the best basketball player in the school. He's kind of a local legend as he has been playing with older kids, even adults, since elementary school. Part of it is his size. He's six foot four and growing but there's more to the story. His skills are so polished that if the rules permitted, he'd be playing on the Durfee varsity squad right now. K can shoot with both hands, score from both three-point ranges, muscle in shots from the inside, rebound well, pass, and play great defense and is extremely fast for a kid his size. Plus he is unselfish and passes off the ball so his teammates can score. He regularly scores thirty points per game but could easily be hitting forty, even fifty, if he were more selfish.

"He is a nice kid, polite and an all-around good citizen, which is unusual for kids coming out of his neighborhood; they usually drop out and end up in jail. But there is a downside to his story, as with many of the kids you have. His dad died from an overdose three years ago and his mother took off with a neighbor and hasn't been seen since.

"K lives with an aunt, his father's sister, who also has a drinking and drug problem. His learning skills are very poor, among the lowest in the class, but he is eager to learn. Who knows, your presence may help him.

"Murray is afraid of the kid and I can never figure out why. I think Murray is uncomfortable with kids who are African American, Asian, or immigrant in general. He doesn't like Tommy or Reggie either and is always sending them to the office. Murray is an old-school guy who has spent all his life in Deep River, was born here, went through the schools, joined the Army during the Korean War, and got his degree from Fitchburg State College. Then he returned home and started teaching social studies here at O'Neil. He's been here ever since.

"He retired a few years back but has been filling in as a sub since then. The good news is that he's planning to move to Florida in January. Thank God. He's a real downer, a bitter guy who is always complaining in the faculty room about how bad things have gotten in the district since he was a student. He has an open line to the superintendent, who is his golf buddy, and he never misses a chance to slam the staff, the kids, especially the minority kids, and me.

"But being the coward he is, he never says anything directly to me. He hangs out with a group of teachers who are about to retire and who have spent their whole careers here. They tend to see everything as negative and are forever repeating the old story that 'O'Neil isn't the way it used to be when the teachers were in charge.'

"They sour the new teachers coming in. A few years here listening to these veterans talk about how bad things are and many of the newer teachers become just like them and spend their days complaining, blaming the kids, the parents, me, and the world for kids just being kids and trying to navigate through pre-adolescence. I'll be glad to see them go and get some fresh blood in here, like you. But that's a few years away, so we make do for now.

"Anyway, K will surely benefit from your being here and from having a positive influence around instead of Murray.

"Here's the cafeteria. You drink coffee? Let's sit and forget the kids for a few minutes. Are you married? Got a girl? Where are you living?"

Walking back to Ed's office, De Feo got back to his administrator role and reported that the reason he knew so much about special education students was that he had taught special ed at the school for fifteen years before becoming assistant principal. He said that now, with the budget cuts, one of his added duties was supervising the special education program.

De Feo said, "I've always had a special place in my heart for special needs kids. Most of the kids in the regular program can make it on their own with a little help, but the classified kids like you have need lots of help and mentoring or they simply stop coming to school. Sure, we do everything we can to get them to return to school but it's often a losing battle.

"They may not be old enough to drop out but what they do is simply hide. We've tried everything—home visits, legal action, family court, social services, on and on—but they know how to wear us down and at some point we have to give up because the process is costing us valuable counseling and psychological resources we can put to better use helping the kids who stay in school.

"Take this next kid, Jen Pella. Jen has major medical issues as well as learning problems. It's complicated. Her problems with learning seem to have a negative impact on her medical condition and her medical problems affect her learning. It's a catch-22 situation. You see, she has a major eating disorder, anorexia. She's been in and out of the hospital since she came here in sixth grade. Her hospital stays, often six to eight weeks, work for her but when she returns home and to school, she usually relapses.

"According to Ed Daly, her doctor, social worker, parents, and hospital outreach nurse are trying a new approach. She's on a new medication and instead of being hospitalized she is enrolled in a bi-weekly support group at the hospital and also in a weekly group here.

"The major problem for the school is that she has missed so many days, over 100 last year, so it's been hard for us to get a handle on how best to help her and to find ways to include her in the program. Jen's parents are very supportive but our sense is that they are running out of hope that a solution will be found to help her. However, we are hopeful that this new medication and the support groups will offer a breakthrough.

"Murray—sorry for my seeming to beat him up—has been no help and seems baffled by her disease and how he should relate to her. Jen tells Ed she is afraid of Murray, as he always seems to ignore her. But you seem to have a nice welcoming touch that may be just what the kid needs. So far she is a stranger to these other kids so it's important that you find ways to make her feel comfortable and involved with the other kids.

"The next kid on your roster is Rachel Myers. Rachel's problems are interpersonal. Ed feels the lingering illness of her father has caused her to withdraw into herself and avoid contact with her classmates and teachers. I am sure you noticed how she isolates herself already. She sits by herself, often with her head down, and refuses—and I mean refuses with a capital R—to engage in any dialogue. It's as if she is in a trance.

"Ed feels we should be patient with her and not push her. His reasoning is that her father has a severe case of lung cancer and isn't expected to live through the fall. He's been ill for many years and I doubt Rachel ever had a day in her young life that wasn't filled with worry and concern about his dying. Plus the father, Rocco, is very abusive to Rachel and her mother, and the police have been called to the home many times to warn him about physically abusing his family members.

"Rachel sees Ed twice a week for counseling, and according to him, she is very angry with her father and often speaks about wishing he were dead. Yet she is in great conflict about wishing her father dead and seems just worn out mentally and physically with all the pressures at home and within her psyche.

"The good news is that she comes to school each day, which must be a major hurdle for her as she takes a lot of verbal abuse from some of the other kids, mainly Tommy and Vicki, who say she is a weirdo. But clearly she has an inner strength that is keeping her going in spite of all her problems, so you have something to build on.

"As for interests, I don't think Rachel has any except survival and maybe that's all we can ask of her until her father passes away. Maybe by spring he will be gone. God, here I am wishing the guy dead. But I know in my heart that when he dies life can begin to change for the better for her and her family. Schools, especially junior highs, are crazy places and sometimes you are presented with an opportunity to click with a student who in the past wanted no relationship with you as a teacher. Be ready when that opportunity comes!

"The next kid has a sad story. Steve Landis, a very special kid, kind to a fault, always positive, never misses a day of school. Plus he's a very good athlete. He made the junior varsity football team although he is only a seventh grader. He's extremely fast and has great football savvy. He can hold his own with the older players who are in grades nine and ten. We provide a special bus for him, Mr. K, and a few other junior high kids so they can compete at the high school level.

"But Steve has problems, big ones. Steve was an excellent student in regular classes until last January, when the violent death of his brother shattered his life. Steve had an older brother, Rob, who was in grade twelve. He was a great kid, like Steve, and a fine athlete who starred in football, basketball, and baseball. He had excellent grades and SAT scores as well. He was headed for either an Ivy League school or a large university with a big scholarship.

"But last New Year's Eve he was killed in a hit and run accident, changing a tire in a big snowstorm on a dark road. Someone came along and ran him over, killing him instantly. Maybe the driver didn't even know he or she hit something. It was a big storm with a gale wind blowing, making it almost impossible to see. Talk about sadness. The whole school and community were devastated at the death of this great kid.

"And Steve took it the hardest. He idolized Rob and then suddenly he was dead. Rob's wake and burial were attended by literally thousands of people. We closed the schools that day so our kids could attend. We tried to give the kids a lot of support by bringing in counselors from the mental health department. But let me tell you, Rob's death hit our kids, parents, and staff hard and I don't think we are over it yet.

"These days we don't have a lot of good news in our schools that can boost our spirits, and so it helped our staff to know they were part of Rob's success and their efforts contributed to opening doors for him. That all vanished with his death. It was like we have bad karma in the district and deep down inside we're always wondering what can happen next. Sometimes I feel we are digging in barren soil and hoping a flower will grow from our efforts. But when something does grow, something else comes along and takes it away from us.

"I guess I am venting now. Even with your small class, look at how many deaths and bad things have happened to these kids. I try to keep my spirits and hopes up and be a positive role model but believe me, there are days when I want to pack it in, as you probably are feeling yourself right now. But I digress.

"Let's get back to Steve. When he returned to school he was a shell of himself. He seemed to lose all his spontaneity and motivation. In April Ed suggested we move him into special education to take some of the pressure off him. He's classified as having emotional problems. After the move into special education classes he improved tremendously and by June seemed to be back to his positive self, even with all the teacher issues we were having with the class.

"I think that a great deal of his recovery has been due to Ed's counseling with him and making the football team. I think your interest in sports will give him another mentor besides Ed to whom he can talk. My sense is he'll be ready to return to regular academic classes once he gets through the Christmas holidays and dealing with the one-year anniversary of Rob's death. I think, too, that football will be a way for him to get his mind off Rob. I just hope it works that way rather than Steve being focused on how much football meant to Rob and the other teammates not letting him just be Steve and not another Rob.

"Buck McFarland, the JV football coach, is great with kids who have home troubles and he told me he is going to make a special effort to get close to Steve. With all of us working together, I know good things will happen with Steve.

"Hey, we're almost through. I've probably given you too much information but I figured you need to know what's going on with the kids you'll soon be meeting in class every day. I believe being well prepared will make you a more effective teacher. Between you and me, I despise those teachers who say they don't want to know anything about their students' home lives because they are not in the classroom to be counselors, parent surrogates, or hand holders.

"What they are really saying is that they don't want to hear stories about kids that might somehow make them reach out and help kids. Their not knowing or seeming to be not caring is their way to avoid taking responsibility to help kids resolve their personal problems in addition to being subject teachers. They take the easy way out by calling themselves 'academic teachers,' which translates into 'don't count on me to help kids in need.' OK, let's get on with it. Two more kids to go.

"Karen Santucci is next. Karen's got a lot going against her. She is slightly retarded and needs a lot of attention and mentoring. She is a great kid and tries so hard, but the schoolwork is very difficult for her and sometimes she just gives up. That results in her missing school for weeks at a time and that puts her even further behind.

"We work closely with the child protective agency to make sure we do everything in our power to get her back to school and somehow not to become a dropout when she turns sixteen. She is the oldest one in the class at fifteen and she's ready to call it quits on her birthday in May. She has three older sisters, all of whom dropped out before they got to high school.

"Part of the problem is that her parents have no interest in the children receiving an education. They want Karen to be at home where she can run the house while they work. In a sense Karen is like a slave. She's not afraid to tell you that it's her job to do the laundry, make dinner, clean the house, and do the shopping. And what does she get for it? Nothing. No allowance, no recognition.

"The child protective agency has tried to get the parents to just let Karen be a teenager, come to school, have friends, and lead a life with a little fun in it. However, the parents are shrewd and cover up the problem by saying they are trying to get Karen to go to school but Karen refuses, which Karen says isn't true. It's just a lot of lies and promises they never carry out.

"The only way we will ever break this cycle is to help Karen learn that she needs an education and she needs to stand up to her parents and stop being a slave, as were her sisters, who are now married, on welfare, and living in poverty.

"So again, you have an important role with Karen, helping to convince her to keep coming to school, develop some goals and dreams, and improve her self-concept so she feels she has some worth. Most important, she must learn to fight back against her parents, and she needs someone to be there as an advocate, even if you have to make home visits yourself. Ed has tried to counsel her but the parents are against it; they think he is interfering in their family life.

"Karen is very overweight and doesn't have much of a wardrobe, so she comes off as looking very different and becomes a victim of bullying and name calling. But for her, school—your class—is the only place she is going to get support, and we are running out of time. May will be here before we know it and believe me, the parents are counting the days until she can be a full-time slave with no school interference.

"One more. You are probably ready to resign right now, Smitty. But don't let all these problems scare you. That's middle school life here. No, this is not a cushy teaching job like you might find in some upscale community. You know the difference between those schools and ours? Sure, kids in the rich suburban schools have problems, even some big-time problems like our kids.

"But here you can see the problems on the kids' faces. Their pain comes through for us to see. It's a raw pain, on the edge, sending a message that things are not going well. It's often a message asking, 'Please, someone help me.'

"In rich suburban schools kids with pain have to keep it covered, not let it show. They are supposed to send the message, 'I shouldn't have problems. I live in a great neighborhood and a fine house and attend a fine school. I should be thankful for that, shouldn't I? But I'm being smothered with being too good, trying to achieve too much, dealing with all the expectation on me from everyone around me because I have it made, have it all, and no reason I shouldn't succeed. So there's no one for me to talk to about my parents yelling and drinking, school being too hard, not having friends I can talk to, and putting my all into sports I hate. I just want my parents, teachers, and friends to just let me be. But they won't let me and there's no one to help me.' But, while things here may be bad for many kids, we are blessed because our kids are raw and needy and they want help.

"So remember, being here, you have the wonderful opportunity to help kids who need your help. Many of them have no one else in their lives to guide them through their early adolescent stage with all the issues they face. You are the man now and my sense is that you are up to the challenge.

"Enough. The last kid is Cindy Citella. Cindy is another one who has emotional problems, lots of them. She didn't start school until she was nine years old. She lived with her mother, who was divorced from her father, and her mother's boyfriend. They lived way out of the city on a small farm. Ed indicated they pretty much kept to themselves, and the neighbor reported hardly ever seeing Cindy or noticing that she wasn't going to school.

"According to Ed the local postman thought something strange was going on with the girl and alerted Child Protective Services. As it turned out, the boyfriend was physically, emotionally, and sexually abusing both the mother and Cindy and kept them as prisoners, telling them he'd kill both of them if they ever tried to move out or tell the police. The boyfriend was arrested and is now serving twenty years at Walpole State Prison.

"With the help of Child Protective Services, Cindy and her mother got excellent medical and psychiatric attention at the UMass Medical Center in Worcester, plus training for the mother to become a medical assistant. It seems the mother had a college degree in chemistry from UMass at Amherst but fell in with this guy after she divorced Cindy's dad.

"Child Protective Services also found a clean rental right near the school on West Adams Street. So we've been trying to bring Cindy up to speed with both her academics and personal relationships. All those years of being a prisoner have taken their toll, but she has improved tremendously and shows a real zest for learning and leadership. Bright kid. I wouldn't be surprised if she was in regular academic class by the end of the year.

"That's really our goal for every one of your kids, but Ed says we must be careful and not push them too hard and let them go at their own pace.

"As we talk I'm beginning to think that maybe the best help I can give you may be to move Murray completely out of your class and use him as a permanent sub when teachers are absent. I'll talk it over with your UMass supervisor and see if I can get him to OK your operating on your own. He needs to understand that Murray is a big obstacle to your success and has nothing to offer you in terms of assistance. Plus the kids don't like him. Kids are very intuitive. Especially those kids who have been failures. They can smell teachers like Murray who don't like them and look at them as losers.

"Yes, the more I think about it, you and the kids are better off with Murray gone to another class. I'll tell Moreno and Murray that I've made the decision. Consider it a done deal starting next Monday.

"Moreno won't complain because he needs our school to place student teachers, plus he has a lousy track record of showing up. I've mentioned his many absences to him so he knows I won't hesitate to let the dean know. He'll go along with whatever I say. So that's the heads-up on your students.

"One question: have you had any kind of personal struggles that may help you relate to these kids? I ask you this in confidence and we'll keep it between you and me."

Smith shared his own story of growing up in an abusive home and finding his way through sports and achieving in school. De Feo seized on Smith's story and said, "Look, you found your way out and the key for you appears to be that playing sports gave you a special niche and allowed you to become a positive contributor. You were able to fit in and be successful as a student and it opened up the door to college and brought you here today. Your job is to help do the same thing for your students. Help them to learn the skills to open up new doors so they don't give up and drop out. Keep in mind that each of these kids is involved in some aspect of sports or wants to be. Maybe your interest in sports can be a way to help you engage them on a personal level and get them to understand that you are 100 percent committed to helping them.

"And again, while I offer no guarantees, if you get the class to gel, you have a good chance of becoming their regular teacher beginning in January. The deal is selling the class on the idea that you and they are in this together. If they succeed, you succeed. If they fail, you will as well. You might even tell them that you are guaranteed a job if you win them over.

"Believe me, they have a stake in your staying on at O'Neil. They've experienced a long line of poorly trained teachers and if you are half as good as I think you're going to be, they are going to fall in line and show they can learn and behave. They may do it so you'll stay but you'll be helping them in the process. It's amazing what kids will do to show their appreciation for a teacher who believes in them. I have a stake in you as well.

"You do your job and I'll talk up your teaching skills with the superintendent and the board. If you succeed, so do your students and so do I. It's that simple. Good luck, be strong, be creative, and don't expect miracles. This first month or two will be tough, and you are going to be called on to address many issues that you haven't experienced before. Take a lot of vitamins."

After his meeting with De Feo, Smith felt better. He wasn't on his own and felt confident he could turn to De Feo and Daly even though they were very busy. He felt that teaching and working in a real school were not exactly what he expected, but he was not about to give up. Smith understood that his survival depended on finding a way to bring his thirteen students together as a team. Right now they were thirteen individuals doing their own thing, and he needed some kind of intervention to have them understand that they too, like Smith, were not alone. Being part of a team would improve their academic and personal lives.

Smith knew they needed a positive identity as a class that they could be proud of and that would send the message to the whole school that they weren't just a bunch of troubled kids. He didn't blame the kids for not trusting him at first. They had been drifting and aimless for a long time and were not about to put their trust in the new guy without checking him out. Smith understood they were challenging him to deliver some new and exciting approach and not the usual boring classroom activities, which turned them off. They were asking Smith to "show me the money," as the saying goes.

This vignette provides an example of the kind of big-brother, let-me-take-you-under-my-wing, spontaneous mentoring opportunities that can occur with novice teachers. They are precious moments in time that offer many lessons to be learned, quickly—teachable moments, as the saying goes.

Here, De Feo had options. He could let Smith sink or swim on his own or try to respond by offering the gift of himself, his experience, and his knowledge of the situation at hand. It was also an opportunity for De Feo to get to know Smith and assess his promise as a teacher.

In fact, De Feo was impressed by the fact that Smith was wise enough to know he was in trouble and that he asked for help. He sensed danger, possibly failure, and he was right. So it was Smith who seized the moment.

De Feo was also wise in choosing a Saturday morning so he had time to give Smith what he needed—information, encouragement, and support. It was technically his day off but as usual he was at school, trying to keep ahead of the paperwork and answer the endless e-mails and phone calls. Meeting with Smith provided him with a break and a needed human interaction, a chance to do what he did best—help people. And here, he did it well. He, like Smith, seized the moment, and he succeeded in helping Smith.

They both gained from the experience. For example, the meeting provided Smith with valuable information and insights about how to approach his students: their family lives, personal and school problems, interests, achievements, and hopes for the future. This conversation with De Feo helped him to see his students as real people and reflect on how he could engage them as individuals and as a group. For the first time he understood the reality he faced if this class was to become *his* class.

As De Feo suggested, it was going to be a challenge, but at least he was not starting from scratch. While he understood that he had De Feo in his corner, it was now up to him to win the kids over. It was Smith's responsibility, his game to win or lose. In a way it was still a sink-or-swim situation, but the good news is that Smith had been given a lifeline by De Feo, albeit a tentative one, to hang onto.

The lifeline didn't mean he was certain of being saved. Rather, it provided him with a temporary respite. Smith knew that during the coming week he would be called upon to use his newly acquired information to bring his class together as a group. He realized he would be challenged and would have to demonstrate his mettle and resolve. This is the path novice teachers need to follow.

Help such as mentoring goes only so far. Yes, it's a critical and necessary process, but in the end novice teachers like Smith still have to earn their place. There are no guarantees. It goes day by day, learning the lessons needed to become a competent teacher as well as learning how to survive in an often hostile, sometimes unforgiving environment.

Chapter Ten

Making the Case for a Whole-School Mentoring Program

This final chapter is a summary of the important issues involved in planning a whole-school mentoring program in our nation's schools. Three important principles guide these issues. First, there is a great need for mentoring teachers in our nation's schools. Second, the mentoring program described can be implemented without the addition of staff or major resources. Third, mentoring skills can also be taught to students, thereby creating a whole-school mentoring program in which no teacher or student falls through the cracks. Here are six issues administrators need to understand:

1. The pressing need to provide mentoring for teachers at all levels of their career development—novice, midcareer, and veteran teachers.
2. The need for administrators to play a leadership role in the mentoring process.
3. The need for the mentoring team to accurately assess the school's willingness to welcome change and new programs.
4. The need to understand what educational leaders and researchers say about mentoring: do they favor the kind of mentoring model this book recommends?
5. The need to learn from examples of mentoring programs now in action around the country.
6. The need to understand mentoring as a vital part of building a strong school community.

ISSUE 1: THE NEED TO PROVIDE MENTORING FOR TEACHERS AT ALL LEVELS OF CAREER DEVELOPMENT

The mentoring model presented here, and the accompanying potential to expand learning opportunities for support staff and students, presents a positive and cost-effective way for administrators to respond to their staff's need for ongoing renewal. This model addresses the learning needs not only of novice teachers like Shawn Mallory and Tom Murray but also veterans like Ellen Turner, Myra Fryman, Harry Walker, and Jim McDonald.

It also addresses the need and opportunity for skilled educational leaders like principals Ralph De Feo and Brad Foley, teacher Frank Bronkowski, department chair Randy Edwards, assistant principal Linda Alvarez, and counselor Ivy Harrison to become mentors, creating not only a vehicle to help and support teachers but also an exciting new career alternative.

Mentoring can make a difference in the professional and personal lives of teachers who want to be effective but who may encounter bad times. Teachers lose their way sometimes, even the best and the brightest of them. New teachers usually struggle to learn the ropes. Some of the lessons, as we saw in the cases of Tom Murray and Shawn Mallory, are subtle and difficult to learn. Teachers often naively assume that if they survive their first few years, they are set for life.

As we saw in the cases of Ellen Turner, Myra Fryman, and Jim McDonald, new issues frequently emerge for teachers, professional and personal issues that throw them off course and cause them to question their effectiveness. Without intervention and mentoring, they can become another case of attrition, professional lives lost that might have been saved.

Tom, Shawn, Ellen, Myra, and Jim do not represent the most at-risk teachers. They have been formally trained as teachers, have been part of a teacher induction program, have had successful classroom experience, and now, if problems emerge, have the support and safety net of a trained mentoring team, an easily accessible school-based help and support mechanism that can assist them.

As the need for new teachers accelerates nationally, a growing number of teachers enter the field with little or no formal education, internship experience, or induction program, and no mentoring team available to intervene. These new teachers are often not education majors; they may be retirees or college graduates who enter the classroom as a second or third career. They begin teaching with little or no training and support in how to manage a classroom and interact with students. Are they doomed to failure? Not all of them, but clearly the odds are not in their favor.

We might rightfully ask why school boards and administrators go along with such a situation, allowing well-intentioned but poorly trained would-be teachers to be exposed to the hazards and risks of the classroom. In a sense, school boards and administrators are encouraging a process that props up a warm body in front of the classroom and hopes for the best while knowing that the would-be teacher, the students, and the school could lose. What follows is a vivid description of how two unprepared and unsupported teachers fared in the classroom.

Bill Gaulman and Erica Lavrack had little or no formal training, no induction, and no mentoring. Bill Gaulman's teaching career began in early August in an old brick two-story school north of Ybor City. It ended in September. In a matter of weeks Bill fell prey to a punishing combination. The hours were too long and not enough students were interested in learning. He developed a knot in his stomach that wouldn't go away.

The word that came to mind was "overwhelmed," said Gaulman, a man whose background included being a Marine and a New York City firefighter. "People told me to just get through the first year," he said. "I thought, I don't know if I can get through this week."

Erica Lavrack also started teaching at the beginning of the school year. She resigned on her second day. She was given a class of emotionally handicapped children, although she had never handled a classroom before. Her qualifications? A degree in psychology and the fact that the Hillsborough schools desperately needed teachers for special education classes.

She reports, "The kids were nice enough but they were running all over the place. There was no way I could teach them anything if I couldn't get them to sit down. I didn't know what to do."

The stories of Gaulman and Lavrack are surprisingly common. Florida desperately needs to attract teachers; an estimated 12,500 teachers are needed each year. But Florida has another problem—keeping teachers from quitting. Many new and veteran teachers become disillusioned and start planning their exit. As Martha Howell, assistant superintendent for the Pinellas County schools, suggests, "If we don't give them the support they need, we lose them."[1]

One can argue that if Bill Gaulman and Erica Lavrack had pre-service training they would have been better prepared to face the realities of the classroom. But Florida school districts are increasingly hiring noneducation majors, retirees, and college graduates who enter the classroom as a second or third career. They begin teaching without the benefit of internships and training to handle classroom situations.

Teachers like Bill Gaulman and Erica Lavrack are growing in number as schools' need to have warm bodies in front of the classroom reaches the level of a national crisis. These would-be teachers need effective intervention and mentoring, probably more than Tom, Ellen, Shawn, Myra, and Jim, because of their lack of preparation. They are, in a sense, the most at-risk teachers.

ISSUE 2: THE NEED FOR ADMINISTRATORS TO PLAY A LEADERSHIP ROLE IN THE MENTORING PROCESS

In making the case that mentoring is needed in our schools, concerned building administrators cannot do the job alone. They have a lot on their plates already. With the recent national emphasis on reform and producing effective teachers, their job definitions may be shifting away from a management and problem-solving role to a role as instructional leaders and facilitators.

Mentoring requires time for observations, follow-up one-on-one conferencing, and ongoing support. Realistically, a school-based team is required. A progression of steps needs to be successfully followed to reach our goal of implementing a school-wide mentoring process.

Interestingly enough, three important elements in the mentoring model presented in this book—newly mentored teachers becoming mentors, transferring mentoring skills to support staff, and transferring mentoring skills to students—are rarely addressed. Their significance in helping develop a supportive school community should not be underestimated.

Administrators need to follow these important steps:

1. Become sold on the mentoring process and how it can help you, the principal, as well as assistant principals, department chairs, counselors, teacher leaders, teachers, support staff, and students.
2. Assess your mentoring skills and train yourself in areas in which you need improvement.
3. Form and train your mentoring team and sell the program to staff.
4. Intervene and mentor teachers.
5. Encourage newly mentored teachers to become mentors themselves.
6. Transfer mentoring skills to support staff.
7. Transfer mentoring skills to students.

ISSUE 3: THE NEED FOR THE MENTORING TEAM TO ACCURATELY ASSESS THE SCHOOL'S WILLINGNESS TO WELCOME CHANGE AND NEW PROGRAMS

This process requires an understanding of how new programs have fared in the school in the past. In many schools, there is a graveyard full of failed programs begun with good intentions, commitment, and resources that faltered along the way. They were torpedoed by not anticipating resistance, by inadequate community building and political skills, and by ignoring problems that arose. Pam Robbins suggests that program planners understand those critical factors that can have a major effect on program design, implementation, and maintenance.[2]

While Robbins' focus is on coaching, the same critical factors apply to mentoring. Robbins' suggestions serve to reinforce a plea that administrators who set out to develop mentoring programs had best be aware of the school's history in developing new programs, where resistance to change will likely arise, and possess a finely honed set of political, planning, and communication skills to help navigate the program through expected and unexpected barriers.

While the vignettes offer a vision of Brad Foley as a supportive and skilled principal, there are many schools in which the potential program leaders need to be tested with the following questions:

- What is the pre-existing climate of collegiality? Is there a history of staff working together and supporting each other? Is this fertile territory to begin growing a new program? If not, building collegiality will take time, patience, and support.
- Are there norms supporting risk taking and experimentation? For mentoring to succeed, the school culture must encourage teachers to take risks and try new approaches. Risk-taking needs to be modeled throughout the school by the principal and school leaders. Administrators can't ask teachers to risk trying out new approaches while they remain safe in one spot.
- Has the supervisory experience been a pleasant or unpleasant one for teachers? Mentoring has a focus of assisting, not evaluating or assessing. It is useful to remember that a teacher's experience with teaching in front of another adult affects his or her feelings about teaching in front of a colleague and mentor. If the previous experience has not been rewarding and nurturing, mentors will have to develop new, supportive conditions.
- What is the school's track record regarding staff development? Has there been a series of failed efforts to bring about change and reform? Is the school's graveyard of failed education programs running out of space? Mentoring needs to be seen by staff as useful, growth promoting, and enjoyable, not as just one more task added to the day. Staff need to be sold on the process and their input valued. Teachers tend to remember staff development interventions that did little for them.
- What are the core values of the school? What do members of the school community think is important? Is rugged individualism prized or is value placed on working together, sharing ideas, and supporting each other? Mentoring has a good chance to thrive in a school community that respects lifelong learning, creativity, and working together.
- Does leadership support mentoring? Administrative support is a major factor in developing the success of mentoring programs. Support needs to be long-term. Administrators who are initially sold on mentoring may get

cold feet when confronted by problems and resistance. New programs need to be able to count on the leader for cover as well as for participation and funding.

- What else is going on? As Robbins wisely suggests, it is useful to examine what the program must compete with in terms of time, focus, and resources. There is a right and wrong time to begin a new program, such as mentoring, that will have a great impact on the way teachers interact and behave. Administrators need to weigh the odds for success and failure of such projects. They need to take a critical look at how many projects are already going on in the school and determine if the staff has the psychological and physical energy required for the new effort. They also need to consider if the school has the necessary resources. Successful administrators usually have a good sense of timing and know when the school needs a new focus. The key is to look for ways to integrate new programs such as mentoring with other efforts, such as restructuring.
- Can the bureaucratic structure of the school support mentoring activities? To what extent can the bureaucratic structure promote or inhibit the program?
- What are the existing structures of collaboration in the school? If the staff has a history of working together, mentoring does not represent a major departure from the norm.
- What is the nature of decision making in the school? Does the staff have ownership in the school? Are they used to working together and being involved in shared decisions? Is it real participation that seeks the collective input of every staff member, or is it only on paper?
- How flexible is the school culture? Do new ideas like mentoring have a chance to be incorporated into the school? Good ideas and intentions don't survive in a culture that is not open to change and fresh ideas.

These questions, if answered honestly, help pave the way for action. They provide a useful antenna on how to proceed by helping sharpen mentors' vision as to where potential problems and opportunities lie. Considering these questions can move the mentoring team beyond good ideas and good intentions to the real issues they can expect to confront. It's good to know what is possible, and it's good to know where the barriers lie.

ISSUE 4: THE NEED TO UNDERSTAND WHAT EDUCATIONAL LEADERS AND RESEARCHERS SAY ABOUT MENTORING

Let's hear what educational leader Lee Shulman, mentor advocate James Rowley, and practitioning mentor Mary Brooks say about mentoring.

In an interview with Carol Tell, Lee Shulman, president of the Carnegie Foundation for the Advancement of Teaching, makes the following points regarding mentoring and the changing role of administrators.[3]

Carol Tell questions Shulman about his view of teacher evaluation: "As you know, a perennial debate in education involves the connection between evaluation and improvement. Some argue that evaluation needs to be treated separately to enhance teachers' knowledge and skills. Others think that given the current emphasis on measurable results, we must align evaluation with professional development and school improvement. How do you feel about making these distinctions? Do you think there will always be tensions?"

Shulman replies, "Somebody once asked me, why are there tensions between theory and practice in the education of professionals? And my answer is that there have to be tensions. One of the ways we make the tension worse [for educators] is to put both the job of nurturer and the task of monitor in the hands of the same person. . . . When evaluating teachers and tying rewards to those evaluations, we should try, within limits of responsibility, to separate and delegate the twin functions of monitor and mentor to different individuals."

Tell also asked Shulman, "So a mentor should never have an evaluative role?"

Shulman replied, "Well, never say never. If you were my mentor, and it was your job to help me learn to be a really accomplished teacher, you would have access—through observations and conversations—to views and perspectives of me that nobody else had. . . . There is a point at which it would be unethical for you to withhold information from those who represented the accountability side of the equation. But as mentor, you would have to explain that to me. You would have to explain to me that 99 percent of the time you are my buddy, my friend, my supporter. But there could be a case in which you observed me doing or not doing something that so violated the fundamental expectations of the role that you would have no recourse but to make the observation part of the general evaluative data."

Tell queries Shulman about the evaluation of principals. "We talk a lot about the evaluations of teachers, but not so much about the evaluation of principals and administrators. Do you know of any moves afoot to revamp the evaluation of those educators?"

Shulman answers, "With regard to principals, my own view is that the principal is the lead teacher. The word *principal* is not only a noun, but also an adjective, the first word of a two-word title: principal teacher. Principals, therefore, should be highly accomplished teachers who have the capacity to manage, organize, lead, and develop the capabilities of other teachers."

Shulman's comments about mentoring and his vision of a mentoring program fit well with the mentoring model and vision of the changing role of administrator and principal suggested in this book. In this model the mentor is available to assist the protégé. Shulman suggests the mentor is available to nurture and to be a friend and a supporter. Mentors are available to help the protégé learn to be a very accomplished teacher, to be nurturing and not solely to monitor, assess, or evaluate.

In the vignettes in this book, principal Brad Foley is available to assist and support Tom Murray; it's a helping role and one that lacks a formal evaluation component. In this model, as represented in the vignette focusing on teacher Shawn Mallory and department chair Randy Edwards, mentoring and close observation can help prevent a situation that could have dire consequences for a teacher's career and the well-being of his or her students. Without the quick and skilled intervention of Randy Edwards, the innocent relationship between Shawn and Aileen could have moved beyond professional boundaries into a romantic relationship. Mentoring and heeding early warning signs proved to be an effective mechanism for help.

Shulman also offers cautionary advice about the limits of some aspects of the mentoring role when he responds to Tell's query, "So a mentor should never have an evaluative role?" Shulman answers, "But as a mentor you would have to remind me that 99 percent of the time you are my buddy, my friend, my supporter. But there could be a case in which you observed me doing something or not doing something that so violated the fundamental expectations of the role that you would have no recourse but to make that observation part of the more evaluative data."

Let's use the example of Shawn to reinforce Shulman's point. Shawn, a new and inexperienced teacher, did not foresee the hazards involved in getting too close to a student. But thanks to Randy's observations and skillful intervention, Shawn learned an important lesson about student–teacher relationships: keep a professional distance. Don't become a friend or surrogate parent.

Shawn's experience easily could have had an unhappy or even career-thwarting ending. For example, what if Shawn rebutted Randy's interventions and continued to become involved with Aileen as a friend, surrogate parent, or even a lover? Eventually, Randy would have had to approach principal Brad Foley and share his situation.

As Shulman suggests, "he would have no recourse but to make the observations part of the general evaluative data," in other words, of Shawn's formal record—a record that could lead to Shawn's dismissal if the behavior continued. Ninety-nine percent of the time mentors like Randy are friends and supporters of their protégés, but when information surfaces that involves the safety and well-being of teachers, students, and parents, it needs to be addressed. In this case, Randy's mentoring served as a deterrent to Shawn's perceived or real risky behavior.

James B. Rowley, associate professor at University of Dayton, suggests that good mentors have the following qualities:[4]

- Good mentors are committed to the role of mentoring. They are highly committed to the task of helping beginning teachers find success and gratification in their work. Committed mentors understand that persistence is as important in mentoring as it is in classroom teaching. Such commitment flows naturally from a resolute belief that mentors are capable of making a significant and positive impact on the life of another.

  The belief is not grounded in a naive conception of what it means to be a mentor. Rather, it is anchored in the knowledge that mentoring can be a challenging endeavor requiring significant investments of time and energy. Good programs require formal mentor training as a prerequisite to mentoring.

- Good mentors are accepting of the beginning teacher. They recognize the power of accepting the beginning teacher as a developing person and professional. Accepting mentors do not judge or reject mentees as being poorly prepared, overconfident, naive, or defensive. Mentors view these traits as changes to overcome in their efforts to deliver meaningful support.

  How can we encourage mentors to be more accepting of new teachers? A training program that engages prospective mentors in reflecting on the qualities of effective helpers is an excellent place to begin. It should be training that helps prospective mentors understand the problems and concerns of beginning teachers as well as teachers at all other stages and ages, training that can cause mentors to revisit their own first years of teaching.

- Good mentors are skilled at providing instructional support. They are willing to coach beginning teachers to improve their performance. Many mentors stop short of providing quality instructional support. Among the factors contributing to this problem is a school culture that does not encourage teachers to observe one another in the classroom. What can be done to prepare mentors to provide instructional support? Mentor training should equip mentors with knowledge, skills, and dispositions for effective coaching. We need to give mentors and mentees the opportunity to participate in pre-conferences, classroom observations, and postconferences that lead to quality clinical support.

- Good mentors are effective in different interpersonal contexts. They recognize that each mentoring relationship occurs in a unique interpersonal context. Just as good teachers adjust their teaching behaviors and communications to meet the needs of individual students, good mentors adjust their mentoring communications to meet the needs of individual mentees. To make such adjustments, good mentors must possess a deep understanding of their own communication styles and a willingness to objectively observe the behavior of the mentee.

  How can we help mentors acquire such self-knowledge and adopt a positive disposition toward adjusting their mentoring behaviors? Mentor training programs that engage mentors in completing and reflecting on self-inventories that provide insight into their leadership or supervisory styles are particularly helpful.

- Good mentors are models of continuous learning. Good mentors are transparent about their own search for better answers and more effective solutions to their own problems. They model this commitment by their openness to learn from colleagues, including beginning teachers, and by their willingness to pursue professional growth through a variety of means.

    How can we ensure that mentors continue their own professional growth and development? Quality entry-year programs establish clear criteria for mentor selection that include a commitment to initial and ongoing mentor training. Program leaders work hard to give veteran mentors frequent opportunities to participate in high quality professional growth experiences that can enhance their work as mentors.

- Good mentors communicate hope and optimism. They capitalize on opportunities to affirm the human potential of their mentees. They do so in private conversations and in public settings. Good mentors share their own struggles and how they overcame them, and always they do so in a genuine and caring way that engenders trust.

    What can we do to ensure that beginning teachers are supported by mentors capable of communicating hope and optimism? Quality programs take the necessary precaution of avoiding the use of veteran teachers who have lost their positive outlook. If teachers and administrators value mentoring and take it seriously, mentoring will attract caring and committed teachers who demonstrate hope and optimism for the future by their willingness to help new teachers discover the same joy and satisfaction that they have found in their own careers.

Rowley's comments regarding the qualities of a good mentor fit well with the mentoring model presented in this book. Brad Foley, Frank Bronkowski, Randy Edwards, Linda Alvarez, and Ivy Harrison are all committed to their mentoring work. They realize the endeavor requires a significant investment of time and energy. The mentor training program and self-inventories helped them focus on the need to take care of themselves and to be physically and emotionally up to the task. Their knowledge of the importance of self-care was easily transferred to their protégés who were neglecting their well-being.

This mentoring model also calls for the mentor to be an effective listener, to be nonjudgmental, to provide useful feedback, to be accepting, and to act as a guide for teacher improvement. For example, Frank Bronkowski refrains from making judgments about Ellen Turner's rapidly deteriorating professional and personal life. He listens and gives useful and accurate feedback. He provides breathing space in which Ellen can gather herself, acquire new awareness, and plan, with Frank, concrete ways to take back her classroom and professional and personal self.

This mentoring model calls for the mentor to be skilled in providing instructional support. Brad Foley, as a good mentor, is quickly able to identify Tom Murray's strengths and the areas that need improvement. He is able to show Tom how to improve some methods of instruction that if left unattended would hinder Tom's classroom success. Brad communicates these thorny issues in a non-threatening, supportive way, more as a friend than a supervisor.

This mentoring model also highlights Rowley's advice that good mentors are accepting of the beginning teacher. Accepting mentors do not judge or reject mentees as being poorly prepared, overconfident, naive, or defensive. When novice teacher Gary Smith becomes overwhelmed with the problems he is facing, Principal Ralph De Feo listens, understands, and accepts his precarious situation and offers him a lifeline that provides Smith with momentary respite, counsel, and information—a needed opportunity to survive in his turbulent world.

For example, De Feo offers Smith the gift of knowing and understanding his students' backgrounds in great detail. He gives Smith both a sense of their past struggles and what he needs to do to get them on board and to help them want to improve and be part of Mr. Smith's class. De Feo understands that he can best support Smith in two ways: help him grasp the reality of the risky situation he is in and then provide the counsel and information he needs to take control of his class. This sends the message that Smith's challenge is not easy, but doable.

As a veteran building principal De Feo knows that acquiring the needed skills to survive quickly is the winning ticket. One of those skills is toughness. There are no soft landings for the majority of novice teachers.

This mentoring model also fits well with Rowley's suggestion that each mentoring relationship is unique and good mentors need to adjust their mentoring communications to meet the needs of individual mentees. We need to look no further than mentors Randy Edwards, Linda Alvarez, and Ivy Harrison to see that each protégé brings his or her own professional and personal issues to the mentoring relationship.

Teachers Shawn Mallory, Myra Fryman, and Jim McDonald are each in a unique experience. The same approach, Mentoring 101, cannot be used in every case. Protégés, with their unique stories and needs, force mentors to adjust and sometimes learn new skills or use an intervention approach they are reluctant to call on.

For example, Linda Alvarez must strongly confront Myra Fryman to make her see her dilemma. Soft words, going along quietly, being nice— these things don't work with Myra. Fastballs have to be thrown in order for

Myra to see that her star role is, in reality, not very satisfying. Mentors need many different skills to fit their many different protégés.

Mentors are also continuous learners. They seek out and create learning opportunities and hubs, not only for their protégés but for themselves as well. Randy Edwards pursues his connection with a local university medical school and his interest in research about teacher sexual abuse. Ivy Harrison becomes an adjunct professor in counseling in exchange for internship help. Linda Alvarez champions issues related to diversity and inclusion. Brad Foley creates ongoing learning networks with community and educational resources. Frank Bronkowski coauthors books on teen issues. These mentors were chosen not only for their excellent track record, skills, and commitment, but also for their intellectual curiosity. They are learners.

Finally, in this model, mentors know how to bring a sense of joy, energy, humor, and lightness to the mentoring relationship. In many of the vignettes, the mentors involved are able to offer hope and optimism and the message that things can improve. Brad Foley lets Tom Murray know that he can deal with hostile situations like the confrontation with Jim's father. Be optimistic, he tells Tom.

Frank Bronkowski does the same for Ellen Turner: he tells her "shift weight; things can change; lighten up; do simple things like bringing in flowers and pictures of your family; create a little joy for yourself. "

Randy Edwards, responding to Shawn Mallory's sudden concern for his career, says he'll provide cover for Shawn. "Lighten up," he says. "This has been a valuable learning experience."

Ivy Harrison, representing the truly empathetic and caring mentor, tells Jim McDonald "you are doing OK; keep expectations low; take it one day at a time; this too will pass; keep working on the issues; I'll be here with you."

Mary Brooks is site coordinator for the Beginning Teacher Mentor Program in West Des Moines, Iowa community schools. She describes the responsibilities of mentors in the following ways:[5]

- Get involved in solving specific problems about curriculum, instruction, and relationships, offering plenty of feedback.
- Provide opportunity for classroom visits with follow-up feedback.
- Express positive feelings about teaching and help beginning teachers attain those same feelings. Address the new teacher's thoughts about being a teacher.
- Assist with the new teacher's understanding and management of authority.
- Listen to daily concerns, progress, and questions.
- Serve as a source of ideas.
- Be easily accessible, trustworthy, and understanding.
- Offer assistance on classroom management.
- Demonstrate professional competence.

- Help expand the beginning teacher's repertoire of teaching strategies.
- Show awareness of, commitment to, and familiarity with the new teacher's classroom.
- Schedule time willingly with the beginning teacher.
- Provide a task-oriented focus established through a two-way interchange about goals and procedures.

Brooks also provides a job description of a mentor that includes what she calls "demonstrated skills: professional competency, effective verbal and non-verbal communication, and interpersonal skills of caring, kindness, and understanding."

The mentoring model presented in this book includes many of the same responsibilities and job descriptions as Brooks'. In this training model and the vignettes, mentors use the full arsenal of skills available to them: problem solving, classroom observations and feedback, expression of positive feelings about teaching, pointing out positive activities of teachers, helping teachers cope with practical details, serving as a source of ideas, remaining accessible and trustworthy, and being generally caring, kind, and understanding.

As Brooks suggests, this process produces a win-win situation. It need not be limited to offering support to beginning teachers. Teachers at every stage of development need support and sometimes intervention.

Kathleen Devaney offers an inclusive list of leadership skills that teachers might be called upon to exercise in emerging school organizations. Clearly, these areas are consistent with my notion of mentors as school leaders:

- Continuing to teach and improve one's own teaching
- Organizing and leading peer reviews of school practice
- Providing curriculum development knowledge
- Participating in school-level decision making
- Leading in-service education and assisting other teachers

Certainly the successful teaching experiences of mentors Frank Bronkowski and Randy Edwards prepared them for advising and guiding veteran teacher Ellen Turner and novice Shawn Mallory. Mentoring presents an emerging opportunity for teachers to assume such a leadership role. It's a positive career opportunity for both skilled teachers and those in need of support.

Nathalie Gehrke also supports the use of teachers, department chairs, and counselors in assuming a leadership role in mentoring teachers. Gehrke suggests mentors must be able to provide not only good role modeling, but also offer the kind of help necessary to establish the beginner as a competent professional. They must know about teaching children and about teaching adults. They must have a level of expertise that goes beyond being a comforter and a source of practical information.[6]

Holly Bartunek also offers support to the notion of classroom teachers as school-based teacher educators. She suggests that school-based teacher educator positions open an avenue of teacher growth. In this role, the classroom teacher is offered opportunities that expand and enhance professional development. Bartunek suggests the following strategies:

- Promote and support peer teacher growth.
- Experience empowerment by facilitating local change.
- Assume a leadership role without leaving the classroom.
- Develop teaching behaviors that blend clinical skills with practitioner-translated research and history.[7]

This revitalization of the teaching role with new responsibilities benefits the school process and its participants. In terms of mentoring as a potential school-based teacher educator role, Bartunek suggests that mentoring programs are rooted in the belief that adults have the capacity for continued growth and learning and that this development can be influenced by specific types of interventions that both support and challenge them.

A critical focus of her argument is the understanding of the teacher's career as moving within a cycle that includes distinct stages: pre-service, induction, competency building, enthusiastic and growing, career frustration, stable and stagnant, career wind-down, and career exit. These stages are dynamically influenced, either singularly or in combination, by personal environmental factors such as family demands, crises, cumulative experience, and individual dispositions and by organizational environmental factors such as administrative style.

Clearly mentors Frank and Randy have added vitality and novelty by becoming school-based teacher educators, with one foot in the classroom and one foot in the mentoring program. Their mentor training program has helped focus them on the important role that aging and career development issues play in teachers' lives, both personally and professionally.

As seen in Ellen Turner's case, family demands and crises do happen. A career that was once enthusiastic and growing winds up with career frustrations. Ellen is lucky, unlike Florida teachers Bill Gaulman and Erica Lavrack. Ellen has access to a well-trained mentor in Frank Bronkowski.

The same holds true for Jim McDonald. The counselor and mentor Ivy Harrison, while not a classroom teacher, also has a new opportunity for professional growth, with one foot in the counseling office and one foot in the mentoring program. She, too, is well trained and ready to help Jim with his "career frustration."

Roland Barth also adds credence to the argument that mentoring creates a unique opportunity for teachers to assume a leadership role in their schools, a role that offers a career alternative, novelty, and, as Barth rightfully points out, an element of risk. [8]

Barth suggests that teachers who become leaders experience personal and professional satisfaction, a reduction in isolation, a sense of instrumentality, and new learning. They become investors in the school rather than mere tenants; they become professionals. Barth describes attributes of teachers who are leaders:

- They get to sit at the table with grown-ups as first-class citizens rather than remain the subordinate in a world full of subordinates.
- They enjoy variety, even relief, from the often relentless tedium of the classroom.
- They have an opportunity to work with and influence the lives of adults as well as youngsters.

Barth also points out that moving from classroom teacher, a subordinate role equal with peers, to a leadership position such as mentoring can be unsettling and even risky.

Barth suggests that in a very real way teachers who choose to confine their work as educators to the classroom win. They have more time and energy to devote to their teaching, to each of their students, and to their responsibilities outside of school. They are immune from interpersonal conflicts with other teachers and the principal. They also enjoy a measure of safety in the relatively risk-free sanctuary of the classroom, where they may be accountable for pupil achievement but not their own achievement as a leader. And they may enjoy a measure of sanity each day in the often turbulent and chaotic world of the school.

For teachers who assume leadership, the outcome is less clear. They choose to supplement their work as classroom teachers by taking on responsibility, some of the time, for some of the issues that are integral to the health and character of the entire school.

By participating in a larger arena, these teachers lose what the larger group wins: time, energy, freedom from interpersonal hassles, and immunity from public criticism for efforts that may not succeed. They probably lose, as well, a measure of their sanity in their days at school and at home.

But Barth suggests that the risks are worth it. The teachers who assume a leadership role such as mentoring win something more important. They experience a reduction in isolation, the personal and professional satisfaction that comes from improving their schools, and a sense of instrumentality, investment, and membership in the school community, and they gain knowledge about schools, the process of change, and themselves. All of these positive experiences spill over into their classroom teaching. Again, these teachers become owners and investors in the school rather than mere tenants. They become professionals.

Yes, the mentoring model presented in this book does have elements of risk and isolation in it. It's new territory. Mentors are no longer just one of the crowd. In becoming mentors they are in a way leaving their school family. The routines, professional and personal boundaries, and rewards all change. Dissonance and anxiety may ensue. Leaving a role they know well for something new does, and should, make them feel they may be losing something in the process.

As mentor Frank Bronkowski says, he is new at the game and still learning, but he wants to help. The way is not clear or known but he is on the road, seizing a new opportunity for growth and service. He has a good track record and the will to succeed. These resources help as he searches for the new rewards that a leadership role such as mentoring can provide.

Barth reminds us that with our nation's schools under relentless scrutiny, a remarkable space exists for teachers to fill. Many teachers want to lead, and schools badly need their ideas, intervention, energy, and leadership.

ISSUE 5: THE NEED TO LEARN FROM EXAMPLES OF MENTORING PROGRAMS NOW IN ACTION AROUND THE COUNTRY

Mentoring teams and school administrators can learn from several examples of mentoring programs in action throughout the country. Administrators considering implementing a mentoring program do not have to reinvent the wheel. They can tap into many excellent mentoring programs in action throughout the country. Establishing contact with leaders of these programs also provides an instant resource for information and networking. What follows is just a sampling of the many fine programs in place.

Rochester, New York

The tidal wave that washes over first-year teachers when they dive into the classroom for the first time can be enough to throw them back on the beach and send them home. The lifesavers for these aspiring educators are often their union colleagues, especially their teacher mentors.

Few do it better than the Rochester Teachers Association, a critical part of the Rochester Public Schools Career in Teaching Program. The mentor–intern program was established in 1986 by the Rochester Teachers Association in cooperation with the city school district and has become a national model for improving teacher retention and preparing new teachers for urban schools.

The 2000 school year produced the largest program in its fifteen-year history, with 205 lead teacher mentors serving more than 600 interns. Nearly all of the interns had no prior teaching experience. The support helped maintain a 93 percent retention rate during the year. Even more impressive, 86 percent of all the 2,000 teachers who have been interns in the program since 1986 are still teaching. Before the program began, the district's retention rate was around 60 percent.

In the Rochester program, aspiring mentors need recommendations. Mentors also need seven years in the district, a desire to continue learning, respect for the profession, and the quality of empathy. Carl O'Connell, Rochester Teachers Association mentor program coordinator, reports, "Can you imagine how many teachers would have been lost to the district and city if we hadn't been here? I've never seen a program that has done so much for our kids, for our administration, and for our colleagues. . . . We've had thirteen years to put this all together. We have a list of warning signs we watch for— a lack of confidence, discouragement, frequent absences, etc. We always try to fix the problem, not blame."[9]

North Bellmore, New York

The North Bellmore Teacher Center on Long Island offers a mentoring program that holds training sessions twice a month on communication, adult learning styles, peer coaching, and weaning.

Susan Weinstein, director of the teacher center, stresses the need to provide training for mentors. She wisely suggests, "Just because you are a good teacher doesn't mean you [will be] a good mentor."

Dumont, New Jersey

Dumont has a mentoring program for first-year teachers at the Honiss Elementary School. It is a program to help new teachers weather the classroom, which school principal Richard S. Sterberg describes vividly: "There is this onslaught, what I call the violation of expectations, the minute they arrive. There is no way to experience it except by living through it."

It's a support program for teachers like new eighth-grade science teacher Pam Nathan, who quickly discovers the gap between idealism and reality. Asking students to pass papers up to the front of the room can be an invitation to chaos. Students, some as tall as she, sass back when she asks for quiet. Many teachers, some of whom taught not only her but her mother, "tsk-tsk" when she tries something new. Asking for new textbooks becomes more work than seeking a presidential pardon.

There are plenty of days when Nathan feels like quitting. That she has not is in no small measure thanks to seventh-grade science teacher Linda Merschtina, who was assigned as her mentor when Nathan arrived in September. Merschtina quickly became her confidential source of reassurance and tips on how to deal with parents, colleagues, and unruly students.

The program at Dumont is part of a statewide requirement of a year of formal, structured mentoring for new teachers, a program that state officials are now proposing to extend to two years. Already fifteen school districts in Bergen County, including Dumont, have started pilot two-year mentoring induction programs.

The job description for a mentor at Dumont includes terms like "coach, prober, empathizer, communicator, promoter of risk-taking, diplomat, nurturer, observer, counselor, motivator, and goal-setter."[10]

Centerville, Ohio

The success of the Centerville mentoring program for new teachers depends on systemic support of the mentoring program. For Mindy Cline, a kindergarten teacher, that support takes the form of mentor Barb Roberts, who smoothed her initial transition into teaching. From the mundane to the philosophical, Roberts lent a hand—and an ear—in Cline's new classroom. She helped Cline arrange her room, reviewed the early lesson plans, and introduced her to other school staff.

Even though Cline had participated in a five-year preparation program with a year-long internship, she still benefited from Roberts' gentle guidance. As a requirement of the Centerville program, Roberts and Cline observed each other's teaching. They also had four days of release time, which they used to visit other schools and gather instructional ideas.

During the course of her induction year, Cline frequently sought Roberts' input on her classroom practices. "Barb made me feel really successful, but she also let me fall a few times. . . . She supported me yet she gave me the space to try new things and see how they worked."

At one point, Cline experienced classroom management difficulties and sought Roberts' assistance. Together they devised a new classroom management program and within three weeks Cline's class exhibited significant improvement.

"Barb also helps me to avoid burning out. She saw that I was constantly working quite late; she advised me to go home. She told me that I might have flawless bulletin boards, but if I was physically exhausted, I wouldn't be very good for students."

Roberts, who serves on the Centerville school district mentoring committee, believes the success of mentoring hinges on systemic support. The union local negotiated release time and a $1,000 stipend for mentor teachers. Roberts says the stipends and incentives are real boosts for mentors, and formalizing the program gives it credibility and communicates that the program is valued. For Cline the stipend also makes a difference. "Knowing she was being paid kept me from feeling I was imposing on her."

Roberts also believes mentors require specialized professional development: "Educators need to be trained to effectively help new teachers." In Centerville, experienced teachers apply to become mentors and participate in course work. Each year the district mentoring committee gives careful consideration to the matches between mentors and new teachers. Mindy Cline believes she benefited from the careful selection process: "As a reading resource teacher, Barb really understood my content concerns, but because she wasn't a member of my teaching team I felt comfortable seeking her advice on my team's dynamics."[11]

Glastonbury, Connecticut

The school day ended for Tom Griffin's twenty-six students nearly an hour ago, but the fourth-grade teacher is still in his classroom. He sits at a squat table across from his mentor, Elaine Ahnell. Ten weeks into his first teaching job, the twenty-nine-year-old rookie has a lot on his mind.

In short order, the two educators cover the logistics of parent-teacher conferences and how to divide the students into different reading groups based on their ability. Ahnell, a twenty-nine-year veteran at Hebron Avenue Elementary School, shares examples of her students' work from a lesson Griffin plans to replicate in the coming days.

These weekly sessions make a long day even longer, but Griffin says he wouldn't want to go through his first year without them. "Elaine is my keel. If I didn't have this, I'd be up until two o'clock in the morning, scared."

But these mentoring meetings are more than hand-holding sessions. They're a part of Connecticut's comprehensive program for inducting teachers into the profession. By providing them with ample support and guidance, the state is betting that new teachers like Griffin will not only survive their first year but will also grow to be highly skilled educators.

This program, Beginning Educators Support and Training (BEST), is part of the $300 million comprehensive Education Enhancement Act passed in 1986. New teachers must successfully complete the program within three years of beginning their first jobs before they can move beyond Connecticut's initial license.

BEST requires that districts give each new teacher a mentor or team of mentors for at least the first year of the program. In terms of training, the state gives each of its mentors three days of workshops in which the educators learn what the program requires of new teachers, such as Connecticut's

Common Core of Teaching, a set of standards spelling out the skills and knowledge expected of teachers in each subject area and grade level.

Tom Griffin says having a mentor across the hall who is also a fourth grade teacher has been a major asset as he tries to find the right balance in setting expectations that are big enough for his students but not so high that they become lost. Although his first year has been a lot of work, more than he expected, he's convinced he made the right choice of a career. [12]

Other Programs

The mentoring programs in Rochester, Dumont, Centerville, and Glastonbury represent some of the many mentoring programs that are being developed throughout the country. The state of California has a beginning teacher support and assessment program in which mentors, called "providers," develop trusting relationships with their novices by meeting formally and informally on a regular basis. The providers are selected for their competency in the classroom and for their communication skills. [13]

The state of Kentucky Teacher Internship Program also represents a major effort to provide mentoring. Legislation passed in 1985 requires all first-year teachers to receive a level of support that develops a strong, life-long career foundation. The program guides each new teacher through a structured process of assistance and assessment with the active involvement of a committee of seasoned educators, a mentor teacher, a university representative, and the school principal. [14]

In Columbus, Ohio, public schools established the Peer Assistance and Review (PAR) Program in 1986. The PAR Program was developed collaboratively by representatives from the teachers' union and district administrators to help new teachers and those experiencing difficulty on the job become effective. PAR mentors, called "consultants," are experienced teachers who remember what it is like to be new.

A panel of administrators, teachers, and union officials select these consultants and release them from their classroom teaching duties for up to three years. All new teachers are required to enroll in PAR. Interns must successfully complete the one-year program to have their contracts renewed. The mentors conduct pre-school orientation meetings, and once school starts make weekly visits to the interns' classrooms and keep in touch through individual conferences. The goal is to establish a supportive relationship that can provide an avenue to help improve teaching strategies and solve non-teaching problems. [15]

Research concerning these mentoring programs had shown positive results. In the California program, researchers Barbara Storm, Jean Wing, Theresa Jinks, Kathleen Banks, and Patricia Cavazos found that most of the program's teachers said that mentoring played a significant role in the professional growth of new teachers.

Specifically, the program's design helped new teachers hone their practice—planning lessons, for example—and reflect on the effectiveness of instruction. Mentors also found that working with beginning teachers engaged them in reflection about their own instructional practices.[16]

Some words of caution need to be said in terms of implementing mentoring programs. In spite of the growing need for mentoring teachers at all levels of career development and some early evidence that effective mentoring reduces attrition, we still must heed the early warning signs cited in previous chapters. Problems can occur if program members do not pay attention to the hazards and risks involved in the selection and training of mentors and establishing a philosophy and process that focus on assisting teachers. Be alert to the following risks:

- Not every experienced master teacher can become an effective mentor. Working intimately with colleagues demands an entirely new set of skills. Selecting veteran teachers on the basis of popularity, political power, and desire alone isn't enough.
- Mentors require well-planned training in how to help and support colleagues. Not recognizing the pitfalls that can occur in intimate relationships and not being trained in how to respond can leave new mentors at risk and vulnerable.
- Mentoring programs that confuse assistance with assessment can quickly backfire. Mentoring programs that initially set out to assist and support teachers through a trusting, loyal, and collegial relationship can sometimes take on an evaluative role—a role that monitors performance.
- The mentoring team needs to be sure of their program's goals and state them clearly. Don't tell protégés that mentors are there to assist and then begin making classroom observations part of a formal evaluation process. Loyalty can be abused in a pressured school climate. When loyalty goes down the drain, so does the mentoring program.

ISSUE 6: THE NEED TO UNDERSTAND MENTORING AS A VITAL PART OF BUILDING A STRONG SCHOOL COMMUNITY

In *Habits of the Heart,* Robert Bellah and colleagues suggest that a community is a "group of people who are socially interdependent, who participate together in discussions and decision making, and who share certain practices that both define the community and are nurtured by it."[17]

Building a strong community cannot occur in schools where teachers are isolated and lack ways to come together in positive fashions that build self-esteem and encourage learning and renewal throughout their careers. How can they be positive role models or mentors for students, support staff, and parents when they lack experienced guides and mentors to offer them support?

A mentoring program that focuses on the mentor as a loyal and trustworthy friend, advisor, coach, and teacher can reshape our schools and can create a caring community that fosters the notion that we are all our brothers' and sisters' keepers. We are responsible and responsive to the glaring problems of teachers like Ellen Turner and students like Jim Moriarty. We are responsible and responsive to the subtle but just as pressing problems of teachers like Myra Fryman and Shawn Mallory and students like Aileen Lopez.

Mentoring, when offered as real assistance and support, is a mechanism to reduce isolation and apathy and, as Bellah and colleagues suggest, create a "certain practice that both defines the community and is nurtured by it." It is a way for both staff and students to be connected.

Mentoring shifts a school from being a community that defines itself by grade level and subject taught to a community of unique but coupled citizens who bring their own gifts and needs to school each day, eager to share, learn, and be supported. This community encourages each member's voice to be heard and stand for something, and values service to others by becoming involved when its members see troubled colleagues or students.

Offering assistance and support, and sometimes requiring tough love and feedback, may be a more powerful tool than formal assessment and evaluation. Promoting conditions that create trust, encourage risk, allow for an experience of failure, and focus on the need to improve, even an inch at a time, can pay off in the long run with improved performance for every member of the school community—administrators, department chairs, counselors, teachers, support staff, students, and even parents.

When people like Mindy Cline are helped and given space to test their own wings, they learn many lessons. They become more effective teachers as well as ideally positioned to help colleagues who need renewal. Who can really predict the future in the life of a community? Who knows when Cline's mentor Barb Roberts may also need renewal and rebirth? One hopes Cline would step in to return the care and support she received. One hopes that kind of intervention would be part of the community norm in their school, part of the work ethic and ethos.

Who knows when Glastonbury, Connecticut teacher Tom Griffin might be called on to be a mentor for Elaine Ahnell? His room is across the hall from hers; he'll know if things begin to not go well for her. Will he intervene? Is that kind of behavior encouraged, part of the community norm and work ethic and ethos, at Hebron Avenue Elementary School?

These are the kinds of expectations, responsibilities, and responses we want to create and encourage in our school community, responses that rest on a community norm that calls for action, intervention, and support at all times and for every member of the community.

When students like Jim Moriarty have help and space to test their own wings, they too learn valuable lessons. When gifted students suddenly find themselves at risk, they need the support of peers like Jim who have faced their problems and learned to move on, becoming more independent and self-sufficient and aware of their peers—thanks to the intervention of teachers like Tom Murray. Jim has become a member of a caring school community and is ideally positioned to help a peer in trouble work through tough times.

Is the community norm of the school supportive of students sharing a concern and helping troubled peers? We need the proactive responses of students like Jim to help create and encourage expectations, responsibilities, and responses that support practices, as Bellah suggests, that both "define the community and are nurtured by it," practices that encourage commitment and caring.

In a caring, conscious school community, members learn to be unafraid of the trouble, pain, and struggle of fellow community members. They learn to embrace the human condition in its many forms, even the dark sides. In fact, the dark sides really show the community the curriculum for mentoring intervention, where the troubles lie, and where their intervention should aim.

It may seem easier to ignore the star teacher Myra Fryman because she can be hostile and has political connections and clout. It may seem easier to let Ellen Turner slowly twist in the wind until the rope snaps. By intervening, however, mentors send a powerful message to the whole school community that life and the people in the school are precious and worth caring about, even when the caring may not come easy.

I know mentors like Brad Foley, Frank Bronkowski, Randy Edwards, Linda Alvarez, and Ivy Harrison. They exist in the real world. I also know teachers like Tom Murray, Ellen Turner, Shawn Mallory, Myra Fryman, and Jim McDonald. I have met and observed them, and I know from firsthand experience that mentoring can work.

It can work if two important variables are put into play: the trust of the mentoring relationship and the skills of the mentor. I know students like Jim and Janine who can benefit from a Tom Murray's intervention. They, too, can be part of a cyclical mentoring process that does not stop at the teacher's door. Students and support staff can acquire the same mentoring skills.

Is such a caring, whole-school mentoring program too much to hope for, or pie in the sky? No. Everything suggested in this book is doable by ordinary folks like you and me. It just takes some assessment of helping and mentoring skills, self-training, skill acquisition, and a plan for mentor train-ing and program implementation.

Yes, establishing a successful program takes political skills, the ability to deal with resistance, and selling the program to make it work. However, people like you and me can do these things. Keep it simple. Follow the path.

Education has once again become a top priority for the American people. Proposals for education reform—competency testing for students and teach-ers, creating a system of national standards, reforming or eliminating tenure, school choice options such as charter schools—are sweeping the country.

Critics of public schools say the schools are not capable of reforming themselves and that the public needs alternatives. Many believe that charter schools are the best way to help children who are locked in urban schools that don't work.

Many teachers and administrators say they can manage education reform if critics stop blasting them and undermining their work, and if the public starts providing the level of funding and staffing they need to address the multitude of issues that today's students are bringing into the schools.

Teachers say that charter schools and other education reform proposals are, in reality, efforts to privatize and weaken public education and establish a system of semiprivate schools in America.

The energy behind many of these proposals to improve public schools is welcome and long overdue. Proposals to help urban students and teachers who are locked into schools that are decaying, unsafe, and without computers and science labs are to be applauded.

But the proposals seem far removed from what happens in the daily life of teachers in classrooms throughout the country. Even if all of these education reforms were enacted tomorrow, the reality is that teachers in the class-rooms—whether in a charter school, a magnet school, or a school attended by voucher students—still will be faced with the challenge of how to develop their craft over a lifetime career. They need to learn how to adapt, change, and respond successfully to the students' and their own professional needs.

If educational leaders are truly going to reform our schools, we need ongoing mentoring so that teachers can learn, in easily accessible ways, how to aspire to become, and actually become, skilled and competent teachers, no matter what kind of education reform model takes center stage.

The bulk of this mentoring must go on in local schools, where teachers are found each day and are available for ongoing training. The mentoring process itself has to be led by school administrators who have the power, the position, and the resources to mount such an effort. To really make a dent in improving teacher effectiveness and reaching out to resistant groups, admin-istrators have to form mentoring teams composed of known and respected school leaders, experienced educators who have developed their craft and who can model and demonstrate for their peers how to be an effective teacher.

The danger in rushing to reform is that we may overlook two important factors that are necessary in developing effective teachers. First, teaching is a craft that is developed over a lifetime. A critical question, and one noticeably absent in the debate about which road to take in education reform, is, "What are the characteristics of teachers who master their craft?" How do they, through a process of accumulated classroom experience, often with many failures and some successes, develop a body of knowledge and a special set of skills that work for them, for their students, and for parents?

A second factor that is extremely important to reformers is how to use the experience of successful school leaders—administrators, department chairs, and teacher and counselor leaders—to retrain colleagues who are locked into outmoded and unsuccessful practices. What does it take to translate and transfer what constitutes effective teaching practices to teachers who are less than effective? What are the characteristics of educators who are able to successfully share their knowledge and experience with teachers who aren't quite making it? How do they get these teachers to trust and believe they can start again?

There are teachers in every school who seem to stay the same and never develop their craft, using the same skills and methods learned early in their careers despite a changing world and radically different student needs.

At the same time, many of these teachers are talented and they aspire, in spite of their resistance, to be better at their craft. What is missing for them in the workplace is a mentoring process that connects their aspirations with interventions and training that can open up their classrooms and professional lives to new energy and teaching options.

Again, to quote Stephen Sondheim, "What I found out in my experience is that everyone is talented. It's just that some people get it developed and some don't. Developing your talent takes work." Developing into an effective teacher takes a steady dose of hard work. Teachers must proceed to rekindle the spirit and enthusiasm of subpar teachers so they can once again begin to work hard to raise their level of skill and competency.

Clearly, educators who are successful in their schools and have the skills to mentor and retrain their colleagues are our major resource for rekindling spirits and raising competency. National movements, education department dictates, and attempts to influence the daily work of teachers by experts espousing their own solutions are often seen as threatening, faddish, and self-serving vehicles.

We would be wise to remind ourselves that well-trained educators are ideally positioned to train, not tell, teachers to embrace the notion that developing their craft requires a lifelong process of acquiring knowledge, of adapting or abandoning what falls short of their goal, and of acquiring a new set of skills that works for today's schoolwide community.

In closing, let me reiterate the three important principles that administrators need to keep in mind as they embark on a mentoring program.

First, there is a great need to create a safe and supportive mentoring environment in which teachers at every career stage have the opportunity to learn and in some cases turn their professional lives around. Whenever possible, these mentoring programs should take place in the schools in which teachers work. Easy access and availability for help and support are key components in establishing a mentoring program.

Second, mentoring programs can be implemented without an increase in staff or resources. Staff in place can become skilled mentors if they are provided with the hands-on training I suggest in this book. Many administrators, department chairpersons, counselors, and teacher leaders are looking for exciting career alternatives in which they can learn new skills and offer needed services without giving up their regular positions.

Finally, mentoring skills can be passed on from mentored teachers to their students, creating a whole-school mentoring process. In the aftermath of the terrorist attacks on the World Trade Center in New York, many students are searching for ways to be of service to their peers, school, and community. Learning the skills to intervene and help others is important not only to our students, but to our nation.

In a real sense, an effective mentoring program can help teachers believe in themselves and avoid the trap of defining themselves as just a cog in the wheel, with nothing unique about them. This is a sad state of mind that a wise mentor knows can be avoided with support, insight, self-care, risk, and a belief in and enjoyment of the work of teaching.

A mentoring program in which skills are passed on to students can also help those students who see themselves as having nothing unique about them. Mentoring can change low self-esteem and lack of worth by offering programs in which students can learn to be of use and value—programs in which they are noticed, affirmed, and begin to believe in themselves. Simply put, mentoring provides turnaround opportunities for the whole school community.

NOTES

1. This and the previous two quotes from Stephen Hegarty, "Some Newcomers Find Teaching to Be Too Tough," *Naples Daily News*, 28 January 2001, 8D.

2. Pam Robbins, "How to Plan and Implement a Peer Coaching Program" (Alexandria, VA: Association for Supervision and Curriculum Development [ASCD], 1991), 44–54.

3. Carol Tell, "Appreciating Good Teaching," *Educational Leadership* 58(5) (February 2001): 8–11.

4. James B. Rowley, "The Good Mentor," *Educational Leadership* 56(8) (May 1999): 20–21.

5. Mary Brooks, "Mentors Matter," in Marge Scherer, ed., *A Better Beginning* (Alexandria, VA: Association for Supervision and Curriculum Development [ASCD], 1999), 53–56.

6. Nathalie Gehrke, "Developing Teachers' Leadership Skills," ERIC, 1990, www.naesp.org/misc/edweek_article_2–23-00.html (23 April 2001).

7. Holly Bartunek, "Classroom Teacher as Teacher Educator," ERIC, 1989, www.ericsp.org/pages/digests/classroom_teacher_edu_89–7.html (20 April 2001).

8. Roland Barth, "Teacher Leaders," *Kappan* 86(2) (February 2001): 443–449.

9. Clarisse Butler and Ned Hoskins, "Why Mentoring Really Matters," *New York Teacher* (25 April 2001): 10–11.

10. Kate Zernike, "Helping New Teachers Survive the Hardest Years," *New York Times*, 14 February 2001, B11.

11. Joan Montgomery-Halford, "Easing the Way for New Teachers," *Educational Leadership* 55(5) (February 1998): 34–36.

12. Jeff Archer, "Earning Their Stripes," *Education Week*, January 2000, www.edweek.org/sreports/qc00/templates/article.cfm?slug=onestate.htm&keywords (20 April 2001).

13. Margaret Oleve, Amy Jackson, and Charlotte Danielson, "Investing in Beginning Teachers—The California Model," *Educational Leadership* 56(8) (May 1999): 41–44.

14. Sharon Brennan, William Thames, and Richard Roberts, "In Kentucky . . . Mentoring with a Mission," *Educational Leadership* 56(8) (May 1999): 52

15. Patricia Stedman and Sandra A. Stroot, "Teachers Helping Teachers," *Educational Leadership* 55(5) (February 1998): 37–38.

16. Barbara Storm, Jean Wing, Theresa Jinks, Kathleen Banks, and Patricia Cavazos, "CFASST [California Formative Assessment and Support System for Teachers] (field review) Implementation 1999–2000: A Formative Evaluation Report," Princeton, NJ: Educational Testing Service.

17. Robert Bellah et al., *Habits of the Heart* (New York: Harper & Row, 1985), 333.

Bibliography

Andrews, Fred. "Learning to Celebrate Water-Cooler Gossip." *New York Times*, 25 February 2001, BU6.

Araton, Harvey. "At Age 30, Mullin's World Takes Strange New Twists." *New York Times*, 14 January 1994, C6.

Archer, Jeff. "Earning Their Stripes." *Education Week*. January 2000. www.edweek.org/sreports/qc00/templates/article.cfm?slug=onestate.htm& keywords (20 April 2001).

Balliett, Whitney. "King Louis." *The New Yorker* (8 August 1994): 69.

———. "Cecil." *The New Yorker* (5 May 1986): 104.

———. "Miles." *The New Yorker* (4 December 1989): 156.

Barth, Roland. "Teacher Leaders." *Kappan* 86(2) (February 2001): 443–449.

Bartunek, Holly. "Classroom Teacher as Teacher Educator." ERIC, 1989. www.ericsp.org/pages/digests/classroom_teacher_edu_89–7.html (4 April 2001).

Bellah, Robert, Richard Madsen, William Sullivan, Ann Swidler, and Steven Tipton. *Habits of the Heart*. New York: Harper & Row, 1985.

Berkow, Ira. "The Legend Continues . . . Bird Shoots for Coaching Greatness." *New York Times*, 10 August 1997, sec. 8, p.1.

Berliner, David C. "Improving the Quality of the Teaching Force." *Educational Leadership* 58(8) (May 2001): 10–11.

Blair, Julie. "Teachers' Idealism Tempered by Frustration, Survey Finds." *Education Week*, 31 May 2000, 6.

Brennan, Sharon, William Thames, and Richard Roberts. "In Kentucky . . . Mentoring with a Mission." *Educational Leadership* 56(8) (May 1999): 52.

Brooks, Mary. "Mentors Matter." In *A Better Beginning*, edited by Marge Scherer. Alexandria, VA: Association for Supervision and Curriculum Development (ASCD), 1999.

Butler, Clarisse and Ned Hoskins. "Why Mentoring Really Matters." *New York Teacher* (25 April 2001): 10–11.

Casey, Jean and Ann Claunch. "The Stages of Mentor Development." In Hal Porter, ed., *Teacher Mentoring and Induction*. Thousand Oaks, CA: Corwin Press, 2005.

Ciavonne, Jean. "Dandelions, Pine-Cone Turkey, and Abraham Lincoln." *Kappan* 66(2) (October 1984): 142–143.

Combs, Arthur, Donald L. Avila, and William W. Purkey. *Helping Relationships: Basic Concepts for the Helping Profession*. Boston: Allyn & Bacon, 1971.

Cruickshank, Donald, Deborah Bainer, Joshua Cruz, Jr., Carmen Giebelhaus, Joy D. McCullough, Kim K. Mentcalf, and Richard Reynolds. *Preparing America's Teachers*. Bloomington, IN: Phi Delta Kappa Foundation, 1996.

Dowd, Maureen. "Port Mortuary's Pull," *New York Times*, 1 November 2009, WK9.

Dunning, Jennifer. "Twyla Tharp Finds Value as a Cause for Dancing." *New York Times*, 12 January 1995, C1, C13.

Education Research Service. "Is There a Shortage of Qualified Candidates for Openings in the Principalship? An Exploratory Study." NAESP Online, 1998. www.naesp.org/ misc/ed-week_article_2–23.htm (20 April 2001).

Ellington, Duke. "Do Nothin' Till You Hear from Me." *Louis Armstrong and Duke Ellington.* Capitol Records, 3 April 1961.

Erickson, Steve. "Neil Young . . . On a Good Day." *New York Times*, 30 July 2000, sec. 6, p. 26.

Etzioni, Emitai. *The Spirit of Community*. New York: Crown, 1993.

Faulkner, David. "For Yastrzemski, the Fire Still Burns." *New York Times*, 14 October 1986, C3.

Ferrandino, V. L. and G. N. Tirozzi. "Our Time Has Come." NAESP Online. www.naesp.org/ misc/edweek_article_2–23-00.html (23 February 2000)

Fibkins, William. *Students in Trouble: Schools Can Help before Failure.* Lanham, MD: Scarecrow Education, 2005.

Ganser, Tom. "Learning from the Past—Building for the Future." In Hal Porter, ed., *Teacher Mentoring and Induction.* Thousand Oaks, CA: Corwin Press, 2005.

Gehrke, Nathalie. "Developing Teachers' Leadership Skills." ERIC, 1990.www.naesp.org/ misc/edweek_article_2–23-00.html (23 April 2001).

Gilman, David A. and Barbara Lanman-Givens. "Where Have All the Principals Gone?" *Educational Leadership* 58(8) (May 2001): 73.

Gladwell, Malcolm. "Designs for Working." *The New Yorker* (11 December 2000): 60–70.

Glauber, Bob. "Simms: I'd Retire If . . . " *Newsday*, 19 October 1991, Newspapers & Newswires Section, p. 85.

Goldberg, Cary. "Betraying a Trust: Teacher Student Sex is Not Unusual, Experts Say." *New York Times*, 21 May 1995, L37.

Goodnough, Abby. "Teaching by the Book, No Asides Allowed." *New York Times*, 23 May 2000, A1, B7.

Hammer, Michael and James Champy. *Reengineering the Corporation*. New York: HarperCollins, 1993.

Hegarty, Stephen. "Some Newcomers Find Teaching to Be Too Tough." *Naples Daily News*, 28 January 2001, 8D.

Holland, Holly. "KERA: A Tale of One Teacher." *Kappan* 79(4) (December 1997): 265–271.

Holloway, John S. "The Benefits of Mentoring." *Educational Leadership* 58(8) (May 2001): 85–86.

Jacobson, Steve. "A Complement to Sutton's Life." *Newsday*, 7 January 1998, A75.

———. "Complex Illness Hits Harnisch." *Newsday*, 6 August 1997, A71.

James, Caryn. "Death, Mighty Thou Art; So Too, a Compassionate Heart." *New York Times*, 23 March 2001, E1.

Keiffer-Brown, Susan and Kathleen Ware, "Growing Great Teachers in Cincinnati." *Educational Leadership* 58(8) (May 2001): 56–58.

King, Matthew. "If These Walls Could Talk." *Educational Leadership* 58(5) (February 2001): 64–65.

Lahr, John. "The Imperfectionist." *The New Yorker* (12 September 1992): 68.

———. "Sinatra's Song." *The New Yorker* (3 November 1997): 77.

———. "Making It Real . . . How Mike Nichols Recreated Comedy and Himself." *The New Yorker* (21 February 2000): 197.

———. "Been Here and Gone . . . How August Wilson Brought a Century of Black American Culture to the Stage." *The New Yorker* (16 April 2000): 49–65.

Lemmon, Jack and Kevin Spacey. "A Couple of Winners Talk Awards and Acting." *New York Times*, 12 March 2000, sec. 2A, 2.

Letters to the Editor, "The Education of Donna Moffett." *New York Times*, 29 May 2001, A14.

Lopate, Phillip. "Learning to Love the Ardent Chaos of Cassavetes." *New York Times*, 10 August 1997, H11.

Macaulay, Alastair. "Happy Hooligan." *The New Yorker* (27 April 1992): 89.

McCay, Elizabeth. "The Learning Needs of Principals." *Educational Leadership* 58(8) (May 2001): 75–76.

Moir, Ellen. "Launching the New Generation of Teachers." In Hal Porter, ed., *Teacher Mentoring and Induction*. Thousand Oaks, CA: Corwin Press, 2005.

Montgomery-Halford, Joan. "Easing the Way for New Teachers." *Educational Leadership* 55(5) (February 1998): 34–36.

NEA Teacher Quality Fact Sheet. "Ready or Not: A National Teacher Shortage Looms." NEA, 2001. www.nea.org/teaching/ shortage.html (19 April 2001).

Margaret Newhouse. "Legacies of the Heart: The Flip Side of Purpose." *The Positive Aging Newsletter* (July/August 2009): 1.

Oleve, Margaret, Amy Jackson, and Charlotte Danielson. "Investing in Beginning Teachers— The California Model." *Educational Leadership* (May 1999): 41–44.

Rehak, Melanie. "Things Fall Together." *New York Times*, 26 March 2000, sec. 6, 36.

Riding, Alan. "The Joy of a Comeback that Leaves the Past Behind." *New York Times*, 29 April 2001, AR3.

———. "Looking at a France That's Seldom Seen." *New York Times*, 27 August 2000, AR17.

Robbins, Pam. *How to Plan and Implement a Peer Coaching Program*. Alexandria, VA: Association for Supervision and Curriculum Development (ASCD), 1991.

Routtencutter, Helen. "Andre Previn." *The New Yorker* (12 January 1983): 43.

Rowley, James B. "The Good Mentor." *Educational Leadership* 56(8) (May 1999): 20–21.

Saint-Exupery, Antoine. *Wind, Sand, and Stars*. New York: Reynolds & Hitchcock, 1939.

Sarason, Seymour. *Creation of Settings*. San Francisco: Jossey Bass, 1972.

Schiff, Stephen. "Stephen Sondheim." *The New Yorker* (8 March 1993): 77.

Seuss, Dr. *Oh, the Places You'll Go!* New York: Random House, 1990.

Solomon, Andrew. "Bruce Nauman." *New York Times*, 5 March 1995, sec. 6, 28.

———. "The Jazz Martyr." *New York Times*, 9 February 1997, sec. 6, pp. 34–38.

Sondheim, Stephen. "I'm Still Here." In the Broadway musical *Follies*, 1972.

Spacey, Kevin. "An Example, A Mentor, An Actor Above All." *New York Times*, 4 January 2001, AR6.

Stedman, Patricia and Sandra A. Stroot. "Teachers Helping Teachers." *Educational Leadership* 55(5) (February 1998): 37–38.

Steinbeck, John. *East of Eden*. New York: Viking Press, 1952.

Steinberg, Jacques. "Class Wars: Clashing over Education's One True Faith." *New York Times*, 14 December 1997, sec. 4, 1.

Storm, Barbara, Jean Wing, Theresa Jinks, Kathleen Banks and Patricia Cavazos. "CFASST [California Formative Assessment and Support System for Teachers] (field review) Implementation 1999–2000: A Formative Evaluation Report." Princeton, NJ: Educational Testing Service, 2000.

Teachout, Terry. "Still Full of Jazz, Still Pouring It Out." *New York Times*, 19 December 1999, AR44.

Tell, Carol. "Appreciating Good Teaching." *Educational Leadership* 58(5) (February 2001): 8–11.

Temes, Peter. "The End of School Reform." *Education Week*. 4 April 2001. www. edweek.org/ ew/ewstory.cfm?Slug=29temes.h20.

Thomas, George. "Jets Discover Their Coach's Joyful Energy." *New York Times*, 17 May 2001, D5.

Wadsworth, Deborah. "A Sense of Calling." *Public Agenda* (2000).

Weintraub, Bernie. "Looking Back at Two Classics." *New York Times*, 23 January 1998, E8.

Zernike, Kate. "Helping New Teachers Survive the Hardest Years." *New York Times*, 14 February 2001, B11.

Zipkin, Amy. "In Tight Labor Market Bosses Find Value in Being Nice." *New York Times*, 31 May 2000, C1.

About the Author

William L. Fibkins is an author and educational consultant specializing in training administrators, teachers, and counselors. He holds degrees on school administration and counselor education from Syracuse University and the University of Massachusetts. His other publications include *Teen Obesity: How Schools Can Be the Number One Solution to the Problem, Innocence Denied: A Guide to Preventing Sexual Misconduct by Teachers and Coaches, Students in Trouble: Schools Can Help before Failure, An Educator's Guide to Understanding the Personal Side of Students' Lives, What Schools Can Do to Stop Kids from Smoking, The Teacher-As-Helper Training Manual, The Empowering School: Getting Everyone on Board to Help Teenagers*, and *The Work Experience of Teacher and Professional Burnout*. His web page can be found at WilliamFibkins.com.

Breinigsville, PA USA
02 March 2011
256799BV00002B/1/P